D0316383

Progress in Reading Literacy in National and International Context

Studies in International Comparative and Multicultural Education

edited by

Wilfried Bos, Dortmund
Marianne Krüger-Potratz, Münster
Jürgen Henze, Berlin
Sabine Hornberg, Bayreuth
Botho von Kopp, Frankfurt (Main)
Hans-Georg Kotthoff, Freiburg
Knut Schwippert, Hamburg
Dietmar Waterkamp, Dresden
Peter J. Weber, München

Volume 13

Waxmann 2012
Münster / New York / München / Berlin

Knut Schwippert, Jenny Lenkeit (Eds.)

Progress in Reading Literacy
in National and International Context

The Impact of PIRLS 2006 in 12 Countries

Waxmann 2012
Münster / New York / München / Berlin

Bibliographic information published by die Deutsche Nationalbibliothek
Die Deutsche Nationalbibliothek lists this publication in the
Deutsche Nationalbibliografie; detailed bibliographic data
are available in the internet at http://dnb.d-nb.de.

PIRLS 2006
Progress in International Reading Literacy

A study under the auspices of International Association
for the Evaluation of Educational Achievement

**Studies in International Comparative
and Multicultural Education, Volume 13**
ISSN 1612-2003
ISBN 978-3-8309-2666-5

© Waxmann Verlag GmbH, 2012
Postfach 8603, 48046 Münster, Germany
Waxmann Publishing Co.
P. O. Box 1318, New York, NY 10028, U. S. A.
www.waxmann.com
info@waxmann.com

Cover Design: Pleßmann Design, Ascheberg
Print: Hubert & Co., Göttingen
Printed on age-resistant paper, acid-free as per ISO 9706

Contents

Foreword

The ability to read is universally regarded as a key foundational skill, the lynch-pin to future social and economic well-being for individuals as well as for nation states. The International Association for the Evaluation of Educational Achievement (IEA) has been at the forefront of large-scale assessments of student achievement in reading and other subject matter areas for more than 50 years. The aim of these assessments, as it was for the Progress in Reading Literacy Study of 2006 (PIRLS 2006), is to provide policymakers, educators, researchers, and the public with key insights into the scholastic performance of Grade 4 students and into the contextual and background variables apparently associated with excellence. The ultimate goal for these assessments is to provide part of the empirical basis that contributes to educational debate, improvement, and reform.

This volume examines empirically the ways in which participation in the PIRLS 2006 assessment has made an impact in 12 of the countries that participated in the study. Despite the limited number of country essays, the authors, among them, identify a wide range of influences that participation in large-scale assessments such as PIRLS tend to have. These reported impacts range from structural changes to education systems, including the establishment of dedicated research and evaluation units, to policy change (the elevation of concerns about quality in the educational debate) and curricular reforms. The country chapters also illustrate how the achievement data and the antecedent factors potentially implicated in explanations of achievement outcomes can be used not only to inform policy dialogue within institutions responsible for educational reform but also to generate public discourse on education.

While the authors provide compelling evidence that the goal of large-scale assessments—influencing educational reform and improvement—can be realized, they also identify challenges that may mitigate impact. These include the ease with which educational stakeholders, the media, and the public can access the information embedded in complex data and the need to invest in ways to communicate study outcomes more effectively.

This book is a useful contribution to the growing body of literature focused on the impact of large-scale assessments of student achievement. IEA values the work that Dr Knut Schwippert, Jenny Lenkeit, and their colleagues continue to make to our understanding of that impact.

Hans Wagemaker,
Executive Director, IEA

Chapter 1
Introduction

Knut Schwippert and Jenny Lenkeit

1.1 Overview

The *Impact of PIRLS 2006 in 12 Countries* is the second book portraying the apparent influence of the findings of the Progress in Reading Literacy Study (PIRLS) surveys in different national contexts. The book, which follows the conceptual design of its predecessor (Schwippert, 2007), presents a compilation of insights from 12 of the 35 countries that participated in PIRLS 2006. These insights relate to the impact of PIRLS on the systemic, governmental, administrative, and school-level aspects of the 12 education systems featured.

Ten years have passed since PIRLS was first conducted in 2001. These years have provided a considerable period of time for transformative processes to establish and become visible as changes in educational institutions, and in students' achievement evident in the results of the 2006 study. This book provides in-depth information on the various aspects of the national education systems represented in this book that have originated, been restructured, or otherwise been modified as a direct or indirect consequence of the results from the two PIRLS surveys.

Our intention in this introductory chapter is to give readers a basic description of the PIRLS program and its purpose, and to provide preliminary information about the countries that participated in the two surveys. We also outline the relevance of large-scale assessments for understanding and enhancing students' literacy achievement. We finish the chapter by setting out the purpose and the methodological approaches of the Impact of PIRLS 2006 project.

1.2 PIRLS 2001 and 2006

The PIRLS program encompasses a cycle of trend studies designed to monitor progress in reading achievement in an internationally comparative context (Wagemaker, 2001). PIRLS 2001, the first international reading literacy study conducted in the new millennium, assessed students in the primary school; the target grade in most participating countries was (and continues to be) Grade 4.

The second cycle of PIRLS in 2006 saw an increase in the number of participating countries (from 35 to 45), as depicted in Figure 1.1. However, as the figure also makes apparent, seven of the countries that participated in the 2001 cycle decided not to participate in the 2006 study. The overall increase nevertheless reflects a growing interest in the information that large-scale assessments such as PIRLS provide.

Figure 1.1:   Countries participating in PIRLS 2001 and 2006

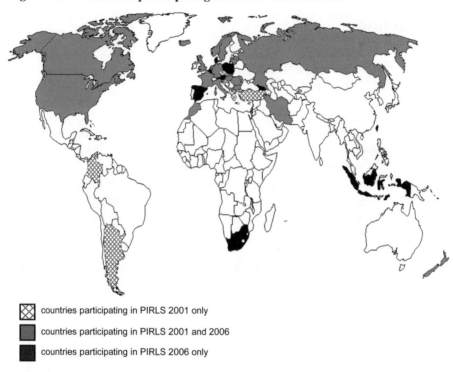

⊠   countries participating in PIRLS 2001 only

▨   countries participating in PIRLS 2001 and 2006

■   countries participating in PIRLS 2006 only

PIRLS 2001 and 2006 (28 countries)

Bulgaria	Canada (Ontario, Québec)[1]	England	France
Germany	Hong Kong SAR	Hungary	Iceland
Iran, Islamic Rep. of	Israel	Italy	Kuwait
Latvia	Lithuania	Macedonia, Rep. of	Moldova, Rep. of
Morocco	Netherlands	New Zealand	Norway
Romania	Russian Federation	Scotland	Singapore
Slovak Republic	Slovenia	Sweden	United States

PIRLS 2001 only (7 countries)

Argentina	Belize	Colombia	Cyprus
Czech Republic	Greece	Turkey	

PIRLS 2006 only (16 countries)

Austria	Belgium (Flemish)	Belgium (French)	Canada (Alberta)
Canada (British Columbia)	Canada (Nova Scotia)	Chinese Taipei	Denmark
Georgia	Indonesia	Luxembourg	Poland
Qatar	South Africa	Spain	Trinidad and Tobago

1   Canada is represented by the provinces of Ontario and Québec only.

PIRLS 2006 was conducted in autumn 2005 (southern hemisphere) and spring 2006 (northern hemisphere), five years after the first cycle in 2001. The findings were published in an international report the year following the survey (Mullis, Martin, Kennedy, & Foy, 2007). The study was directed by Ina V. S. Mullis and Michael O. Martin of the TIMSS and PIRLS International Study Center at Boston College in the United States and by members of the IEA Secretariat in Amsterdam, the Netherlands. They were supported in this task by Statistics Canada in Ottawa, the IEA Data Processing and Research Center in Hamburg, Germany, and Educational Testing Service in Princeton, the United States.

Large-scale assessments such as PIRLS do not focus on the individual student but on entire education systems. The instruments used to collect data from students, their parents, teachers of the sampled classes, and school principals are therefore designed to capture detailed information about the various contexts in which students learn to read. The PIRLS database thus provides extensive information on students' family backgrounds and on students' classroom and school environments, all of which feature factors known to significantly contribute to the development of reading literacy. An encyclopedia of reading education in the participating countries assembled by Kennedy, Mullis, Martin, and Trong (2007) provides information on the national contexts in which students learn to read.

Figure 1.2 depicts the interrelationship of national, home, school, and class contexts relative to reading literacy. Figure 1.3, in turn, gives an example of this interrelationship by depicting the various factors within these contexts that appear to have influenced the reading literacy outcomes of the German Grade 4 students who participated in PIRLS 2001 and 2006. Both figures illustrate not only that a variety of contextual factors inside and outside educational structures influence achievement outcomes but also that the outcomes themselves retroactively influence the system.

Figure 1.2: Contexts within which students develop reading literacy

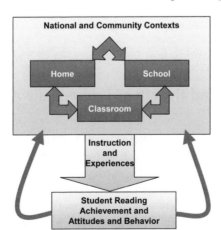

Source: Mullis et al. (2007).

Figure 1.3: **Theoretical framework used to depict the two-way relationship between input and process factors and student achievement in reading literacy in Germany as determined through analysis of PIRLS data**

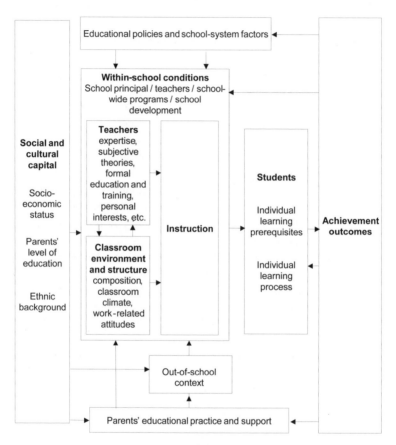

Source: Adapted from Bos et al. (2007, p. 22).

1.3 Relevance and Benefit of Large-Scale Assessments in Education

Awareness of the relevance of international comparative studies has increased markedly in recent years. Although these studies have been and still are criticized for various reasons relating to, for example, methodology and conceptualization (Arnold, 1999; Bos & Schwippert, 2003; Brügelmann & Heymann, 2002), the essential benefits of them are obvious. The fact that many of the countries participating in the Impact of PIRLS project have taken part in international large-scale surveys for a good length of time (see Table 1.1) indicates that policymakers, experts, and researchers in participating countries see merit in such participation.

In line with the use of standardized tests as an important mechanism for monitoring educational achievement, evidence-based decisionmaking has become, in many countries, an increasingly accepted part of educational innovation (Arbeitsgruppe Bildungsforschung/Bildungsplanung, 2007). The data collected during the PIRLS surveys on the reading achievement of students in Grade 4 and on students' home, classroom, and school environments have provided policymakers, researchers, and practitioners with information useful for identifying and then remedying structures and processes across the various levels of the education system that limit children's reading acquisition.

Table 1.1: **Participation in international large-scale surveys conducted by various organizations from 1959 to 2009 of countries taking part the Impact of PIRLS 2006 study**

Year(s) of data collection[+]	Name of survey	Organization in charge	Countries
1959–1962	The Pilot Twelve-Country Study	IEA	Belgium, England, Germany (FRG)
1963–1967	First International Mathematics Study (FIMS)	IEA	Belgium, England, Germany (FRG), Netherlands
	Six-Subject Survey		
1968–1972	First International Science Study (FISS)	IEA	Belgium (FL), England, Germany (FRG), Hungary, Netherlands, New Zealand
1968–1972	The Study of Reading Comprehension	IEA	Belgium (FL), England, Hungary, Netherlands, New Zealand,
1968–1973	The Study of Civic Education	IEA	England, Germany (FRG), Netherlands, New Zealand
1968–1973	The Study of French as a Foreign Language	IEA	England, Netherlands, New Zealand
1968–1973	The Study of English as a Foreign Language	IEA	Germany (FRG), Hungary, Netherlands
1968–1973	The Study of Literature Education	IEA	Belgium (FL), England, New Zealand
1977–1981	Second International Mathematics Study (SIMS)	IEA	Belgium (FL), England, Hong Kong, Hungary, Netherlands, New Zealand
1980–1985	Classroom Environment Study	IEA	Hungary, Netherlands, Germany (FRG)*
1982–1986	Second International Science Study (SISS)	IEA	England, Hong Kong, Hungary, Netherlands
1983–1988	Written Composition Study	IEA	England, Germany (FRG),# Hungary, Netherlands, New Zealand

Year(s) of data collection[+]	Name of survey	Organization in charge	Countries
1989	Computers in Education Study (COMPED)	IEA	Austria, Belgium (FL), Germany (FRG), Hungary, Netherlands, New Zealand
1992	Computers in Education Study (COMPED)	IEA	Austria, Germany, Latvia, Netherlands
1985–1994	Reading Literacy Study (RLS)	IEA	Germany (FRG), Germany (GDR), Hong Kong, Hungary, Netherlands, New Zealand
1991	International Assessment of Educational Progress-II (IAEP-II)	Educational Testing Service	England, Hungary, Russian Federation ##
1993–1996	Language Education Study	IEA	Austria, England, Hong Kong, Hungary, Latvia,** Netherlands, Russian Federation, Republic of South Africa
1995	Third International Mathematics and Science Study (TIMSS)	IEA	Austria, Belgium (FL), England, Germany, Hong Kong, Hungary, Latvia, Netherlands, New Zealand, Republic of South Africa, Russian Federation, Slovak Republic
1999	Third International Mathematics and Science Study Repeat (TIMSS-R)	IEA	Belgium (FL), England, Hong Kong, Hungary, Latvia, Netherlands, New Zealand, Russian Federation, Slovak Republic, Republic of South Africa
2003	Trends in International Mathematics and Science Study (TIMSS)	IEA	Belgium (FL), England, Hong Kong, Hungary, Latvia, Netherlands, New Zealand, Russian Federation, Slovak Republic, Republic of South Africa
2007	Trends in International Mathematics and Science Study (TIMSS)	IEA	Austria, England, Germany, Hong Kong, Hungary, Latvia, Netherlands, New Zealand, Russian Federation, Slovak Republic
1998–2004	Third International Mathematics and Science Study Repeat Video Project (TIMSS-R Video)	IEA	Hong Kong, Netherlands
1994	International Adult Literacy Survey (IALS)	OECD	Germany, Netherlands
1996	International Adult Literacy Survey (IALS)	OECD	Belgium (FL), England, Germany, Netherlands, New Zealand
1998	International Adult Literacy Survey (IALS)	OECD	Belgium (FL), England, Germany, Hungary, Netherlands

Year(s) of data collection[+]	Name of survey	Organization in charge	Countries
1996/1997	Civic Education Study (CivEd)	IEA	England, Germany, Hong Kong, Hungary, Netherlands
1999/2000	Civic Education Study (CivEd)	IEA	England, Germany, Hong Kong, Hungary, Latvia, Russian Federation, Slovak Republic
1997–1999 (Module 1)	Second Information Technology in Education Study (SITES)	IEA	Hong Kong, Hungary, Latvia, New Zealand, Russian Federation, Slovak Republic, Republic of South Africa
1999–2002 (Module 2)	Second Information Technology in Education Study (SITES)	IEA	England, Germany, Hong Kong, Latvia, Netherlands, Slovak Republic, Republic of South Africa
2006	Second Information Technology in Education Study (SITES)	IEA	Hong Kong, Russian Federation, Slovak Republic, Republic of South Africa
1999	Monitoring Learning Achievement	UNESCO/ UNICEF	Republic of South Africa
2000	Program for International Student Assessment (PISA)	OECD	Austria, Belgium, England, Germany, Hong Kong, Hungary, Latvia, Netherlands, New Zealand, Russian Federation
2003	Program for International Student Assessment (PISA)	OECD	Austria, Belgium, England, Germany, Hong Kong, Hungary, Latvia, Netherlands, New Zealand, Russian Federation, Slovak Republic
2006	Program for International Student Assessment (PISA)	OECD	Austria, Belgium, England, Germany, Hong Kong, Hungary, Latvia, Netherlands, New Zealand, Russian Federation, Slovak Republic
2009	Program for International Student Assessment (PISA)	OECD	Austria, Belgium, England, Germany, Hong Kong, Hungary, Latvia, Netherlands, New Zealand, Russian Federation, Slovak Republic
2001	Southern African Consortium for the Monitoring of Educational Quality II (SACMEQ)	IIEP, UNESCO	Republic of South Africa
2001	Progress in International Reading Literacy Study (PIRLS)	IEA	England, Germany, Hong Kong, Hungary, Latvia, Netherlands, New Zealand, Russian Federation, Slovak Republic

Year(s) of data collection[+]	Name of survey	Organization in charge	Countries
2006	Progress in International Reading Literacy Study (PIRLS)	IEA	Austria, Belgium (FL), England, Germany, Hong Kong, Hungary, Latvia, Netherlands, New Zealand, Russian Federation, Slovak Republic, Republic of South Africa
2006–2009	Teacher Education and Development Study in Mathematics (TEDS-M)	IEA	Germany, Russian Federation
2009	Citizenship Education Study ICCS	IEA	Austria, Belgium (FL), England, Hong Kong, Latvia, Netherlands, New Zealand, Russian Federation, Slovak Republic

Organization abbreviations: ETS (Educational Testing Service); IEA (International Association for the Evaluation of Educational Achievement); IEEP (International Institute for Educational Planning); OECD (Organisation for Economic Co-operation and Development); UNESCO (United Nations Educational, Scientific and Cultural Organization); UNICEF (United Nations Children's Fund)

Notes:
[+] The time of data collection differed for countries in the southern hemisphere. See the official IEA website for more detailed information: http://www.iea.nl/completed_studies.html
[*] The Federal Republic of Germany conducted the study two years later.
[**] Latvia carried out only the first stage (gathering information on language education at the national level).
[#] Only the federal state of Hamburg participated.
[##] Former Soviet Union.

Another important attribute of studies such as PIRLS is that individual countries can assess the educational achievement of their students against the achievement of students in other countries. This process gives governments as well as educational policymakers and practitioners a better sense of the functioning and effectiveness of their own education systems than they could gain by studying their particular system in isolation (Porter & Gamoran, 2002).

In similar vein, PIRLS and other cross-national studies of educational achievement provide those responsible for developing education systems with opportunity to carefully examine the merit of implemented changes to those systems (Schwippert & Goy, 2008). The cyclical nature of PIRLS also enables the participating countries to gain a snapshot understanding of the state of their education system at one point in time and to follow developments across time.

In addition to gathering an increasing amount of data-based information (from both national and international contexts), many countries have made changes to their education systems that have steered them away from the traditional input orientation of educational governance toward an orientation that is increasingly output focussed (Schwippert & Goy, 2008). The Impact of PIRLS project has also been useful with respect to this change because it documents how the various participating countries have achieved it.

1.4   The Impact of PIRLS Project

The Impact of PIRLS project began when a small group of researchers from 13 of the participating PIRLS countries decided, after the first PIRLS cycle in 2001, to record the reactions of their respective government agencies, researchers, schools, and members of the public to the results of the study. The outcome was the aforementioned report by Schwippert (2007). After the second PIRLS cycle in 2006, researchers again agreed to assess the impact of PIRLS in their national contexts. The 12 countries that contributed to the project in 2006 were:

- Austria
- Germany
- Latvia
- Russian Federation
- Belgium (FL)
- Hong Kong SAR
- Netherlands
- Slovak Republic
- England
- Hungary
- New Zealand
- South Africa.

Of these countries, five had participated in the first impact study. The seven that were new to the impact project were Austria, Belgium (FL), Latvia, the Netherlands, New Zealand, the Russian Federation, and South Africa.

The researchers' work culminated in a report from each participating country, and it is these reports that form much of the content of this present publication. Because the reports are written from an insider perspective, they are each informed by different backgrounds, experiences, and opinions. These differences need to be taken into account when reading the single reports. As is evident from Table 1.2, the home institutions of the authors vary greatly with regard to their influence, interest, and purpose within the respective education systems.

The primary aim of the Impact of PIRLS project has been to explore the opportunities that the findings from PIRLS hold for the development of different education systems. Those of us involved with the present iteration of the project were particularly interested in its potential for yielding information on transformation processes, programs, and initiatives—information that we considered would be even more useful than that obtained from PIRLS 2001 simply because the passage of time has allowed implementation of actions informed by the 2001 data. This lapse in time has, indeed, enabled us to consider if those actions facilitated changes in the 2006 student achievement results.

Table 1.2:   Home institutions of the authors of the country reports

Country	Authors and institutions	Status of institution
Austria	Birgit Suchań, Christina Wallner-Paschon, Cornelia Rieß *Federal Institute for Educational Research, Innovation &* *Development of the Austrian School System (BIFIE)*	Division in the Ministry of Education
Belgium (FL)	Hongqiang Liu, Heidi Knipprath, Jan Van Damme *Research Centre for Educational Effectiveness and* *Evaluation, Katholieke Universiteit Leuven*	University department
England	Liz Twist *Department for Research in Assessment and Measurement,* *National Foundation for Educational Research*	Independent educational research institute
Germany	Knut Schwippert, Jenny Lenkeit *Department for Evaluation of Educational Systems, University* *of Hamburg* Martin Goy *Institute for School Development Research, TU Dortmund* *University*	University department
Hong Kong SAR	Shek Kam Tse *Center for Advancement of Chinese Language Education and* *Research and Faculty of Education, University of Hong Kong* Elizabeth Ka Yee Loh *Faculty of Education, University of Hong Kong*	University department
Hungary	Péter Balkányi *Educational Authority*	Division in the Ministry of Education
Latvia	Antra Ozola *Faculty of Education, Psychology, and Art, University of Latvia*	University department
Netherlands	Andrea Netten *National Center for Language Education*	Independent educational research institute
New Zealand	Megan Chamberlain *Comparative Education Research Unit*	Division in the Ministry of Education
Russian Federation	Isak Froumin *Europe and Central Asia Human Development Unit, The World* *Bank, Institute of Education, National Research University,* *Higher School of Economics* Marina Kuznetsova *Center of Primary Education, Institute of Content and Methods* *of Learning, Russian Academy of Education* Galina Kovaleva *Center for Evaluating the Quality of Education, Russian* *Academy of Education* Andrey Melnikov *ICT in Education Department, National Training Foundation* Marina Pinskaya, Tatiana Timkova, Yulia Tumeneva *Institute for Educational Studies of the University* *Higher School of Economics* Galina Zuckerman *Psychology Institute, Russian Academy of Education*	
Slovak Republic	Eva Ladányiová, Paulína Koršňáková, Daniela Heldová *Department of International Measurements, National Institute* *for Certified Educational Measurements*	Independent educational research institute
South Africa	Sarah Howie, Elsie Venter *Centre for Evaluation and Assessment, University of Pretoria*	University department

The Impact of PIRLS project maintains that improvements to one's own education system are likely to be more effective if they are informed by comparison of and reflection on developments in other countries. To allow this comparison, we provided the authors with an analytical framework for structuring their reports. We asked them to provide the following:

1. A short description of their country and its characteristics;
2. An outline of the structure and nature of their national education system;
3. An indication of their country's experience with national and international large-scale surveys;
4. A summation of their national results for PIRLS 2001 and/or 2006 and a report of the current and the anticipated long-term impact of those results on the education system and on students' reading literacy achievement; and
5. An account of expected future activities, including research.

The first three sections provide readers with contextual information necessary for understanding and interpreting the content of the two remaining sections. These two sections form the heart of each chapter because they cover the PIRLS findings and their reporting, reactions to those findings from different interest groups and policymakers, and the impact of the findings in relation to dissemination, educational governance, and the functioning and work of schools. Readers will note that the emphasis the authors give to each of these sections varies across the chapters. Despite this variation, we consider that the analytical framework is sufficiently robust to enable cross-country comparison of the content in each chapter.

That said, researchers conducting large-scale assessments rarely claim to comprehensively capture the nature of education systems on the basis of methodological research criteria derived to benefit an empirical examination. This claim and approach are, however, fundamental to the comparative tradition in educational research, wherein experts perform in-depth descriptions and comparisons of different education systems (Schwippert & Goy, 2008). Because the Impact of PIRLS project extends the significance of international surveys from mere descriptions of achievement outcomes toward an analysis of historical, societal, and cultural aspects, and because it also endeavors to place PIRLS and its impact within broader national contexts, it embraces both traditions of educational research. The project furthermore has the advantage of highlighting the limited value of viewing the impact of large-scale assessments solely from the perspective of cross-national league tables. Greater understanding about the contexts and conditions that give rise, across countries, to patterns of educational achievement comes from the type of comparative discussion that consideration of the chapters of this book permit.

However enriching it may be to follow and assess the developments of other countries in regard to one's own educational transformation processes, we agree with Fuchs (2005) that borrowing ideas and practices from other education systems when seeking to develop one's own is rarely fruitful. As we have already noted, countries vary markedly in the nature of their political, financial, control, and governmental systems, making it illusory to expect a "one size fits all" response to the educational demands of the different countries (Smith, 2002).

1.5   Structure of the Book

Chapter 2, which follows this introductory chapter, is primarily directed at readers unfamiliar with PIRLS. In it, the authors outline the design and major findings of the two PIRLS cycles, as well as developments in reading achievement evident across the participating countries during the years between the two iterations. The country reports (Chapters 3 to 14) are ordered alphabetically by country name. Chapter 15 presents a summary and discussion of the information contained in the 12 country reports. The last chapter (16) offers a brief reflection on the anticipated and tangible implications that the findings presented in this publication have for policymaking, pedagogy, and research relating to children's literacy achievement.

Readers interested in further reading or background information will find a bibliography of international PIRLS literature toward the end of the book. The final section of the book provides information on the authors of the country reports.

We wish to conclude this chapter by acknowledging the work of the authors who contributed to the book. It is their continuous commitment that makes the Impact of PIRLS project a reality and the publications arising out of it possible. We would also like to thank Paula Wagemaker for proofreading this book with great care, and Juliane Pfeiffer for skillfully assisting us with the layout.

References

Arbeitsgruppe Bildungsforschung/Bildungsplanung. (2007). *Nutzung großflächiger Tests für die Schulentwicklung. Erfahrungen aus England, Frankreich und den Niederlanden* [Application of large-scale assessments for school development: Experiences from England, France and the Netherlands]. Bonn, Germany: Bundesministerium für Bildung und Forschung (BMBF). (Bildungsforschung; Bd. 3).

Arnold, K.-H. (1999). Faire Beurteilung im Schulsystem: Möglichkeiten und Grenzen der Schulleistungsbeurteilung auch am Beispiel PISA [Fair assessments in the school system: Possibilities and limits of the evaluation of educational achievement, using PISA as an example]. *Pädagogische Woche der GEW, 55,* 1–21.

Bos, W., Hornberg, S., Arnold, K.-H., Faust, G., Fried, L., Lankes, E.-M., Schwippert, K., & Valtin, R. (Eds.). (2007). *IGLU 2006: Lesekompetenzen von Grundschulkindern in Deutschland im internationalen Vergleich* [IGLU 2006: Reading competencies of primary students in Germany in an international comparison]. Münster, Germany: Waxmann.

Bos, W., & Schwippert, K. (2003). The use and abuse of international comparative research on student achievement. *European Educational Research Journal*, *2*(4), 559–573.

Brügelmann, H., & Heymann, H. W. (2002). PISA: Befunde, Deutungen, Folgerungen [PISA: Results, interpretations, conclusions]. *Pädagogik*, *54*(3), 40–43.

Fuchs, H.-W. (2005). Leistungsmessungen und Innovationsstrategien in Schulsystemen: Zur Einleitung in den Band [Assessments of achievement and innovation strategies in educational systems: An introduction to the book]. In H. Döbert & H.-W. Fuchs (Eds.), *Leistungsmessungen und Innovationsstrategien in Schulsystemen. Ein internationaler Vergleich* [Assessments of achievement and innovation strategies in education systems: An international comparison] (pp. 9–14). Münster, Germany: Waxmann.

Kennedy, A. M., Mullis, I. V. S., Martin, M. O., & Trong, K. L. (Eds.). (2007). *PIRLS 2006 encyclopedia: A guide to reading education in the forty PIRLS 2006 countries*. Chestnut Hill, MA: Boston College.

Mullis, I. V. S., Martin, M. O., Kennedy, A. M., & Foy, P. (2007). *PIRLS 2006 international report: IEA's Progress in International Reading Literacy Study in primary schools in 40 countries*. Chestnut Hill, MA: TIMSS & PIRLS International Study Center, Lynch School of Education, Boston College.

Porter, A. C., & Gamoran, A. (2002). Progress and challenges for large-scale studies. In A. C. Porter & A. Gamoran (Eds.), *Methodological advances in cross-national surveys of educational achievement* (pp. 3–23). Washington, DC: National Academy Press.

Schwippert, K. (Ed.). (2007). *Progress in reading literacy: The impact of PIRLS 2001 in 13 countries* (Studies in International Comparative and Multicultural Education). Münster, Germany: Waxmann.

Schwippert, K., & Goy, M. (2008). Leistungsvergleichs- und Schulqualitätsforschung [Research on achievement assessment and school improvement]. In W. Helsper & J. Böhme (Eds.), *Handbuch der Schulforschung* [Handbook of research on schools] (pp. 387–421). Wiesbaden, Germany: Verlag für Sozialwissenschaften.

Smith, M. S. (2002). Drawing inferences for national policy from large-scale cross-national education surveys. In N. R. Council (Ed.), *Methodological advances in cross-national surveys of educational achievement* (pp. 295–318). Washington DC: National Academy Press.

Wagemaker, H. (2001). Preface. In J. R. Campbell (Ed.), *Framework and specifications for PIRLS assessment* (pp. v–vii). Chestnut Hill, MA: Boston College.

Chapter 2
PIRLS 2006 in Brief

Martin Goy, Irmela Tarelli, and Wilfried Bos

2.1   Introduction

This chapter provides an overview of the design and several of the main results of the PIRLS 2006 assessment of reading literacy. Our intention, in this chapter, is to give readers unfamiliar with the PIRLS 2006 assessment some background information sufficient to aid their interpretation of the detailed information contained in the 12 national reports included in this book. In the following sections, we briefly describe the theoretical framework used in PIRLS to assess reading literacy, give an account of the population tested in PIRLS, and overview the assessment procedures and central assessment results.

We emphasize that this brief introduction to PIRLS 2006 and its results is relatively general. Our presentation is based on two central PIRLS 2006 publications, the *PIRLS 2006 Assessment Framework and Specifications* (Mullis, Kennedy, Martin, & Sainsbury, 2006) and the *PIRLS 2006 International Report* (Mullis, Martin, Kennedy, & Foy, 2007), which together provide a comprehensive account of the PIRLS assessment. In addition to introducing PIRLS 2006, we cover some aspects of the PIRLS 2001 assessment in order to allow comparisons of the results of both surveys. Readers seeking in-depth information on the 2001 cycle of the PIRLS assessment will find it in the *Framework and Specifications for PIRLS 2001 Assessment* (Campbell, Kelly, Mullis, Martin, & Sainsbury, 2001) and the *PIRLS 2001 International Report* (Mullis, Martin, Gonzalez, & Kennedy, 2003).

We begin this chapter by introducing the theoretical framework that forms the foundation of the PIRLS reading tests. We then describe the PIRLS 2006 target population, provide some additional information on the countries participating in this assessment, and introduce the core findings from PIRLS 2006. We pay particular attention to differences in the distribution of the results for reading ability found between and within the participating countries and regions, which include Belgium, with its two education systems, and Canada, with its five provincial education systems. The differences between the countries are presented with regard to the different subscales of reading comprehension distinguished in PIRLS 2006.

As the *PIRLS 2006 Assessment Framework* details, purposes for reading and processes of comprehension are the foundation of the PIRLS 2006 assessment of reading comprehension (see Section 2.2.2 below). However, in this chapter, we present the results on the subscale of purposes for reading only, as these are the results reported in detail in the national reports contained in this volume. The full set of PIRLS 2006 results relating to comprehension can be found in the *PIRLS 2006 International Report*.

We also present in this chapter the PIRLS 2006 results for a number of factors relevant to discussion on the impact of PIRLS: student gender, immigrant background, and sociocultural and socioeconomic background. Our particular purpose in this regard is that of comparing the results of the two PIRLS surveys in order to provide an initial tentative account of changes in Grade 4 students' reading literacy over time.

2.2   Assessing Reading Literacy in PIRLS 2006

2.2.1   Definition, Relevance, and Dimensions of Reading Literacy

Reading is a fundamental cultural technique that enables students to become competent and successful members of society. Within this sociocultural view, reading refers not only to the ability to decode words but also to the ability to reflect on what is read and to use the understanding gained from that reflection as a tool for attaining individual and societal goals. Accordingly, IEA chose, in their 1991 study of reading achievement, to join the terms *reading* and *literacy* to convey a broad sociocultural notion of reading ability (Mullis et al., 2006). With explicit reference to the reading experience of young children, IEA defines reading literacy as

> ... the ability to understand and use those written language forms required by society and/or valued by the individual. Young readers can construct meaning from a variety of texts. They read to learn, to participate in communities of readers, and for enjoyment. (Mullis et al., 2006, p. 3)

For young readers, acquiring reading literacy, as defined here, is essential to their success in education, and in life in general. Children in their fourth year of formal schooling (i.e., typically 9- to 10-year-olds) are the target population of PIRLS. Most students of this age are at a point in their reading development where they have stopped learning to read and have begun reading to learn. Students who fail to achieve to learn to read—let alone read to learn—experience considerable difficulty coping with the demands of school and society. Only by reading to learn can children become autonomous learners and thereby sustain their participation in a global society that increasingly requires people to engage in lifelong learning.

This view of reading literacy is based on theories that regard reading as a constructive and interactive process. According to this view, readers actively construct meaning from text, employing reading strategies to do so and reflecting on what they read. Literate readers, in this sense, are those who hold positive attitudes toward reading and who read for information as well as for recreation. When endeavoring to acquire knowledge about the world and themselves, literate readers use a range of different types of text, from traditional written books to electronic texts presented on the internet (Mullis et al., 2006).

2.2.2 The Components of the Theoretical Framework

With these considerations in mind, the research team responsible for PIRLS 2006, like the team responsible for PIRLS 2001, designed the study to assess three core aspects of reading literacy (Mullis et al., 2006, p. 4):

1. Processes of comprehension
2. Purposes of reading
3. Students' reading behaviors and attitudes.

The team used tests to assess the first two aspects and administered a student background questionnaire to obtain the third set of information.

Figure 2.1 illustrates the theoretical framework within which the test of reading ability was developed. This figure shows that the PIRLS 2006 reading literacy test rested on two purposes of reading and four processes of comprehension. *Purposes of reading* relate to the two types of reading that students of the age group assessed in PIRLS most commonly engage in across classroom, school, and home contexts. These are (1) reading for literary experience, and (2) reading to acquire and use information. In the test, narrative fiction was used to assess the former while various informational texts were used to assess the latter. *Processes of comprehension* concern how readers construct meaning from a text. Text comprehension involves cognitive processes wherein readers focus on and retrieve specific explicit information, make inferences, interpret and integrate ideas and information, and examine and evaluate content, language, and textual elements (Mullis et al., 2006, pp. 11 ff.).

Under this schema, the German PIRLS group and the TIMSS and PIRLS international study center for PIRLS 2001 conceived reading comprehension as a skill requiring two main abilities: (1) the ability to use text-based information, and (2) the ability to draw upon general or external knowledge (Bos et al., 2003; Bos, Valtin, Voss, Hornberg, & Lankes, 2007; Mullis et al., 2007). The former relies not only on extracting information from the text but also on identifying relationships between the parts and passages of the text. The latter requires ability to reflect on the content and the structure of the text. Each of these abilities, in turn, relates directly to the processes of comprehension (see Figure 2.2). In similar vein, members of the PIRLS international study center distinguished separate scales for the two main processes of comprehension: a scale for retrieval and straightforward inferencing for the two less complex reading processes, and a scale for interpreting, integrating, and evaluating for the two more complex processes (Mullis, Martin, & Gonzalez, 2004; Mullis et al., 2007).

Figure 2.1:   The PIRLS 2006 assessment—reading purposes and processes

Purposes of Reading

Process of Comprehension	Literacy experience	Acquire and use information
Focus on and retrieve explicitly stated information		
Make straightforward inferences		
Interpret and integrate ideas and information		
Examine and evaluate content, language, and textual elements		

Source: Campbell et al. (2001, p. 4). See also Mullis et al. (2006, p. 5).

2.2.3   Testing Reading Achievement

The tests of reading achievement administered in PIRLS 2006 were designed to determine the achievement levels of the tested students and to distinguish relative strengths and weaknesses within the whole population tested and between different subpopulations. The design of the assessment had to take conflicting stipulations into account. The first stipulation was that the tests should be administered on one single school day and not be of a length that would subject fourth-grade students to long testing periods. The second was that the tests should allow for a thorough assessment of the different purposes and processes of reading comprehension.

In order to meet both these demands and provide a comprehensive picture of the reading achievement of fourth-grade students in the participating countries, PIRLS 2006 employed a matrix sampling technique, which meant that although each student would have to work on two reading passages only, the reading achievement of the population tested could still be precisely estimated. Kennedy and Sainsbury (2007) provide further information on the matrix sampling and the time allocated for the reading tests.

The reading tests consisted of both multiple-choice and constructed-response items. For details on item development and scoring procedures, see Kennedy and

Sainsbury (2007). The PIRLS 2006 assessment data were scaled using three distinct item response theory (IRT) models, which were chosen according to item type and scoring procedure. Further details on the test construction and the three IRT models distinguished appear in Foy, Galia, and Li (2007).

Figure 2.2: Reading comprehension abilities assessed in PIRLS and their relationship to the purposes and processes of reading

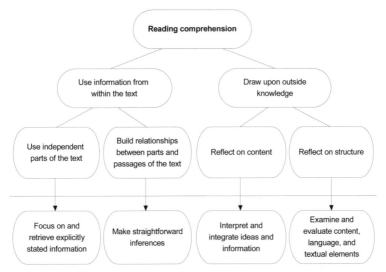

Source: Adapted from Bos, Valtin, Voss, Hornberg, and Lankes (2007, p. 85) and Bos et al. (2003, p. 79). The depicted model was proposed by the German PIRLS group and based on the theoretical framework of reading comprehension assessment used in PIRLS 2001 and 2006.

2.3 The PIRLS 2006 Target Population

The formal definition of the target population of PIRLS 2006 drew on UNESCO's International Standard Classification of Education (ISCED) in order to identify the appropriate target grade. In line with this classification, the target population was defined as:

> ... all students enrolled in the grade that represents four years of schooling, counting from the first year of ISCED Level 1, providing the mean age at the time of testing is at least 9.5 years. (Joncas, 2007, p. 36)

The target grade was thus Grade 4, or its national equivalent, in most of the countries participating in PIRLS. However, because the age of formal school entry and the age at which schools introduce children to formal reading are not the same in all these countries, the selected grade and the average age of the students assessed in PIRLS varied slightly across them.

Table 2.1 shows, for each participating country, the name of the selected grade and the number of years of formal schooling in the schools attended by the tested students. The table also shows the mean age of the tested students in each country. For more detailed information on the school system of each country participating in PIRLS, readers should refer to the *PIRLS 2006 Encyclopedia*, edited by Kennedy, Mullis, Martin, and Trong (2007).

2.4   PIRLS 2006 International Findings

The information presented in this section relates to students' achievement, across the PIRLS 2006 participating countries, in the different reading literacy domains. In the figures in this section (i.e., Figures 2.3 to 2.10), the countries' average scores on the different scales are shown on the achievement distribution graph and listed in the table portion of each figure. Because PIRLS involved a sample design, inferences about the tested population within the countries involve some degree of uncertainty.

Significant differences in performance across the countries can be discerned by comparing the extent to which the confidence intervals overlap. If the confidence intervals of two countries overlap, we can assume that no significant difference was observed. If the confidence intervals do not overlap, we can interpret the observed mean achievement of both countries as significantly different. The *PIRLS 2006 Technical Report* (Martin, Mullis, & Kennedy, 2007) provides details on the calculations of differences and also addresses the issue of adjustments for multiple comparisons such as the Bonferroni procedure. In order to take the clustered sampling design into account, the jackknife repeated replication technique was used to estimate all standard errors reported in Figures 2.3 to 2.10 (for details, see Kennedy & Trong, 2007).

2.4.1   Results for the Combined Literacy Scale

2.4.1.1 Results for PIRLS 2006

Figure 2.3 displays the overall achievement on the combined literacy scale of the students who participated in the PIRLS 2006 reading assessment. In the figure, the participating countries appear in descending order of average reading achievement scores. In PIRLS 2001, the scale was set to have a mean of 500 and a standard deviation of 100, and it was designed to remain constant from assessment to assessment (Mullis et al., 2007, p. 36). This feature meant the international average for PIRLS 2006 of 506 points was slightly above the international average for PIRLS 2001 when measured on the same scale. However, we again caution the need, when interpreting results such as these, to remember that the two sets of countries participating in PIRLS 2001 and 2006 differed (see Chapter 1 of this book).

Table 2.1:   Information about students tested in PIRLS 2006 countries

Country	Country's name for grade level tested	Policy on school entry age	Mean age of students tested
Austria	Grade 4	6	10.3
Belgium (Flemish)	Grade 4	6	10.0
Belgium (French)	Grade 4	6	9.9
Bulgaria	Grade 4	7	10.9
Canada, *Alberta*	Grade 4	6	9.9
Canada, *British Columbia*	Grade 4	5	9.8
Canada, *Nova Scotia*	Grade 4	5	10.0
Canada, *Ontario*	Grade 4	6	9.8
Canada, *Québec*	Second year of elementary cycle 2	6	10.1
Chinese Taipei	Grade 4	6	10.1
Denmark	Grade 4 or 4th form	7	10.9
England	Year 5 (Y5)	5	10.3
France	CM1 = mean course 1st year or 2nd year of the 3rd cycle (Deepening cycle)	6	10.0
Georgia	Grade 4	6.5	10.1
Germany	Grade 4	6	10.5
Hong Kong SAR	Primary 4	6	10.0
Hungary	Grade 4	Between 6 and 8	10.7
Iceland	Grade 4	6	9.8
Indonesia	Grade 4	7	10.4
Iran, Islamic Rep. of	Grade 4	6	10.2
Israel	Grade 4	6	10.1
Italy	Primary school—4th class	5	9.7
Kuwait	Grade 4	6	9.8
Latvia	Grade 4	7	11.0
Lithuania	Grade 4	6	10.7
Luxembourg	5th year of primary studies	6	11.4
Macedonia, Rep. of	Grade 4	Between 6 and 7	10.6
Moldova, Rep. of	Grade 4	6	10.9
Morocco	–	–	10.8
Netherlands	Group 6	6	10.3
New Zealand	Year 5	6	10.0
Norway	Grade 4	6	9.8
Poland	Grade 3 of primary school	6	9.9
Qatar	Grade 4	6	9.8
Romania	Grade 4	7	10.9
Russian Federation	Grade 4	Between 6.5 and 7	10.8
Scotland	Primary 5 / P5	5	9.9
Singapore	Primary 4	6	10.4
Slovak Republic	Grade 4	6	10.4
Slovenia	Grade 4 of 9-year elementary school; Grade 3 of 8-year elementary school	6 for 9-year elementary school; 7 for 8-year elementary school	9.9
South Africa	Grade 5	Year students turn 7	11.9
Spain	Grade 4	6	9.9
Sweden	Grade 4	7	10.9
Trinidad and Tobago	Standard 3 (3)	5	10.1
United States	Grade 4	Varies by state; typically 6	10.1

Notes:
1 The highlighted countries are those participating in the Impact of PIRLS 2006 project.
Data were provided by PIRLS national research coordinators. A dash (–) indicates data are not available.
Source: Mullis et al. (2007, pp. 30–31)

Figure 2.3:   Distribution of average combined reading literacy scale scores of students tested in PIRLS 2006, by percentiles, by country

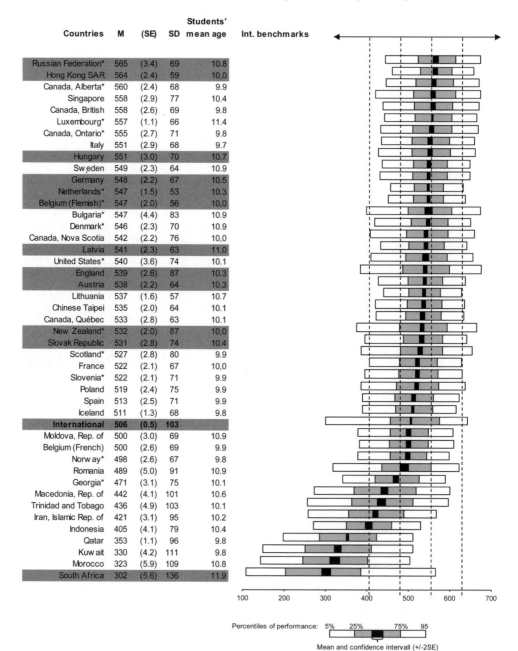

Countries	M	(SE)	SD	Students' mean age	Int. benchmarks
Russian Federation*	565	(3.4)	69	10.8	
Hong Kong SAR	564	(2.4)	59	10,0	
Canada, Alberta*	560	(2.4)	68	9.9	
Singapore	558	(2.9)	77	10.4	
Canada, British	558	(2.6)	69	9.8	
Luxembourg*	557	(1.1)	66	11.4	
Canada, Ontario*	555	(2.7)	71	9.8	
Italy	551	(2.9)	68	9.7	
Hungary	551	(3.0)	70	10.7	
Sweden	549	(2.3)	64	10.9	
Germany	548	(2.2)	67	10.5	
Netherlands*	547	(1.5)	53	10.3	
Belgium (Flemish)*	547	(2.0)	56	10,0	
Bulgaria*	547	(4.4)	83	10.9	
Denmark*	546	(2.3)	70	10.9	
Canada, Nova Scotia	542	(2.2)	76	10,0	
Latvia	541	(2.3)	63	11,0	
United States*	540	(3.6)	74	10.1	
England	539	(2.6)	87	10.3	
Austria	538	(2.2)	64	10.3	
Lithuania	537	(1.6)	57	10.7	
Chinese Taipei	535	(2.0)	64	10.1	
Canada, Québec	533	(2.8)	63	10.1	
New Zealand*	532	(2.0)	87	10,0	
Slovak Republic	531	(2.8)	74	10.4	
Scotland*	527	(2.8)	80	9.9	
France	522	(2.1)	67	10,0	
Slovenia*	522	(2.1)	71	9.9	
Poland	519	(2.4)	75	9.9	
Spain	513	(2.5)	71	9.9	
Iceland	511	(1.3)	68	9.8	
International	506	(0.5)	103		
Moldova, Rep. of	500	(3.0)	69	10.9	
Belgium (French)	500	(2.6)	69	9.9	
Norway*	498	(2.6)	67	9.8	
Romania	489	(5.0)	91	10.9	
Georgia*	471	(3.1)	75	10.1	
Macedonia, Rep. of	442	(4.1)	101	10.6	
Trinidad and Tobago	436	(4.9)	103	10.1	
Iran, Islamic Rep. of	421	(3.1)	95	10.2	
Indonesia	405	(4.1)	79	10.4	
Qatar	353	(1.1)	96	9.8	
Kuwait	330	(4.2)	111	9.8	
Morocco	323	(5.9)	109	10.8	
South Africa	302	(5.6)	136	11.9	

Percentiles of performance: 5%   25%   75%   95

Mean and confidence interval (+/-2SE)

Notes:
* Specific accounts of these countries' samples appear in Martin et al. (2007).
Countries participating in the Impact of PIRLS 2006 project are highlighted.
Israel was not included because the overall student exclusion rate exceeded 20 percent. For further details, see Mullis et al. (2007, p. 292).
Source: Adapted from Valtin, Bos, Buddeberg, Goy, and Potthoff (2008, p. 60).

When considering the descriptions of differences across countries, note that the mean age cited for the national samples varies. This consideration is important because ability to read is positively related to the age of students and to the number of instructional years. These correlations between age, instruction time, and reading achievement can—but do not necessarily have to be—substantial; their sizes depend on the group of PIRLS countries chosen for comparison. This confounding factor is not a problem as long as it is taken into account when interpreting national achievement scores in an international comparison. Therefore, Figure 2.3 (see previous page) includes not only the mean achievement scores and measures of their dispersion, but also the mean age of the students per country. The rather complex relationship between age-within-grade configurations and reading achievement across countries in PIRLS 2006 is illuminated in a recent article by Mullis, Martin, and Foy (2011).

As is evident in Figure 2.3, the highest-performing country was the Russian Federation, followed by Hong Kong SAR and Canada (Alberta). Belgium (Flemish), Bulgaria, the Canadian provinces of British Columbia and Ontario, Denmark, Hungary, Italy, Germany, Luxembourg (the grade tested was 5), the Netherlands, Singapore, and Sweden outperformed the majority of other countries. In total, 31 countries achieved above the international average. The achievement of students in the following countries was clearly below the international average: Indonesia, Iran, Kuwait, Macedonia, Morocco, Trinidad and Tobago, South Africa, and Qatar.

We can also see in Figure 2.3 that the achievement scores for the countries participating in the Impact of PIRLS 2006 project varied greatly. This variation was also evident in the Impact of PIRLS 2001 project, but the authors of the corresponding publication considered it to be a beneficial aspect because it allowed readers, through reference to the different national reports, to identify contexts that aligned with their respective individual, national, and/or international perspectives, tasks, and settings (Schwippert & Goy, 2007). We anticipate that this variation will hold the same advantage for readers of this current publication.

2.4.1.2 PIRLS 2006 and 2001 Compared

PIRLS is designed to provide reliable measurement of trends in reading comprehension over time. In PIRLS 2006, a number of passages and questions from PIRLS 2001 were included in the assessment in addition to newly developed passages and items. Through a transformation of the 2006 proficiency scores to the metric used in 2001, the achievement scores for both study cycles can be directly compared (for further information on the procedures see Foy, Galia & Li, 2007). Countries which participated in both PIRLS 2001 and PIRLS 2006 were required to use the same target grade for PIRLS 2006 that was used in 2001. For an overview of the realized target populations, see the respective table in Mullis, Martin, Kennedy, and Foy (2007, p. 296).

Figure 2.4 displays the achievement scores on the combined reading scale for the 28 countries that participated in both PIRLS 2001 and PIRLS 2006. The table portion of the figure lists the difference in scores across the two time periods. In those cases where the difference is statistically significant, the bars are grey. This mode of shading marks significant differences in the remaining figures in this chapter.

For 13 of the participating countries, the overall reading achievement score was higher in 2006 than in 2001. In nine of these countries, the difference was significant. The increase for Hong Kong SAR, the Russian Federation, and Singapore—which were among the highest-performing countries in 2006—was 30 scale points or more. Other participants with considerable gains in achievement scores (eight points or more) were Hungary, Italy, Germany, Moldova, the Slovak Republic, and Slovenia.

According to Mullis et al. (2007), the increase in achievement in the Russian Federation and Slovenia can be interpreted as the result of the major reforms that these countries made to the primary level of their education systems after 2001. The authors of the Hong Kong SAR and Singapore chapters respectively attribute the achievement increase in the former country to the process of curriculum reform that the country implemented in 2000 and in the latter to the implementation in 2001 of a revised primary school syllabus.

In seven of the countries depicted in Figure 2.4, student achievement on the combined reading scale dropped substantially and significantly between the 2001 and 2006 iterations of PIRLS. These countries were England, Kuwait, Morocco, Romania, Sweden, the Canadian province of Québec, and the Netherlands.

2.4.2   Results for the Reading Purposes Subscales

The reading literacy purposes in PIRLS 2006 were grouped in two scales reflecting the typical purposes for reading that students are engaging in by the end of Grade 4 (see Section 2.2.2 of this chapter): reading for literary experience and reading to acquire and use information. The PIRLS 2006 assessment contained five literary texts and five informational texts; the comprehension processes described above were assessed within each purpose (Mullis et al., 2007). As Mullis et al. (2007, p. 50) point out, the two numerical scale scores cannot be directly compared, as they represent different constructs. In addition, the assessments were slightly different in terms of difficulty. In order to allow comparing the relative performance of each of the PIRLS 2006 participants for each purpose, the international average for each purpose for reading was scaled to be 500, which made it possible to compare relative strengths and weaknesses of countries by examining their relative positions on the two scales. In the following, we report the relative differences between the two scales.

Figure 2.4: Comparison of students' average reading achievement scores on the combined reading scale for PIRLS 2001 and PIRLS 2006, by country

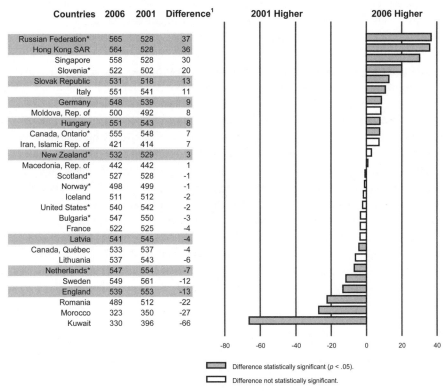

Countries	2006	2001	Difference[1]
Russian Federation*	565	528	37
Hong Kong SAR	564	528	36
Singapore	558	528	30
Slovenia*	522	502	20
Slovak Republic	531	518	13
Italy	551	541	11
Germany	548	539	9
Moldova, Rep. of	500	492	8
Hungary	551	543	8
Canada, Ontario*	555	548	7
Iran, Islamic Rep. of	421	414	7
New Zealand*	532	529	3
Macedonia, Rep. of	442	442	1
Scotland*	527	528	-1
Norway*	498	499	-1
Iceland	511	512	-2
United States*	540	542	-2
Bulgaria*	547	550	-3
France	522	525	-4
Latvia	541	545	-4
Canada, Québec	533	537	-4
Lithuania	537	543	-6
Netherlands*	547	554	-7
Sweden	549	561	-12
England	539	553	-13
Romania	489	512	-22
Morocco	323	350	-27
Kuwait	330	396	-66

Difference statistically significant ($p < .05$).

Difference not statistically significant.

Notes:
1 Inconsistencies in the reported differences are due to rounding errors.
* Specific accounts of these countries' samples appear in Martin et al. (2007).
Countries participating in the Impact of PIRLS 2006 project are highlighted.
Israel is not included because the country's overall student exclusion rate exceeded 20 percent. For further details, see Mullis et al. (2007, p. 292).
Source: Adapted from Bos, Valtin, Hornberg et al. (2007, p. 141).

Figure 2.5 presents the results of the comparison between the two purposes. It shows the mean scores for both subscales as well as the differences in students' achievement between the two reading purposes. The average achievement of students in 18 of the PIRLS participating countries was significantly higher on the reading for literary purposes subscale than on the reading for informational purposes subscale. For countries participating in the Impact of PIRLS 2006 project, this pattern was evident for Germany, Hungary, and the Slovak Republic. Students in 16 countries scored significantly higher on the reading for information subscale. These countries included the following Impact of PIRLS 2006 participants: Belgium (Flemish), Hong Kong SAR, New Zealand, the Russian Federation, and South Africa.

Figure 2.6 presents the comparison of participants' performance in PIRLS 2001 and PIRLS 2006 for the informational reading scale. Countries where students gained significantly higher achievement scores on the informational purposes scale were Canada (Ontario), Germany, Hong Kong SAR, Italy, New Zealand, the Russian Federation, Singapore, and Slovenia. Significantly lower performances were observed in England, France, Kuwait, Latvia, Lithuania, Romania, and Sweden.

Figure 2.7 presents the changes in average achievement in reading for literary purposes. Among those countries that showed significantly higher achievement scores for literary purposes in PIRLS 2006 were these Impact of PIRLS 2006 participants: Germany, Hong Kong SAR, Hungary, the Russian Federation, and the Slovak Republic. Significantly lower performance was evident in the Netherlands.

Figure 2.5: Relative difference in students' achievement between reading for literary and reading for informational purposes in PIRLS 2006, by country

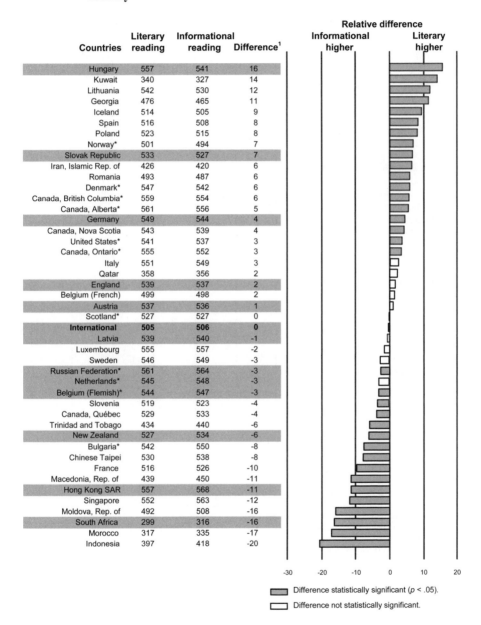

Countries	Literary reading	Informational reading	Difference[1]
Hungary	557	541	16
Kuwait	340	327	14
Lithuania	542	530	12
Georgia	476	465	11
Iceland	514	505	9
Spain	516	508	8
Poland	523	515	8
Norway*	501	494	7
Slovak Republic	533	527	7
Iran, Islamic Rep. of	426	420	6
Romania	493	487	6
Denmark*	547	542	6
Canada, British Columbia*	559	554	6
Canada, Alberta*	561	556	5
Germany	549	544	4
Canada, Nova Scotia	543	539	4
United States*	541	537	3
Canada, Ontario*	555	552	3
Italy	551	549	3
Qatar	358	356	2
England	539	537	2
Belgium (French)	499	498	2
Austria	537	536	1
Scotland*	527	527	0
International	505	506	0
Latvia	539	540	-1
Luxembourg	555	557	-2
Sweden	546	549	-3
Russian Federation*	561	564	-3
Netherlands*	545	548	-3
Belgium (Flemish)*	544	547	-3
Slovenia	519	523	-4
Canada, Québec	529	533	-4
Trinidad and Tobago	434	440	-6
New Zealand	527	534	-6
Bulgaria*	542	550	-8
Chinese Taipei	530	538	-8
France	516	526	-10
Macedonia, Rep. of	439	450	-11
Hong Kong SAR	557	568	-11
Singapore	552	563	-12
Moldova, Rep. of	492	508	-16
South Africa	299	316	-16
Morocco	317	335	-17
Indonesia	397	418	-20

Difference statistically significant ($p < .05$).

Difference not statistically significant.

Notes:
1 Inconsistencies in the reported differences are due to rounding errors.
*Specific accounts of these countries' samples appear in Martin et al. (2007). Countries participating in the Impact of PIRLS 2006 project are highlighted. Israel is not included because the country's overall student exclusion rate exceeded 20 percent. For further details, see Mullis et al. (2007, p. 292).
Source: Adapted from Valtin, Bos, Buddeberg et al. (2008, p. 72).

Figure 2.6: **Comparison of students' achievement on the PIRLS 2001 and PIRLS 2006 reading for informational purposes subscale, by country**

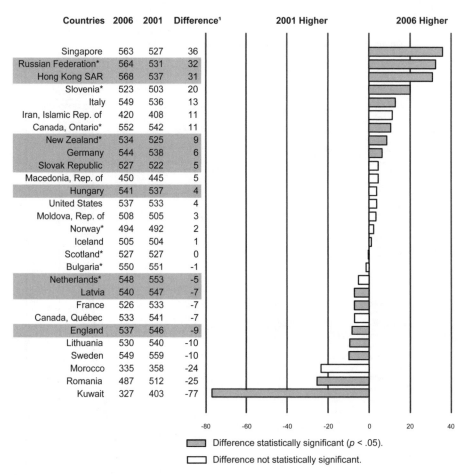

Countries	2006	2001	Difference[1]
Singapore	563	527	36
Russian Federation*	564	531	32
Hong Kong SAR	568	537	31
Slovenia*	523	503	20
Italy	549	536	13
Iran, Islamic Rep. of	420	408	11
Canada, Ontario*	552	542	11
New Zealand*	534	525	9
Germany	544	538	6
Slovak Republic	527	522	5
Macedonia, Rep. of	450	445	5
Hungary	541	537	4
United States	537	533	4
Moldova, Rep. of	508	505	3
Norway*	494	492	2
Iceland	505	504	1
Scotland*	527	527	0
Bulgaria*	550	551	-1
Netherlands*	548	553	-5
Latvia	540	547	-7
France	526	533	-7
Canada, Québec	533	541	-7
England	537	546	-9
Lithuania	530	540	-10
Sweden	549	559	-10
Morocco	335	358	-24
Romania	487	512	-25
Kuwait	327	403	-77

Difference statistically significant ($p < .05$).

Difference not statistically significant.

Notes:
1 Inconsistencies in the reported differences are due to rounding errors.
* Specific accounts of these countries' samples appear in Martin et al. (2007).
Countries participating in the Impact of PIRLS 2006 project are highlighted.
Israel is not included because the country's overall student exclusion rate exceeded 20 percent. For further details, see Mullis et al. (2007, p. 292).
Source: Adapted from Bos, Valtin, Hornberg et al. (2007, p. 145).

Figure 2.7: **Comparison of students' achievement on the PIRLS 2001 and PIRLS 2006 reading for literary purposes subscale, by country**

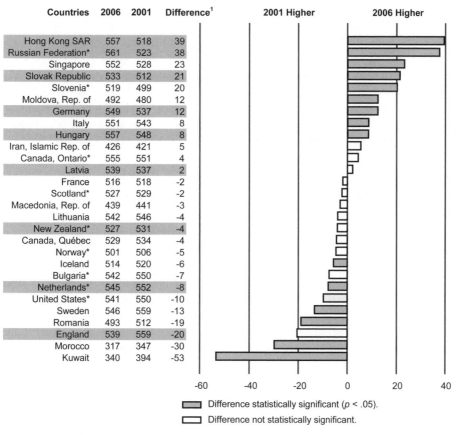

Countries	2006	2001	Difference[1]
Hong Kong SAR	557	518	39
Russian Federation*	561	523	38
Singapore	552	528	23
Slovak Republic	533	512	21
Slovenia*	519	499	20
Moldova, Rep. of	492	480	12
Germany	549	537	12
Italy	551	543	8
Hungary	557	548	8
Iran, Islamic Rep. of	426	421	5
Canada, Ontario*	555	551	4
Latvia	539	537	2
France	516	518	-2
Scotland*	527	529	-2
Macedonia, Rep. of	439	441	-3
Lithuania	542	546	-4
New Zealand*	527	531	-4
Canada, Québec	529	534	-4
Norway*	501	506	-5
Iceland	514	520	-6
Bulgaria*	542	550	-7
Netherlands*	545	552	-8
United States*	541	550	-10
Sweden	546	559	-13
Romania	493	512	-19
England	539	559	-20
Morocco	317	347	-30
Kuwait	340	394	-53

Difference statistically significant ($p < .05$).

Difference not statistically significant.

Notes:
1 Inconsistencies in the reported differences are due to rounding errors.
* Specific accounts of these countries' samples appear in Martin et al. (2007).
Countries participating in the Impact of PIRLS 2006 project are highlighted.
Israel is not included because the country's overall student exclusion rate exceeded 20 percent. For further details, see Mullis et al. (2007, p. 292).
Source: Adapted from Bos, Valtin, Hornberg et al. (2007, p. 144).

2.4.3 Results for Students' Reading Attitudes and Behaviors

The concept of reading literacy used in PIRLS takes into account not only the processes of comprehension and purposes for reading, which are at the core of the PIRLS assessment, but also students' attitudes toward reading and their actual reading behavior, both in and out of school. Researchers have identified that a positive self-concept with respect to reading ability and high reading motivation are closely related to reading achievement: "Students who enjoy reading and who perceive themselves to be good readers usually read more frequently and more widely, which in turn broadens their reading experience and improves their comprehension skills" (Mullis et al., 2007, p. 139).

The PIRLS background questionnaires contain several questions addressing these aspects. In both 2001 and 2006, students were asked to report on their individual attitudes toward reading, their perception of their own reading abilities, their engagement in reading-literacy activities outside of school, how much they personally enjoyed reading, and the time they spent reading for fun. As in PIRLS 2001, two indices were used in the *PIRLS 2006 International Report* to allow for an international comparison of these various aspects. The indices were (1) students' attitudes toward reading (SATR), and (2) students' reading self-concept (SRSC) (Mullis et al., 2007).

2.4.3.1   Attitudes toward Reading

In general, the PIRLS Grade 4 students showed positive attitudes toward reading in both the 2001 and 2006 assessments. Within each country, this positivity is usually closely aligned with students' average reading achievement scores. Comparison of PIRLS 2001 and PIRLS 2006 revealed significantly higher scores in 2006 than in 2001 on the index of attitudes toward reading for only four countries: Germany, Hong Kong SAR, Iran, and Italy (Mullis et al., 2007, p. 141). A comparatively high percentage of students (15% or more) positioned within the low index in PIRLS 2006 was found for Belgium (Flemish) (16%), England (15%), Luxembourg (15%), and the Netherlands (16%). For 10 of the 2006 participants, the percentage of students at the high level of the attitudes index turned out to be significantly lower than the 2001 percentage. Among these countries were England (with a difference of four scale points), the Netherlands (five scale points), and Sweden (nine scale points). All three were countries that showed a high performance on the combined literacy scale in the 2001 assessment.

2.4.3.2   Reading Self-Concept

On average, internationally, half of the students (49%) who participated in PIRLS 2006 scored at the high end of the self-concept scale. The scores of 48 percent of the students placed them at the mid level of the scale. Only three percent were at the low end of this index. In the group of countries participating in the Impact of PIRLS 2006 project, Austria and the Netherlands had the largest percentages of students within the high level of the self-concept index.

As was the case in 2001, there was a close relationship in the 2006 PIRLS data between self-concept and reading achievement. Students with a high level of reading self-concept had an average reading achievement score that was 50 points higher than the average achievement score of students whose reading self-concept placed them at the mid level of the self-concept index. The average achievement of this second group of students, in turn, was more than 40 points higher than the average achievement of students at the low level of the index (Mullis et al., 2007). For all countries, however, the number of students in the lowest group on the reading self-concept index was relatively small.

2.4.3.3   Reading Behavior

The reading behavior of students in terms of quantity and frequency can be considered a point of intersection between reading attitudes and reading achievement (Bos, Valtin, Hornberg et al., 2007; Mullis et al., 2007). Internationally, 40 percent of the PIRLS 2006 students reported that they read for fun outside school daily or almost daily (Mullis et al., 2007, p. 155). In contrast, the proportion of students who said they never or almost never read for fun when outside school was 18 percent (Bos, Valtin, Hornberg et al., 2007, p. 137). Of the countries participating in the Impact of PIRLS 2006 project, those in which low numbers of students (under 15%, on average) never read for fun outside school were Germany, Hong Kong SAR, Hungary, the Russian Federation, and the Slovak Republic (Bos, Valtin, Hornberg et al., 2007, p. 137).

Comparison of the results of the two PIRLS assessments pertaining to engagement in reading literacy activities outside school identified five countries where the percentages of students reporting frequent engagement (daily or almost daily) were significantly higher in 2006 than in 2001. These countries were the Canadian province of Ontario, Germany, Hong Kong SAR, Hungary, and Italy (Mullis et al., 2007, p. 155). Across the two time periods, students in six countries were significantly less likely to report frequent engagement in reading for fun in 2006 than in 2001. These countries were Iceland, Latvia, Norway, Singapore, Slovenia, and Sweden.

2.4.4   Reading Achievement of Boys and Girls

In all of the countries that participated in PIRLS 2001, girls' achievement on the combined literacy scale was significantly higher than the achievement of boys. Except for Luxembourg and Spain, a comparable result emerged for the countries that took part in PIRLS 2006 (Mullis et al., 2007, p. 48).

In Figure 2.8, the tabular portion of the figure shows the advantage (in scale score points) that girls in the Impact of PIRLS 2006 countries held over boys in each PIRLS cycle. The first nine countries listed in the figure are the Impact of PIRLS 2006 countries that participated in both the 2001 and 2006 assessments. Data for the three Impact of PIRLS countries that participated in 2006 only—that is, Austria, Belgium (Flemish), and South Africa—appear at the bottom of the figure. (This same mode of presentation is used in Figures 2.9 and 2.10.) As can be observed in Figure 2.8, the advantage was significantly higher for four countries in 2001, namely, Germany, Hong Kong SAR, Hungary, and the Netherlands.

Figure 2.8: **Girls' higher reading achievement scores advantage over boys' achievement in PIRLS 2001 and 2006, by country**

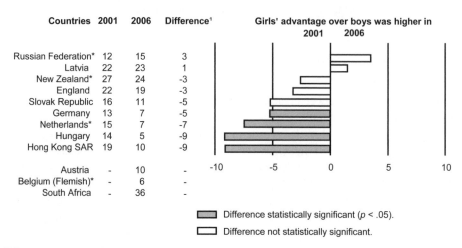

Countries	2001	2006	Difference[1]
Russian Federation*	12	15	3
Latvia	22	23	1
New Zealand*	27	24	-3
England	22	19	-3
Slovak Republic	16	11	-5
Germany	13	7	-5
Netherlands*	15	7	-7
Hungary	14	5	-9
Hong Kong SAR	19	10	-9
Austria	-	10	-
Belgium (Flemish)*	-	6	-
South Africa	-	36	-

▨ Difference statistically significant (*p* < .05).
☐ Difference not statistically significant.

Notes:
1 Inconsistencies in the reported differences are due to rounding errors.
The countries included are those that participated in the Impact of PIRLS 2006 project.
* Specific accounts of these countries' samples appear in Martin et al. (2007).
Source: Adapted from Hornberg, Valtin, Potthoff, Schwippert, and Schulz-Zander (2007, p. 218).

2.4.5 Reading Achievement of Students with/without Immigrant Background

In order to determine whether or not the students participating in PIRLS came from an immigrant background, both the 2001 and 2006 student questionnaires asked students to state which country or countries their parents were born in. Researchers analyzing the PIRLS achievement data took this information into account when endeavoring to explain the dispersion of students' scores on the reading subscales.

Across the countries that participated in PIRLS 2006, 76 percent of the students said their parents were born in the country of current residence (i.e., the country where the students took the PIRLS test), 14 percent said either their mother or father was born outside the country of residence, and 10 percent stated that both parents were born outside the country of residence (Mullis et al., 2007, p. 136). Among the countries participating in the Impact of PIRLS 2006 project, Hungary and the Slovak Republic had the greatest percentage of students without a migration background (i.e., both parents born in the country of residence), while Hong Kong SAR and New Zealand had the highest percentages of students with a migration background. In a majority of participating PIRLS 2006 countries, students with nonimmigrant backgrounds gained higher reading scores than students from migration backgrounds.

The advantage in reading achievement for children whose parents were born in the country of residence over those whose parents were both born abroad was significantly higher in 2006 than in 2001 in six countries, among which were two Impact of PIRLS countries—England and the Slovak Republic; see Figure 2.9. For six countries, of which two were Impact of PIRLS countries (Germany and the Russian Federation), the advantage in favor of students from nonimmigrant backgrounds was significantly higher in 2001.

Figure 2.9: Higher reading achievement scores of students whose parents were both born in the country of residence over students whose parents were both born abroad in PIRLS 2001 and 2006, by country

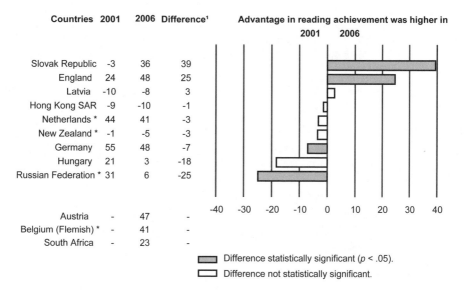

Countries	2001	2006	Difference[1]
Slovak Republic	-3	36	39
England	24	48	25
Latvia	-10	-8	3
Hong Kong SAR	-9	-10	-1
Netherlands *	44	41	-3
New Zealand *	-1	-5	-3
Germany	55	48	-7
Hungary	21	3	-18
Russian Federation *	31	6	-25
Austria	-	47	-
Belgium (Flemish) *	-	41	-
South Africa	-	23	-

Difference statistically significant ($p < .05$).
Difference not statistically significant.

Notes:
1 Inconsistencies in the reported differences are due to rounding errors.
The countries included are those that participated in the PIRLS 2006 project.
* Specific accounts of these countries' samples appear in Martin et al. (2007).
Source: Adapted from Schwippert, Hornberg, Freiberg, and Stubbe (2007, p. 265).

2.4.6 Reading Achievement of Students from Different Sociocultural and Socioeconomic Backgrounds

PIRLS 2006 revealed a close association between the average reading achievement scores of the PIRLS students and the sociocultural and socioeconomic backgrounds of their families. As was the case in a number of other IEA studies, including Reading Literacy, TIMSS, and PIRLS 2001, the PIRLS 2006 research team used number of books in students' homes as an indicator of the status of each student's educational, social, and—to some extent—economic background. Bos et al. (2003), drawing on

PIRLS 2001 data, showed that this indicator is a reliable means of representing these aspects of home background (see also Schwippert & Goy, 2007).

Across the countries participating in the PIRLS assessments, students from families with more than 100 books at home tended to gain higher reading achievement scores than students from families with fewer than 100 books at home (Bos, Schwippert, & Stubbe, 2007, p. 234). In the Slovak Republic and Hungary, the advantage with respect to average reading achievement that students from families with 100-plus books at home held over students from families with fewer than 100 books at home was significantly higher in 2006 than in 2001 (see Figure 2.10).

Figure 2.10: Higher reading achievement scores of students from families with 100-plus books at home over students from families with fewer than 100 books at home in PIRLS 2001 and PIRLS 2006, by country

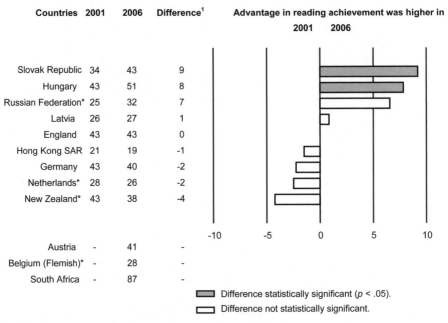

Notes:
1 Inconsistencies in the reported differences are due to rounding errors.
The countries included are those that participated in the Impact of PIRLS 2006 project.
* Specific accounts of these countries' samples appear in Martin et al. (2007).
Source: Adapted from Bos et al. (2007, p. 235).

2.5   Conclusion

In this chapter, we provided a brief overview of PIRLS 2006. The first sections of the chapter were given over to a description of the main aspects of the concept of reading literacy underpinning the PIRLS assessment. The PIRLS 2006 results given in the second part of the chapter were those deemed most useful for providing readers with a frame of reference when interpreting the PIRLS 2006 findings and their impact presented in the national reports that follow this chapter.

We also, in this chapter, summarized differences in student performance between the reading achievement subscales and test cycles of PIRLS and looked at differences in achievement between boys and girls, between students with and without an immigrant background, and between students from different sociocultural and socioeconomic backgrounds. Readers endeavoring to understand and interpret the reading achievement diversity within and across countries described in the following chapters may find it useful to consider this diversity from similar perspectives.

References

Bos, W., Lankes, E.-M., Schwippert, K., Valtin, R., Voss, A., Badel, I., et al. (2003). Lesekompetenzen Deutscher Grundschülerinnen und Grundschüler am Ende der vierten Jahrgangsstufe im internationalen Vergleich [Reading competencies of German primary school students at the end of fourth grade in international comparison]. In W. Bos, E.-M. Lankes, M. Prenzel, K. Schwippert, G. Walther, & R. Valtin (Eds.), *Erste Ergebnisse aus IGLU. Schülerleistungen am Ende der vierten Jahrgangsstufe im internationalen Vergleich* [First results from PIRLS Germany: Students' achievement at the end of fourth grade in international comparison] (pp. 69–142). Münster, Germany: Waxmann.

Bos, W., Schwippert, K., & Stubbe, T. C. (2007). Die Koppelung von sozialer Herkunft und Schülerleistung im internationalen Vergleich [The link between social origin and student achievement in international comparison]. In W. Bos, S. Hornberg, K.-H. Arnold, G. Faust, L. Fried, E.-M. Lankes, K. Schwippert, & R. Valtin (Eds.), *IGLU 2006: Lesekompetenzen von Grundschulkindern in Deutschland im internationalen Vergleich* [PIRLS 2006: Reading competencies of primary school students in Germany in international comparison] (pp. 225–247). Münster, Germany: Waxmann.

Bos, W., Valtin, R., Hornberg, S., Buddeberg, I., Goy, M., & Voss, A. (2007). Internationaler Vergleich 2006: Lesekompetenzen von Schülerinnen und Schülern am Ende der vierten Jahrgangsstufe [International comparison 2006: Students' reading competencies at the end of fourth grade]. In W. Bos, S. Hornberg, K.-H. Arnold, G. Faust, L. Fried, E.-M. Lankes, K. Schwippert, & R. Valtin (Eds.), *IGLU 2006: Lesekompetenzen von Grundschulkindern in Deutschland im internationalen Vergleich* [PIRLS 2006: Reading competencies of primary school students in Germany in international comparison] (pp. 109–160). Münster, Germany: Waxmann.

Bos, W., Valtin, R., Voss, A., Hornberg, S., & Lankes, E.-M. (2007). Konzepte der Lesekompetenz in IGLU 2006 [Concepts of reading competence in PIRLS 2006 in Germany]. In W. Bos, S. Hornberg, K.-H. Arnold, G. Faust, L. Fried, E.-M. Lankes, K. Schwippert, & R. Valtin (Eds.), *IGLU 2006: Lesekompetenzen von*

Grundschulkindern in Deutschland im internationalen Vergleich [PIRLS 2006: Reading competencies of primary school students in Germany in international comparison] (pp. 81–108). Münster, Germany: Waxmann.

Campbell, J. R., Kelly, D. L., Mullis, I. V. S., Martin, M. O., & Sainsbury, M. (2001). *Framework and specifications for PIRLS assessment 2001* (2nd ed.). Chestnut Hill, MA: Boston College.

Foy, P., Galia, J., & Li, I. (2007). Scaling the PIRLS 2006 reading assessment data. In M. O. Martin, I. V. S. Mullis, & A. M. Kennedy (Eds.), *PIRLS 2006 technical report* (pp. 149–172). Chestnut Hill, MA: Boston College.

Hornberg, S., Valtin, R., Potthoff, B., Schwippert, K., & Schulz-Zander, R. (2007). Lesekompetenzen von Mädchen und Jungen im internationalen Vergleich [Reading achievement of girls and boys in international comparison]. In W. Bos, S. Hornberg, K.-H. Arnold, G. Faust, L. Fried, E.-M. Lankes, K. Schwippert, & R. Valtin (Eds.), *IGLU 2006: Lesekompetenzen von Grundschulkindern in Deutschland im internationalen Vergleich* [PIRLS 2006: Reading competencies of primary school students in Germany in international comparison] (pp. 195–223). Münster, Germany: Waxmann.

Joncas, M. (2007). PIRLS 2006 sample design. In M. O. Martin, I. V. S. Mullis, & A. M. Kennedy (Eds.), *PIRLS 2006 technical report* (pp. 35–48). Chestnut Hill, MA: Boston College.

Kennedy, A. M., Mullis, I. V. S., Martin, M. O., & Trong, K. L. (Eds.). (2007). *PIRLS 2006 encyclopedia: A guide to reading education in the forty PIRLS 2006 countries*. Chestnut Hill, MA: Boston College.

Kennedy, A. M., & Sainsbury, M. (2007). Developing the PIRLS 2006 reading assessment and scoring guides. In M. O. Martin, I. V. S. Mullis, & A. M. Kennedy (Eds.), *PIRLS 2006 technical report* (pp. 9–22). Chestnut Hill, MA: Boston College.

Kennedy, A. M., & Trong, K. L. (2007). Reporting student achievement in reading. In M. O. Martin, I. V. S. Mullis, & A. M. Kennedy (Eds.), *PIRLS 2006 technical report* (pp. 173–193). Chestnut Hill, MA: Boston College.

Martin, M. O., Mullis, I. V. S., & Kennedy, A. M. (Eds.). (2007). *PIRLS 2006 technical report*. Chestnut Hill, MA: Boston College.

Mullis, I. V. S., Kennedy, A. M., Martin, M. O., & Sainsbury, M. (Eds.). (2006). *PIRLS 2006: Assessment framework and specifications* (2nd ed.). Chestnut Hill, MA: Boston College.

Mullis, I. V. S., Martin, M. O., & Foy, P. (2011). Age distribution and reading achievement configurations among fourth-grade students in PIRLS 2006. In M. von Davier and D. Hastedt (Eds.), *IERI monograph series: Issues and methodologies in large-scale assessments* (Vol. 4, pp. 9–33). Hamburg, Germany, and Princeton, NJ: IEA-ETS Research Institute.

Mullis, I. V. S., Martin, M. O., & Gonzalez, E. J. (2004). *International achievement in the processes of reading comprehension: Results from PIRLS 2001 in 35 countries.* Chestnut Hill, MA: Boston College.

Mullis, I. V. S., Martin, M. O., Gonzalez, E. J., & Kennedy, A. M. (2003). *PIRLS 2001 international report: IEA's study of reading literacy achievement in primary schools in 35 countries*. Chestnut Hill, MA: Boston College.

Mullis, I. V. S., Martin, M. O., Kennedy, A. M., & Foy, P. (2007). *PIRLS 2006 international report: IEA's Progress in international reading literacy study in primary schools in 40 countries*. Chestnut Hill, MA: Boston College.

Schwippert, K., & Goy, M. (2007). PIRLS 2001 in brief. In K. Schwippert (Ed.), *Progress in reading literacy: The impact of PIRLS 2001 in 13 countries* (pp. 21–36). Münster, Germany: Waxmann.

Schwippert, K., Hornberg, S., Freiberg, M., & Stubbe, T. C. (2007). Lesekompetenzen von Kindern mit Migrationshintergrund im internationalen Vergleich [Reading competencies of students with immigration backgrounds in international comparison]. In W. Bos, S. Hornberg, K.-H. Arnold, G. Faust, L. Fried, E.-M. Lankes, K. Schwippert, & R. Valtin (Eds.), *IGLU 2006: Lesekompetenzen von Grundschulkindern in Deutschland im internationalen Vergleich* [PIRLS 2006: Reading competencies of primary school students in Germany in international comparison] (pp. 249–270). Münster, Germany: Waxmann.

Valtin, R., Bos, W., Buddeberg, I., Goy, M., & Potthoff, B. (2008). Lesekompetenzen von Schülerinnen und Schülern am Ende der vierten Jahrgangsstufe im nationalen und internationalen Vergleich [Students' reading competencies at the end of fourth grade in national and international comparison]. In W. Bos, S. Hornberg, K.-H. Arnold, G. Faust, L. Fried, E.-M. Lankes, K. Schwippert, & R. Valtin (Eds.), *IGLU-E 2006. Die Länder der Bundesrepublik Deutschland im nationalen und internationalen Vergleich* [PIRLS–German extension 2006: The federal states in Germany in national and international comparison] (pp. 51–101). Münster, Germany: Waxmann.

Chapter 3
The Impact of PIRLS in Austria

Birgit Suchań, Christina Wallner-Paschon, and Cornelia Rieß

3.1   Austria at a Glance[1]

Austria, situated in Central Europe, borders on eight countries: the Czech Republic, Germany, Hungary, Italy, Liechtenstein, Slovakia, Slovenia, and Switzerland. Extending 249 kilometers from north to south and 573 kilometers from east to west, Austria is a relatively small country. The total surface area is about 83,879 square kilometers. Approximately 60 percent of Austrian territory is mountainous and belongs to the Eastern Alps. The biggest river is the Danube, which flows 350 kilometers through Austria—about one eighth of the river's total length.

The population of Austria is 8,331,930 (2008 figures), and the average population density is 99 residents per square kilometer. About one fifth of the population (1,677,867 people) lives in the capital city, Vienna, where the average population density of 4,046 people per square kilometer greatly exceeds the average density countrywide. Vienna is the only city in Austria with more than one million inhabitants. About 56 percent of Austria's population lives in towns with up to 10,000 inhabitants.

Austria is a federal parliamentary republic that consists of nine provinces (*Bundesländer*), each of which has its own provincial government. Responsibility for legislation and its implementation is divided between the federation (*Bund*) and the provinces. Austria is a member of numerous international organizations, among them the International Monetary Fund, the Organisation for Economic Co-operation and Development, the United Nations, and the World Trade Organization. In 2008, Austria's gross national income per capita of US$46,260 ($37,680 PPP international dollars) positioned the country, under the World Bank classification, as a high-income country. Austria is also ranked on the international Human Development Index (HDI) as a highly developed country (HDI ranking of at least 0.8).

3.2   Austria's Education System as a Context for PIRLS

The Austrian education system is hierarchically organized, highly centralized, and one of the few school systems that is selective at a very early stage. The Federal Ministry for Education, Arts and Culture (the Bundesministerium für Unterricht, Kunst und Kultur or BMUKK) is responsible for primary, secondary, and non-university tertiary education. The Austrian Federation has centralized control and oversight of the

---

1   This text is based on the Austrian part of the *PIRLS Encyclopedia* (Kennedy, Mullis, Martin, & Trong, 2007).

education system. Its responsibilities include supervision of all areas of school management, organization of school instruction in public and private schools, and compliance with the legal regulations governing the remuneration and retirement of educational staff. The provinces are mainly responsible for providing public-sector compulsory education and for apportioning and administering the funding that local communities need to establish and maintain their schools. Each of the nine provinces has a complement of provincial school inspectors. They are assisted by district school inspectors for compulsory schools and subject inspectors for intermediate and upper secondary schools.

Through reference to proposals drafted by curricular task forces, the BMUKK establishes the curricular framework, consulting as it does so with various agencies, including district and provincial education bodies and teacher associations. Schools enjoy some autonomy with respect to budgetary management and have some measure of freedom to adapt the curriculum to local needs.

Eighty-nine percent of schools in Austria (and 97% of all primary schools) are public. These schools are free of charge for all children.

Pre-primary education is available to children up to six years of age, but it had not been compulsory up to fall 2010 ("last compulsory year of kindergarten"). The Austrian Federation does not govern this section of education; instead, each province sets its own governance legislation. In 2007, 73 percent of three-year-old children, 92 percent of four-year-old children, and 94 percent of five-year-olds attended pre-primary education in private or public day nurseries and kindergartens. The pre-primary sector does not have a set curriculum but is guided by a general educational objective for institutional childcare. This calls on providers in these facilities to advance and support children in their social, emotional, motivational, linguistic, and physical development.

Children begin their compulsory education at age six, and it lasts for a total of nine years. This stage of education begins with primary education (*Grundschule* or *Volksschule*), which encompasses Grades 1 to 4 (children aged 6 to 10 years).[2] Six-year-old children who are considered insufficiently "mature" to go to school have to attend preschool for one year before they begin primary school. Most primary schools are half-day schools but some offer supervision in the afternoon.

After completing primary school, children and their parents can apply for entry to either a secondary general school (*Hauptschule*) or a lower-level secondary academic school (*Allgemein bildende höhere Schule/AHS-Unterstufe*; the short name for this school type is *Gymnasium*). Both school types include Grades 5 to 8 and cater for children 10 to 14 years of age. In order to be admitted to a lower-level secondary academic school, students have to fulfill certain criteria in their school performance: the grades for the subjects "German, reading, writing" and "mathematics" must be at least "good" (in some schools the criterion is even higher). If they are not, students

---

2   Normally, children attend *Grundschule/Volksschule* from Grades 1 to 4. However, there are some school locations where *Volksschule* also includes the upper-primary Grades 5 to 8.

have to pass a qualifying examination. There are no admittance criteria for *Hauptschule*. During school year 2007/2008, about 64 percent of Austrian schoolchildren attended *Hauptschule* and 34 percent attended *Allgemein bildende höhere Schule (Gymnasium)*. The remaining children attended special education schools or were still at primary school.

The practice of selecting children into different educational tracks relatively early in their school careers (i.e., at the end of their fourth year of compulsory schooling) is a distinguishing feature of the Austrian education system. Bacher (2008) showed that the determination of which child goes where is associated (along with other variables, such as the population density of the surrounding community and the child's grades in primary school) with parents' level of education: the higher the educational qualification of the parents, the higher the probability that their child will attend a lower-level secondary academic school instead of a secondary general school. Social selectivity within the school system is not a feature peculiar to this first point of selection. The school career of Austrian children is, in general, strongly related to the education, occupations, and income of their parents (Bacher, 2008).

Having realized that this early segregation of Austrian children into either an "academic" secondary school or a more "practical" general school has pedagogical and social flaws, Austria began, in 2008/2009, a pilot project designed to enhance education throughout all secondary schools. The project, called *Neue Mittelschule* ("new secondary school"), mixes elements of academic secondary school and general secondary school provision. In these schools, children are taught the academic secondary school curriculum by academic school teachers and by general secondary school teachers. Schools have not been obliged to participate in this pilot project; instead, they have been able to decide for themselves if they want to take part.

After completing their lower secondary education, students can choose to attend prevocational school, which lasts only one year, vocational school (a one- to three-year program of study), or upper secondary school. The latter, which encompasses four or five years, ranges from Grades 9 to 12 or 13 and thus caters for students from age 14 to age 18 or 19. There are several types of upper secondary school: general secondary academic school, polytechnic school, and commercial school. The goal of these school types is a certificate (*Matura*) that allows students to gain access to higher (tertiary) education.

In Austria, preservice teachers wanting to teach Grades 1 to 8 have access to two kinds of training. Teachers destined for primary school and *Hauptschule* receive their preservice education at special colleges of education called *Pädagogische Hochschulen*. They graduate after completing a three-year Bachelor of Education degree. Teachers intending to work in lower-level secondary academic schools are trained at general universities. They graduate with a Master's degree.

In addition to completing coursework, primary school and *Hauptschule* teachers are required to complete a school-based practicum, where they observe and engage in teaching under the supervision of experienced teachers. They also receive complementary training in seminars. The primary school teacher is a generalist who is able to teach all subjects of the primary school curriculum. *Hauptschule* teachers specialize in two subjects. They have to choose a "first subject" (German, English, or mathematics) and a "second subject" (i.e., another compulsory subject, from a list that includes physics, chemistry, biology, and so on).

Teachers trained to teach at lower-level secondary academic schools complete coursework in two subjects in addition to other educational (didactic) courses. Obtaining their Master's degree does not, however, fully qualify them for employment as a teacher. They first have to spend an internship year teaching the subjects they intend to teach once fully qualified. During their internship year, these individuals work under the supervision of a teacher specially trained to work with trainee teachers, and they have a reduced number of teaching commitments.

3.3   Austria's Participation in Large-Scale Assessments

3.3.1   International Assessments

Austria's experience with large-scale assessments is relatively limited. Responsibility for determining participation in these assessments lies with the BMUKK. The ministry also determines which research institutes in the country will be responsible for conducting any one assessment, and it finances that work. Since 2008, the Federal Institute for Educational Research, Innovation, and Development of the Austrian Schooling System (BIFIE) has undertaken all international (and national) assessments.

Austria's participation in 2000 in the OECD-conducted Programme for International Student Assessment (PISA) began the country's regular collection of data pertaining to the performance of its 15- to 16-year-old students in reading, mathematics, and science. Prior to participating in PISA, Austria had taken part in three IEA international studies of educational achievement:

- The Computers in Education Study (1987–1993);
- The Language Education Study (1993–1996); and
- The Third International Mathematics and Science Study (1993–1997).

In order to complement the PISA data obtained at the end of compulsory schooling with data from the beginning of schooling, Austria's federal government decided to participate in PIRLS and TIMSS as well. Austria thus joined the IEA-conducted studies PIRLS in 2006 and TIMSS in 2007 as well as in 2011.

3.3.2   National Assessments

The tradition of national assessments is relatively poor in Austria. In 2000, the first national large-scale assessment was started with the project called Austrian Educational Standards. Until this time, the Austrian education system had been generally input- rather than output-oriented. As implied above, only the participation in the international assessments TIMSS, PIRLS, and PISA made apparent the necessity for national assessments. The following paragraphs provide an overview of the development of educational standards in Austria.

In the mid 1990s, a process was initiated in Austria that focussed on empowering schools to operate more autonomously, especially with respect to their curricula. While schools were still required to provide government-stipulated core subjects, they could define further emphases. This autonomy, however, pointed out the need to have nationally standardized achievement targets for these core subjects. The Federal Ministry of Education (BMUKK) commissioned representatives of the ministry and school inspectorate as well as teachers and designated researchers to develop national educational standards. These standards include the subjects German, reading, writing, and mathematics in primary school and German, mathematics, and English in secondary school. For these subjects, the Austrian Educational Standards determine the basic competencies students normally should have acquired by the end of Grade 4 (primary school) and by the end of Grade 8 (secondary school).

Austrian standards are based on the concept of average standards, not minimal or maximal standards. A main function of educational standards is to provide information that shows whether and to what extent schools fulfill their responsibility to impart competencies that are generally understood as being necessary. Those planning and teaching lessons thus need to keep in mind acquisition of the determined basic competencies. This also means that teachers have to consider the systematic structure of competencies against the related standards when planning and conducting their lessons. By comparing students' actual acquired competencies against the standards, teachers can identify the best possible way to further improve their students' learning outcomes. The educational standards, by bringing in competence-oriented teaching that is focussed on students and their educational outcomes, introduced a paradigm shift in the Austrian education system from inputs to outputs.

In 2008, subsequent to a piloting phase of six years, the Austrian School Court Act made the standards mandatory nationwide. In January 2009, the government issued its Ordinance on Educational Standards. This determines the functions of the standards and states that all types of public schools as well as private schools with public status must be evaluated every three years.

The standards essentially bring together three areas of responsibility within the Austrian school system—implementation, monitoring, and evaluation. The implementation of standards requires more student-based competence-orientation in teaching. Monitoring students' performance by way of standardized tests indicates whether and to what extent students have acquired the designated skills. Ongoing evaluation observes the standards' influence on teaching and learning culture.

A main purpose behind the standards is to give the participants in the learning process (students, teachers, schools) as well as educational policy- and decisionmakers feedback about educational outcomes. This educational monitoring strives to enable continuous quality assurance and quality improvement in the school system.

Teachers and schools therefore receive regular external feedback about testing results. The implementation process also includes providing teachers with diagnostic instruments to encourage internal evaluation. However, the testing results are not allowed to influence the teachers' individual gradings of their students. Rather, educational standards are intended to serve as a tool for orientation and for more self-responsibility among teachers and schools.

3.4   PIRLS 2006: National Results

The Austrian students who participated in PIRLS 2006 gained an average of 538 score points on the general reading comprehension scale, a result that put the performance of these Grade 4 students on par with their counterparts in the European Union (EU) and OECD countries that participated in PIRLS.

The proportion of Austrian students who performed at the high end of the scale was relatively low (8%). Sixteen percent of the Austrian students performed at the lower end of the scale, an outcome which means that, on average, by the end of primary school, every sixth Austrian student is or has the potential to be functionally illiterate. In 8 of the other 14 EU-analogue countries, proportions of students falling into this "at risk" category were significantly lower than the proportion of such students in Austria. The performance of the Austrian students on texts read for literary purposes and texts read for informational purposes was similar. However, when it came to reading for comprehension purposes, the Austrian students were significantly better at retrieving information and at straightforward inferencing than they were at interpreting, integrating, and evaluating information.

In Austria, as in most of the PIRLS countries, the girls' reading achievement was significantly better than the boys'. However, the difference was relatively moderate in Austria, with only 10 score points separating the two gender groups on the general reading comprehension scale.

Gender differences were also observed in relation to reading activities outside school. While, in Austria, girls and boys did not differ in the frequency with which they read informational texts, girls appeared to read literary-type texts more frequently in their leisure time than did boys. Twenty-nine percent of the girls said they read stories or novels daily or nearly every day, while only 16 percent of the boys reported doing so. The biggest gap, however, related to reading for pleasure: more than half of the girls (55%) read every day or nearly every day for pleasure, but only one third of the boys (36%) did this.

A closer look at the reading habits of 9- to 10-year-old Austrian students as a group (i.e., both boys and girls) revealed that the most popular reading material was non-fiction books—36 percent of students said they read them daily or nearly every day. Literary-type texts, such as storybooks and novels, along with instructional-type texts were being read daily or nearly daily by at least one fifth of the students.

The PIRLS data for Austria also showed a strong association between the students' reading achievement and their socioeconomic background, as measured by parents' level of attained education and occupational status. Children from a low socioeconomic background were, on average, significantly more likely to receive a low score on the reading achievement test than were students from a high socioeconomic background. Another disparity could be observed with respect to migration status: the performance of students with a migrant background was significantly poorer than that of students without such a background.

Another interesting pattern to emerge from the PIRLS data for Austria concerned children's socialization into reading within their families. The association between socioeconomic background and reading achievement can mostly be explained by certain conditions in the family, such as the reading habits of the parents, the parents' attitudes toward reading, the number of books at home, and the extent to which the children received early linguistic support from family members. The last of these variables had a particularly strong association with the reading motivation and the reading achievement of the Austrian 10-year-old students. Despite the weak association between gender and reading achievement, we detected a strong association between gender and reading motivation. However, we found no significant difference between boys and girls with respect to their early reading socialization in the family.

The association between reading habits and reading achievement highlighted a paradoxical pattern not only in Austria but also in most of the EU countries that participated in PIRLS. Whereas frequent reading of literary-type texts was positively correlated with reading achievement, frequency of reading informational-type texts was negatively associated with reading achievement, suggesting that weaker readers are more likely than good readers to focus their reading on informational texts.

Three particularly interesting implications of the PIRLS data for the Austrian education system concern teachers' ability to assess their students' reading achievement, the extent of specialist reading support available to students, and equity of educational opportunity. When analyzing the data relating to Austrian teachers' judgments of their students' reading proficiency, we found, with regard to the first implication, that teachers in one out of every five classes, on average, underestimated the proportion of poor readers in their respective classes. We also found that in one out of every four classes, teachers judged students who recorded a low level of proficiency on the PIRLS assessment to be reading at a level 10 percentage points higher than that actually recorded on the PIRLS scale. This finding has particular relevance when we acknowledge that the proportion of specialist reading support teachers (especially those trained to work separately with weak readers) within the teaching body of the higher-performing EU countries that participated in PIRLS is twice as much (at 44%) as the proportion in the Austrian teacher cohort.

The PIRLS results also highlighted the selective nature of the Austrian school system and what this means for equity of educational opportunity. As noted above, Austrian students are required to choose between two types of school—secondary general and secondary academic—on completing Grade 4, a stage when students are typically 10 years of age. Once again, the findings pointed out that children from lower socioeconomic backgrounds tend to enter the first type of school and children from higher socioeconomic backgrounds to enter the second. As the PIRLS results showed, this pattern held even if students from both backgrounds exhibited comparable reading proficiency. We also observed that students from higher SES backgrounds gained higher grades for their schoolwork overall than did students from lower SES backgrounds, and that this pattern again held even if the reading achievement of members of both groups was the same.

We are currently undertaking other, deeper secondary analyses of the PIRLS 2006 data. These findings will be presented at research conferences, and we also plan to publish, in educational research journals, articles based on the PIRLS 2006 report prepared by the Austrian national expert team (see next section).

3.5   PIRLS 2006 Publications

Austria, in line with all practice relating to the international assessments in which the country participates, has published four reports on PIRLS 2006. The first three publications comprise the following:

- *An overall account of the study directed at the general public:* The publication's content, presented by the report's authors (Suchań & Wallner-Paschon, 2007) in a brief, easily understood way, covers the aims and the organization of the study, general technical information, details about the assessment framework and associated questionnaires, examples of test items, methods of data collection, and quality assurance issues.

- *A report directed at people interested in gaining a deeper appreciation of the technical details of the study:* The content of this "national technical report," edited by Haider and Suchań (2007), is similar in structure to the first publication, but it is far more detailed in scope. The report can be downloaded for free from the BIFIE homepage (http://www.bifie.at).

- *A presentation of the initial findings of PIRLS 2006:* Edited by Suchań, Wallner-Paschon, Stöttinger, and Bergmüller (2007), the report contains the most important information arising out of the cross-national comparisons of students' scores on the reading scales. Relationships between reading achievement and variables such as gender, migration background, and socioeconomic status are also documented and analyzed.

These three publications provided the basis for the fourth publication, known as the "national experts report." Edited by Suchań, Wallner-Paschon, and Schreiner (2009), and published one and a half years after the initial findings report, this publication sets out insights gained from deeper analyses of the PIRLS data, and explores issues made evident by the results. It also contains different points of view (garnered from Austrian educationists with expert knowledge in relevant fields) on the findings, especially those pertaining to Austria. Implications of the findings for Austrian educational policy are another important feature of this publication.

The releases of the two reports containing results were each accompanied by press conferences. During the press conference for the report detailing the initial findings from PIRLS 2006, journalists received a portfolio containing a PowerPoint presentation of the results in print format as well as a leaflet providing a summary of the main results. During the press conference accompanying the release of the fourth report (the expert report), journalists again received a portfolio that included a PowerPoint presentation in print format, a leaflet with information about the four main issues addressed by the press conference, and the contact addresses of the respective experts.

The aforementioned BIFIE, which, as part of its work, conducts international and national assessments in Austria, also organized at that time a symposium that focussed on the issues raised in the report. Educational researchers, educational policymakers, and other interested members of the educational community attended.

Since the release of the initial findings from PIRLS 2006, we have been in contact with reading organizations and colleges of education. Our aim is to present the results personally to each of these places and to be available for discussions, especially those relating to teacher education, in general, and professional development for teachers in the area of reading, in particular.

3.6   The Impact of PIRLS 2006

In order to gain an extensive insight into the impact of PIRLS 2006 in Austria, we conducted interviews with people involved in educational policy, an approach that provided us with perspectives additional to those held by ourselves.

It was apparent from these interviews that international studies are having a considerable impact on current educational policy in Austria. The policymakers we interviewed said that it is essential for Austria to know how its school system stands in an international context, and that this information also has important relevance for ensuring students are equipped to enter today's labor market. More particularly, the individuals we interviewed stressed the necessity of having empirical data to inform understanding of how the education system is performing, to provide a rationale for reforms to it, and to confirm or negate assumptions held about issues relating to that system.

The PIRLS 2006 results have not been as evident in the public eye as the results of PISA, which were released around the same time. When the first PIRLS press conference took place (November 2007), public attention and discussion were heavily focused on other political topics. One week after the PIRLS press conference, the PISA results were published and attracted considerable media coverage. Because Austria's experience with international assessments started with PISA 2000, the study has a high public profile, and its results attract considerable discussion and debate. This is why the media coverage of PIRLS decreased as soon as the PISA results were released.

PIRLS data are not only picked up by those engaged in public debates (in plenums, committees, press releases, presentations, speeches, and panel discussions). The results also inform educational practice and the development of concrete measures (e.g., teacher training in the Coordination Center for Reading, *Koordinationsstelle Lesen*). The PIRLS results that appear to attract the most frequent attention are those relating to the association between socioeconomic status and student reading performance, the reading achievement of students with a migration background, early reading socialization within the family and (connected with this) within preschool education, and reading socialization within school. Another area of particular interest is how other countries not only identify students with low levels of reading proficiency and those with high levels of reading proficiency but also cater to the needs of these two groups.

Within the jurisdiction of the BMUKK, PIRLS has led to some changes designed to have impacts on the efficacy of the national education system. One such development arose out of the realization that reading-based monitoring and support needs to be provided not just for those children for whom German is a second language, but for all children with reading-related problems, deficits, and learning disorders. The ministry is also reviewing its approach to reading education. It intends to establish a steering group made up of representatives from all sections of the ministry that are involved in reading education. This change will make this area of education a cross-sectional concern instead of a matter handled separately by each section.

The ministry also plans to address three issues relevant to primary schools. They intend to evaluate present policy regarding school entrance (assessment of school readiness), consider notions and practices relating to individualized instruction, and determine what else can be done to support children's reading abilities.

The establishment of the aforementioned Coordination Center for Reading in the ministry is an outcome of PIRLS. The center coordinates a network of education colleges throughout Austria, thereby bringing together not only individuals with expertise in preservice and inservice teacher education but also teachers and others with expertise in the area of school supervision. One essential purpose of the center is to disseminate the PIRLS results among primary school teachers. The center has been working closely with the Austrian national study center for PIRLS to achieve this aim. The PIRLS results have also had relevance, within the ministry, with respect to identifying topics relevant to the reading-related professional development for teachers offered by pedagogical colleges. It should also be mentioned that PIRLS brought up crucial arguments relevant to the debate about educational standards in Austria.

These overall activities at the ministry have been accompanied by several smaller local projects or initiatives that have been established in connection to the PIRLS findings. Examples include midwives endeavoring to make expectant mothers aware of their important role in early reading socialization, the establishment of reading partnerships (adults reading aloud to students), the establishment of libraries within schools, and advising teachers on how to make effective use of different types of reading material in their classrooms.

Although political discussion about educational issues arising out of PIRLS and effort to address those issues have been relatively limited, the findings of PIRLS and the other international studies that Austria has participated in have influenced the political discussion. These large cross-national studies bring a new quality to discussions on education not only because they are free from ideology but also because they provide empirical, and therefore objective, information. The studies have definitely had the effect of making education a prominent political issue and drawing attention to areas of concern.

In recent years in Austria, children's written and spoken German language acquisition and competency has become an area of significant interest and disquiet in educational circles. The federal government has begun implementing holistic initiatives in the sector of pre-primary education. For example, preschool facilities can now use a diagnostic tool to assess the linguistic competence of children in the year before they start primary education (Breit, 2009). An "education plan" (*BildungsRahmenPlan*) was developed in 2009 by the BMUKK (http://www.sprich-mit-mir.at). One part of the plan focuses on language and language improvement in pre-primary education. Since the beginning of the 2010 school year, the federal government, acting in concert with the provinces, has required all five-year-old children to attend one year of kindergarten. This provision is free of charge.

3.7 Future Activities

Austria is participating in the PIRLS and TIMSS iterations of 2011, even though concerns have been expressed that the intervals between the different international assessments are not long enough to establish and bed in the adaptations and reforms prompted by the results of these studies. At the same time, implementation of the national educational standards (see section 3.3.2 of this chapter) will continue. The first round of regular assessments of children against these standards will be carried out in 2012 in secondary schools and in 2013 in primary schools. As we noted earlier in this report, this regular testing will allow assessment of student achievement outcomes by the end of Grade 4 and Grade 8 and, consequently, in the long run, supposedly encourage continuous quality improvement.

In 2009, the BIFIE synthesized the data gained from the various international and national studies in which Austria had participated, and published this information in a national education report. The BIFIE intends to publish corresponding reports every three years. Each report will serve two main purposes. The first is to add, on an ongoing basis, to the database of knowledge pertaining to the school system. This database is an important repository of information for those involved in educational policy- and decisionmaking. The second is to keep the public and Austria's legislature informed about issues and problems facing the country's school system. This information, in turn, will provide both rationales and incentives for educational reforms. Finally, the findings of PIRLS 2006 are continuing to provide valuable information for people involved in current discussion about bringing in a new form of teacher training in Austria.

3.8   Concluding Remarks

For Austria, PIRLS 2006 provided a first opportunity to engage in a large-scale international study of the reading achievement and reading activities of primary school children. The study also marked the first time that Austria obtained empirical data on the reading achievement of its primary school students. The findings from PIRLS, and from TIMSS, complement the data that Austria has obtained relative to its secondary school students through its participation in PISA. Taken together, these studies have allowed us to build valuable empirical databases on the competencies of Austrian students in reading, mathematics, and science at the end of primary school as well as at the end of compulsory education.

Austria's participation in international assessments, such as PIRLS, has also highlighted weaknesses in Austria's education system. By emphasizing the same problems, the data from PIRLS, TIMSS, and PISA, as well as those obtained from Austria's participation in the OECD Teaching and Learning International Survey (TALIS), have made evident the need for reform. This is happening, but is still relatively small scale. Nonetheless, the changes that are being made, including those presently being piloted, represent a change of national perspective about the effectiveness of the Austrian education system. The *neue Mittelschule* and the compulsory year in kindergarten for all five-year-olds are among the encouraging changes to date, while organizations concerned with reading acquisition and remediation are becoming more prevalent and are having a stronger positive impact within the education system.

As we move ahead, we need to hold to our course by regularly monitoring the competencies of our students and comparing their achievement with the achievement of students from other countries. This approach will allow us not only to continue monitoring and detecting strengths and weaknesses in our school system but also to sensitize politicians and the public to them. For Austria, the raised consciousness brought about by the country's participation in international surveys of educational achievement such as PIRLS is, we believe, a key to driving forward improvements in our educational landscape.

References

Bacher, J. (2008). Soziale Ungleichheit, Schullaufbahn und Testleistungen [Social inequalities, schooling and test scores]. In B. Suchań, C. Wallner-Paschon, & C. Schreiner (Eds.), PIRLS 2006: *Die Lesekompetenz am Ende der Volksschule: Österreichischer Expertenbericht* [Reading at the end of primary school: A report from Austrian experts] (S. 79–101). Graz, Austria: Leykam.

Breit, S. (Ed.). (2009). *Frühkindliche Sprachstandsfeststellung: Konzept und Ergebnisse der systematischen Beobachtung im Kindergarten* [Early childhood language skills assessment: Concept and results of systematic observation in the nursery]. Graz, Austria: Leykam.

Haider, G., & Suchań, B. (Eds.). (2007). *PIRLS 2006: Internationaler Vergleich von Schülerleistungen: Technischer Bericht: Lesen in der Grundschule* [PIRLS 2006: International comparisons of student performance. Technical report: Reading in elementary school] [Electronic version]. Salzburg, Austria: ZVB Österreichisches Projektzentrum für Vergleichende Bildungsforschung. Retrieved from http://www.bifie.at/publist-07-11-28-1

Kennedy, A. M., Mullis, I. V. S., Martin, M. O., & Trong, K. L. (Eds.). (2007). *PIRLS 2006 encyclopedia: A guide to reading education in forty PIRLS 2006 countries.* Chestnut Hill, MA: Boston College.

Suchań, B., & Wallner-Paschon, C. (2007). *PIRLS 2006: Internationaler Vergleich von Schülerleistungen: Die Studie im Überblick. Lesen in der Grundschule: Ziele und Organisation, Methoden und Tests, Aufgabenbeispiele* [PIRLS 2006: International comparisons of student performance: The study at a glance. Reading in elementary school: Aims and objectives, methods and tests, activity examples]. Graz, Austria: Leykam.

Suchań, B., Wallner-Paschon, C., & Schreiner, C. (Eds.). (2009). *PIRLS 2006: Die Lesekompetenz am Ende der Volksschule: Österreichischer Expertenbericht* [PIRLS 2006: Reading at the end of primary school. A report from Austrian experts]. Graz, Austria: Leykam.

Suchań, B., Wallner-Paschon, C., Stöttinger, E., & Bergmüller, S. (Eds.). (2007). *PIRLS 2006: Internationaler Vergleich von Schülerleistungen. Erste Ergebnisse: Lesen in der Grundschule* [PIRLS 2006: International comparisons of student performance. First results: Reading in elementary school]. Graz, Austria: Leykam.

Chapter 4
The Impact of PIRLS in Belgium (Flemish)

Hongqiang Liu, Heidi Knipprath, and Jan Van Damme

4.1 Belgium and Flanders at a Glance

Belgium, a country in northwestern Europe, covers an area of 30,528 square kilometers. It shares borders with France, Germany, Luxembourg, the Netherlands, and the North Sea. The country has a population of around 10 million, with a high population density of 344 people per square kilometer. Its population consists of two large linguistic groups—Dutch speakers and French speakers, mostly Walloons, and a small group of German speakers. There are thus three (language) communities. Belgium's territory also includes three regions that partly overlap these three communities:

- The Dutch-speaking region in the north, called Flanders, which is inhabited by 59 percent of the Belgian population;
- The French-speaking region in the south, called Wallonia,[1] which has 31 percent of the Belgian population; and
- The Brussels-capital region, which, although officially bilingual, is mostly French-speaking and has 10 percent of the population.

Belgium's linguistic diversity and related political and cultural differences define a complex governmental system consisting of the federal government, the three regions, and the three communities. As a result, the Belgian constitution allows for seven parliaments and governments.

The federal state is responsible for matters of national importance. Regions have authority in fields that can be broadly associated with their territory. Communities exercise their authority, within linguistically determined geographical boundaries, over matters such as culture (including audiovisual media) and education. The Flemish community includes both Flanders and the Dutch-speaking people of the Brussels-capital region. Flanders has five provinces—Antwerp, East Flanders, West Flanders, Flemish Brabant, and Limburg. Flemish politicians decided to merge the institutions of the region of Flanders and the institutions of the Flemish Community when the communities and regions were created in 1980. Therefore, Flanders has only one parliament and one government, which together are responsible for the Flemish Community and region.

Belgium is highly integrated with Europe and with the rest of the world. It is a member of the United Nations, the European Union, NATO, and the OECD. Because

---

1   Wallonia also has a small area that is inhabited by German speakers.

of its location at the heart of industrialized countries and its highly productive workforce, Belgium has a GDP per capita of €31,414 (National Bank of Belgium, 2010). The Belgian economy is very much service oriented. It is also asymmetric in that the Flemish economy is dynamic and the Walloon economy lags behind it. Flanders has a GDP per capita of €31,067, in contrast with €22,868 in Wallonia (National Bank of Belgium, 2010). The Flemish Community invests heavily in education, with its per capita spending placing it among the top five countries with respect to educational expenditure in Europe and considerably above the European Union average (Flanders Investment & Trade, 2010). In 2007, the Flemish education budget was €B8.86, a sum that accounted for 40 percent of the total Flemish budget and represented an average nominal increase of 3.75 percent per year since 1995 (De Ro, 2008).

4.2   The Education System in Flanders

In 1989, the federal state transferred responsibility for education to the communities. The only areas for which the state still has responsibility are determining the start and end of compulsory education, setting minimum requirements for obtaining a school qualification (diploma), and overseeing the pension scheme for teachers. As a result, each of the Flemish-, French-, and German-speaking Communities has its own education system. In Flanders, the Ministry of Education and Training is responsible for almost all aspects of education policy across all levels of the education system (i.e., from preschool through to higher and adult education).

The Belgian Constitution states that every child has a right to education. Accordingly, all children residing in Belgium must attend education from the age of 6 to the age of 18. Young people can engage in education on a part-time basis from ages 15 or 16, but only if they combine this provision with work or workplace-based learning. Most young people, however, complete full-time secondary education.

4.2.1   Educational Networks

Under the Belgian Constitution, Belgians are guaranteed the right to provide and/or attend education of their choice. There are three types of educational provision: community education, subsidized public education, and subsidized private education.

In Flanders, community education (in Dutch, this form of education is known as GO!) is organized by the Autonomous Council for Community Education and is financed by the Flemish Community. The constitution stipulates that community education must be secular. Approximately 14.5 percent of elementary school students and 16.5 percent of secondary school students attend schools run by the Flemish Community (Hostens, 2009).

Subsidized public education (known as OGO in Dutch) is organized by municipal and provincial authorities and is subsidized by the Flemish Community. Schools in this network can be denominational or secular. Over 22 percent of all elementary school students and nearly 8 percent of secondary school students attend OGO (Hostens, 2009).

Subsidized private education (known as VGO in Dutch) is run by private persons or organizations. This network includes denominational (Catholic, Jewish, Protestant), non-denominational, and "independent" schools. Independent schools encompass those that embrace specific modes of education, such as Freinet, Waldorf, and the like. Most subsidized private schools are Catholic schools. Just over 63 percent of elementary school students and approximately 76 percent of secondary school students attend subsidized private schools (Hostens, 2009). The small number of private schools that operate in Flanders are neither recognized nor subsidized by the Flemish government. Parents can homeschool their children, but this provision is also not subsidized by the government.

4.2.2 Education Levels

Basic education in Flanders consists of preschool (nursery) and primary education. This provision is further subdivided into mainstream preschool and primary education, and special preschool and primary education. Children are eligible to attend nursery education from two and a half to six or seven years of age. During school year 2006/2007, 233,344 children were enrolled in mainstream nursery education. About 63 percent of preschoolers at this time were attending publicly subsidized but privately run nursery schools (De Ro, 2008).

Mainstream primary education provides schooling to children from 6 to 12 years of age and thus includes six consecutive years of study. Officially, children can spend a minimum of four years and a maximum of eight years in primary education. During school year 2006/2007, 387,157 children attended mainstream primary schools; approximately 64 percent of them attended privately run schools (De Ro, 2008).

Special nursery and primary education serves children with physical or mental disabilities, serious behavioral or emotional problems, and/or serious learning difficulties. During school year 2006/2007, the 1,907 children attending special nursery schools accounted for almost one percent of all preschoolers. During the same period, the number of students enrolled in special primary schools was 27,794, which accounted for 6.5 percent of all students of primary school age.

Mainstream and special nursery and primary schools also cooperate to provide integrated nursery and primary education. Under this provision, children with special needs attend classes or activities in a mainstream school but also receive assistance from special education providers. During 2006/2007, 1,103 students attended integrated nursery education and 3,617 attended integrated primary education.

The tracking (streaming) system in Flanders first comes into effect at the beginning of secondary education. Students who successfully complete the require-ments for graduation from primary education go on to Grade 7, A-stream. The remaining students enter the B-stream. From Grade 9, the second stage of tracking comes into operation. At this time, students enter one of the following: general secondary education (*algemeen secundair onderwijs*—ASO), technical secondary education (*technisch secundair onderwijs*—TSO), artistic secondary education (*kunstsecundair onderwijs*—KSO), or vocational secondary education (*beroeps-secundair onderwijs*—BSO). B-stream students usually attend vocational secondary education while A-stream students have the option of entering any of the four tracks. Although the four types of secondary education give access to higher education, many students who attend vocational secondary education find it difficult to move beyond this provision because what they learn there does not readily align with the content of university education. According to researchers and scholars such as Dupriez, Dumay, and Vause (2008), the secondary school tracking system contributes to a situation in which young people's further educational and later work-related opportunities are determined relatively early in their schooling, a situation that, in turn, contributes to inequities in society.

4.3 Experience with Large-Scale Assessments

Flanders has ample experience of international and national student assessments. In this section, we first consider the international studies and then the national studies. In the third part, we focus on PIRLS 2006.

4.3.1 International Perspectives

Belgium has been one of the most active members of the International Association for the Evaluation of Educational Achievement (IEA) since the association's inception. IEA was actually established as an international organization in accordance with Belgian law in 1967. Flemish schools and French-speaking schools in Belgium have always participated separately in international assessments. Flemish schools began their participation with IEA around 1970. In the four decades since, Flanders has participated in 10 international assessments organized by IEA, and four studies conducted by the Organisation for Economic Co-operation and Development (OECD). Three of the four OECD assessments are iterations of the Programme for International Student Assessment (PISA) survey. The fourth is the International Adult Literacy Survey (IALS).

4.3.2 National Perspectives

Since 2002, the Flemish Ministry of Education and Training has organized national assessments in primary and secondary education. Table 4.1 lists the assessments that have been conducted over the intervening years. The primary goal of these assessments is to determine the extent to which Flemish students reach, by the end of particular educational levels, achievement targets that mostly pertain to a specific domain of study or subject matter. The ministry asks a representative sample of schools to participate anonymously and on a voluntary basis in these assessments. Researchers then estimate the percentages of students within these schools who have reached the attainment targets. Researchers also analyze the achievement data with respect to variables relating to characteristics of students, classes, and schools. Their aim is to determine if and to what degree these variables explain variation in achievement scores across students, classes, and schools.

The government, in association with educational researchers and policymakers, uses the results of the national assessment studies to detect shortcomings in the education system. After publishing the results of each assessment, the Flemish Ministry of Education and Training holds a conference that allows participants, and schools in general, to reflect on the results and to look for ways of improving educational practice.

Schools that take part in an assessment receive feedback on the average performance of their students, with the feedback taking into account the individual characteristics of the students. This feedback is for the benefit of the schools only and is not made public. Because a limited sample of schools participate in each national assessment study, the schools that are not included but want to assess their students can access tests equivalent to those used in the national assessments. In 2009, schools were able to download these tests for the first time and receive a feedback report on their students' achievement from a website provided by the Ministry of Education and Training. In this report, information on the "value added" by the school is included to indicate the effects of the school on students' school achievement.

Table 4.1: National assessments of educational achievement conducted in Belgium (Flemish)

Year of data collection	Subject	Educational level
2002	Mathematics and comprehensive reading	Grade 6
2004	Acquisition and processing of information	Grade 8 (A stream)
2005	World studies: nature	Grade 8 (A stream)
2006	Biology	Grade 8 (A stream)
2007	Dutch: reading and listening	Grade 6
2007	French: reading, listening, and writing	Grade 8
2008	French: reading, listening, writing, and speaking	Grade 6
2008	Mathematics	Grade 8 (B stream)
2009	Mathematics	Grade 6
2009	Mathematics	Grade 8 (A stream)

University-based research centers in Flanders also conduct large-scale studies of educational achievement. Between 1990 and 1999, the LOSO-project,[2] which received funding from the Flemish Ministry of Education and Training, followed one cohort of secondary school students from a sample of Flemish secondary schools. The main objective of this project was to describe and explain the "school careers" of secondary school students in Flanders. The researchers regularly assessed students' language skills, mathematics competency, and some non-cognitive outcomes. They also collected data on student, school, and classroom characteristics in order to aid explanation of differences in outcomes between students, classes/teachers, and schools (Van Damme, De Fraine, Van Landeghem, Opdenakker, & Onghena, 2002; Van Damme, Opdenakker, Van Landeghem, De Fraine, Pustjens, & Van de gaer, 2006).

A similar project, called SiBO,[3] has been assessing the language skills, mathematics skills, and other scholastic outcomes of one cohort of primary school students since 2002. These students were first assessed during their last year in kindergarten and then assessed repeatedly thereafter. The main objective of this longitudinal project, which will finish in 2011 and which has also received funding from the Flemish Ministry of Education and Training, is to describe and explain the school careers of primary school students in Flanders.

The Flemish School Feedback Project, launched in 2006 by the Catholic University of Leuven (Center for Educational Effectiveness and Evaluation), the University of Gent, and the University of Antwerp, has been assessing the mathematics attainment and reading comprehension of secondary school students from a representative sample of Flemish schools. The data collected are being used to develop a school feedback system. This system will also be available to primary schools, but the data informing it will come from the achievement tests registered in the SiBO project.

4.3.3   Participation in PIRLS 2006

Neither the Flemish Community nor the French Community participated in PIRLS 2001. In 2006, the Flemish government remained reluctant to participate in PIRLS because it considered the PISA assessment was more relevant than PIRLS or TIMSS to the attainment targets of the Flemish education system. PIRLS assesses Grade 4 students, but Flanders has no attainment targets for this grade. The only attainment targets at primary school level are those for the end of Grade 6. Secondary education, however, has attainment targets for Grades 8, 10, and 12. The increase in the number of large-scale assessment studies, budgetary considerations, and the practical relevance of the studies contributed to the ministry's decision not to take part in PIRLS 2006.

---

2   *Longitudinaal Onderzoek Secundair Onderwijs* (Longitudinal Study of Secondary Education).

3   *Schoolloopbanen in het Basis Onderwijs* (Pathways through Primary Schools).

Instead, the Center for Educational Effectiveness and Evaluation of the Catholic University of Leuven took the initiative to conduct the assessment.

The center's decision rested on two considerations. First, it considered the exclusive focus on PISA an inappropriate policy, especially with respect to the widely held belief that the relatively high level of social inequality evident among Flemish students at age 15 relates to the secondary school tracking system. However, others, including staff members of the Educational Center for Educational Effectiveness and Evaluation, consider that social and educational inequality already exists in primary education. PIRLS 2006 provided an opportunity to investigate this premise. Second, the center maintained that if Flanders continued to participate in PIRLS studies, PIRLS 2006 would provide benchmark data against which to evaluate the Flemish policy of equality of educational opportunity.

4.4 National Results and the Impact of PIRLS

4.4.1 National Results

When considering the results, readers need to keep in mind that Flanders did not meet the sampling criterion relating to exclusion of children. As was the case with Flanders' participation in TIMSS, the Catholic University of Leuven research center asked only mainstream schools to participate in PIRLS 2006. However, about six percent of Flemish 10-year-old children (the age of most fourth graders in Flanders) attend schools for special education. The exclusion of these children from the sample may have inflated the Flemish average achievement score and underestimated the extent of educational inequity in primary schools. Therefore, in the future, Flanders will ask schools providing special education to participate in both PIRLS and TIMSS.

The average score on the PIRLS 2006 reading achievement scale of the Flemish fourth graders was 547, a score that was significantly higher than the international average of 506 (Mullis, Martin, Kennedy, & Foy, 2007). Flanders gained 14th ranking among the 45 participants. The Flemish average was also significantly higher than the average of European Union countries (534) and the average of OECD countries (537). Both the standard deviation and the distance between the 5th and 95th percentiles on the PIRLS scale positioned Flanders as a relatively equitable primary education system, second only to the Netherlands.

PIRLS set four points on the scale as international benchmarks: low, intermediate, high, and advanced (level). Almost all Flemish fourth graders (99 percent) scored above the low benchmark, about 90 percent scored above the intermediate benchmark, about 49 percent scored above the high benchmark, and about 7 percent qualified as advanced readers. In addition, the difference of six score points between girls (550) and boys (544) was substantially lower than the international average difference of 13 score points (with the difference favoring girls in nearly all of the participating countries).

In general, the results indicate that the Flemish primary school system is, relative to other countries, doing well in improving reading capacity for its primary school students overall, given that 90 percent of its fourth graders scored above the intermediate benchmark in PIRLS 2006. However, it is not doing so well in cultivating advanced readers.

The PIRLS results also dispute the notion that Flanders is not sufficiently meeting the learning needs of weak learners, especially those from socially disadvantaged families. The results furthermore strongly suggest that the limited differences in educational achievement across Flemish primary schools can be explained almost entirely by student-background differences, a finding that we consider highly noteworthy. Suchań's (2009) secondary analyses of PIRLS 2006 and TIMSS 2007 data confirm that differences in achievement across schools in Flanders tend to be slight.

This high level of educational equity may be a result of the prevalent free preschool education available to Flemish children from two and a half to five years of age. This provision may help to narrow the cognitive gap between socially advantaged and disadvantaged children once they reach school, and thus narrow student achievement differences among schools. However, it is also possible that primary schools in Flanders do little to influence the reading strategies of children. If this is the case, it would provide another possible explanation for the lack of significant net school effects.

In addition to socioeconomic influences, ethnic/cultural factors were also associated with the Flemish children's achievement scores on the PIRLS reading tests. For example, children of Turkish origin scored much lower than children from other ethnic/cultural backgrounds. In general, achievement gaps between children from immigrant backgrounds and children from nonimmigrant backgrounds can be attributed to socioeconomic factors. However, in the case of Turkish children in Flanders, socioeconomic factors do not explain the considerable achievement gap. In the feedback reports that we gave to schools after the release of the PIRLS results, we pointed out that because PIRLS measures socioeconomic factors in a very rudimentary way, we could only provide analyses of the effect of sociocultural factors.

In order to further investigate the influence of socioeconomic (SES) factors on students' reading achievement, Van Damme, Liu, Vanhee, and Pustjens (2010) created a SES index for PIRLS 2006 and regressed student reading achievement upon it. Comparison of the slopes of each country for SES revealed Flanders as the fourth-ranked country among the 14 European industrialized countries that participated in PIRLS (see Figure 4.1). This finding provides further confirmation that Flanders has a fairly equitable primary education system.

Figure 4.1: **Linear regression of reading achievement scores on SES index of students from PIRLS 2006 European industrialized countries**

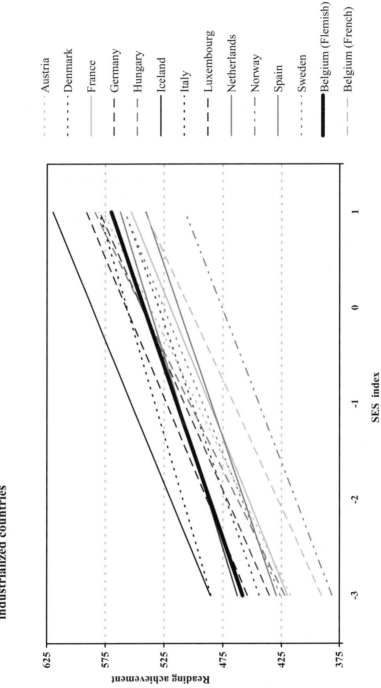

Previous research (e.g., Gustafsson, 2007; Rinderman, 2007) indicates that it is necessary, when conducting cross-national comparisons of school achievement, to take account of differences in the average age of the students in each participating country. Across the PIRLS 2006 countries, the average age of participating students ranged from 9.7 years in Italy to 11.9 years in South Africa. Using data from the findings of several intelligence test studies and student assessment studies, Rindermann (2007) calculated that the increase in achievement of students over a year was, on average, about 42 score points on a scale which, in line with the PIRLS scale, had a mean of 500 and a standard deviation of 100.

Swedish studies show that about a third of this progress is attributable to an extra year of age and two thirds to an extra year of schooling (Gustafsson, 2007), making it justifiable to correct for age differences across countries for ranking purposes. When we adjusted the PIRLS achievement score for all countries according to their students' average ages, the ranking for Flanders moved from 12th to 8th place on the international achievement scale (Van Damme et al., 2010).

4.4.2   Publication of the PIRLS Results in Flanders

As soon as the results were released, we communicated relevant information to media agencies in Flanders. In order to facilitate communication of the PIRLS results, we constructed a website (http://ppw.kuleuven.be/pirls/toets.html) for the general public and, as mentioned previously, produced feedback reports for the participating schools. Some of the information contained in the school feedback reports (http://ppw. kuleuven.be/pirls/voorbeeldrapport.pdf) was produced through multilevel value-added analyses to adjust for intake differences across schools. This process allowed us to determine which schools were more and which schools were less effective in terms of the reading achievement of their students. The feedback report showed each school its respective position relative to other participating schools based on both the PIRLS 2006 raw score and the score adjusted for student background characteristics.

The school feedback reports and the underlying multilevel analyses gave new insights into the national results for PIRLS 2006. The reports showed that most schools did not differ statistically significantly from one another. No school was significantly better or worse than the average school. However, some well-performing schools were statistically significantly more effective than poorly-performing schools. These few significant differences disappeared when we controlled for the effect of background characteristics. These patterns indicate that Flemish primary schools barely differ from one another with respect to the contribution that they make to the reading achievement of students at Grade 4.

4.4.3   The Impact of PIRLS

In general, the PIRLS 2006 findings received little public attention in Flanders, with information related to the study being made available mainly to the participating schools, policymakers, and educational researchers. When the results were first released, a few newspaper reports (e.g., in *De Standaard*) and radio items featuring the findings reached the general public. Later, the fact that only a small percentage of students were positioned as advanced readers attracted commentary in journals (e.g., *Onderwijskrant*) and led to various groups (e.g., parents of gifted children) engaging in actions directed at influencing educational policy.

The PIRLS results have also been mentioned in various other contexts over time, such as in recent discussions on reform of secondary education. In a document setting out government policy for education from 2009 to 2014, the minister of education stated, "Our well-performing children do not perform very well" (Smet, 2009, p. 13). This comment was a direct reaction to the PIRLS 2006 results.

A follow-up study conducted by Driessens and Faes (2008) of the impact of PIRLS 2006 in the participating schools found only limited evidence of influence on school policy and practice relating to reading. Driessens and Faes were particularly interested in how schools interpreted and used the school feedback reports. Based on the findings of their quantitative and qualitative analyses, they concluded that although school principals and some other school staff read the feedback report for their respective schools, the majority of these readers had difficulty interpreting the feedback results. This difficulty may partly explain why only a few principals used these data to adjust school policy. Driessens and Faes also noted that schools generally were only motivated to address issues highlighted by the data when various stakeholders, such as parents, exerted pressure on them to do so.

We consider that the feedback reports would probably have been of more practical value to the schools if their content had been relevant to the specific issues of each school and if they had proposed some solutions. Although consultation was beyond the mission of the feedback project, a short course would have helped the school principals better understand and interpret the content of the report for their school. Another likely and important explanation for the modest reaction to the school feedback reports was that the schools did not receive the reports until after publication of the international results, an event that occurred more than a year after the schools' participation in the PIRLS 2006 data collection.

4.5   Conclusion

In this chapter, we described the Flemish education system and its experiences with large-scale international and national student assessments. We also considered the impact of PIRLS 2006 in Flanders, the only PIRLS study in which Flanders has participated. The PIRLS 2006 findings attracted some media coverage, and each of the participating schools received a feedback report detailing the reading achievement of its Grade 4 students relative to the performance of students at the other participating schools.

The follow-up study conducted by Driessens and Faes (2008) and designed to investigate the influence of the data contained in the feedback reports on school reading-related policy and practice, found few encouraging results. Schools seldom made good use of their respective reports because they did not have the expertise to understand and interpret the reports' relatively academic content. The study findings also indicated that schools were only motivated to address educational issues arising out of the PIRLS 2006 findings when external pressure and incentives required them to do this. The lag between the data-collection phase of PIRLS 2006 and the release of the feedback reports to the schools probably also contributed to schools acting on the information only when pressured.

The fact that only a small proportion of students reached the advanced benchmark presents an important new finding for those engaged in setting and implementing educational policy. This and other issues arising out of the PIRLS findings indicate the need for a more thorough and immediate analysis of the Flemish and international data in order to determine explanations for these findings and thereby provide ideas for ways forward with respect to the reading achievement of primary school children in Flanders. A particular concern that we would like to see addressed relates to the fact that very few Flemish children can read at even a rudimentary level when they start primary school because preschools do not encourage children to read early. Investigating whether all primary schools make an equally insufficient contribution to reading achievement would also be a valuable exercise.

Budgetary constraints may limit Flanders' future participation in PIRLS. Although the Flemish Ministry of Education and Training was interested in participating in PIRLS 2011, the recent global financial and economic crisis compelled the ministry to decide otherwise. We hope that Flanders will participate in PIRLS 2016 so that we can evaluate to what extent changes in policy relating to reading pedagogy have influenced reading achievement. Particularly interesting in this regard will be the effect of Flanders' ongoing policy targeting the reading achievement of immigrant children and schools with a high proportion of immigrant children.

Acknowledgement: The Center for Educational Effectiveness and Evaluation of the Catholic University of Leuven would like to thank the IEA and its executive director, Hans Wagemaker, for their flexibility in accepting the participation of Flanders under rather difficult conditions. The center also thanks their colleagues from the Netherlands, especially Madame Andrea Netten from the Netherlands Expertise Center, Bert Vansteenkiste for data collection and processing, and the Ministry of Education and Training for helping to draw the sample.

References

De Ro, J. (Ed.). (2008). *Education in Flanders: A broad view of the Flemish educational landscape/2008.* Brussels, Belgium: The Ministry of Education and Training. Retrieved from http://www.ond.vlaanderen.be/publicaties/?nr=107

Driessens, A., & Faes, K. (2008). *Schoolfeedback: Analyse van de interpretatie en aanwending van schoolfeedbackrapporten n.a.v. deelname aan het PIRLS-onderzoek* [School feedback: An analysis of the interpretation and use of school feedback reports based on PIRLS 2006]. Unpublished Master's thesis, Catholic University of Leuven, Belgium.

Dupriez, V., Dumay, X., & Vause, A. (2008). How do school systems manage pupils' heterogeneity? *Comparative Education Review, 52*(2), 245–273.

Flanders Investment & Trade. (2010). *Workforce.* Brussels, Belgium: Government of Flanders. Retrieved from http://www.investinflanders.com/en/workforce/default.aspx

Gustafsson, J.-E. (2007). Understanding causal influences on educational achievement through analysis of differences over time within countries. In T. Loveless (Ed.), *Lessons learned: What international assessments tell us about math achievement* (pp. 37–63). Washington, DC: The Brookings Institution.

Hostens, G. (Ed.). (2009). *National summary sheets: Belgium—Flemish Community.* Brussels, Belgium: Ministry of Education and Training. Retrieved from http://eacea.ec. europa.eu/resources/Hostens/pdf/047DN/047_BN_EN.pdf

Mullis, I. V. S., Martin, M. O., Kennedy, A. M., & Foy, P. (2007). *PIRLS 2006 international report: IEA's Progress in the International Reading Literacy Study in primary schools in 40 countries.* Chestnut Hill, MA: Boston College.

National Bank of Belgium. (2010). *Regional accounts 2000–2009.* Brussels, Belgium: National Bank of Belgium. Retrieved from http://www.nbb.be/doc/DQ/N/DQ3/HISTO/NNR09.PDF

Rindermann, H. (2007). The g-factor of international cognitive ability comparisons: The homogeneity of results in PISA, TIMSS, PIRLS and IQ-tests across nations. *European Journal of Personality, 21*, 667–706.

Smet, P. (2009). *Beleidsnota Onderwijs 2009–2014* [Policy note on education 2009–2014]. Retrieved from http://docs.vlaamsparlement.be/docs/stukken/2009-2010/g202-1.pdf

Suchań, B. (2009). *What causes the variance of achievement at the school level? Findings from PIRLS 2006 & TIMSS 2007.* Paper presented at the European Conference on Educational Research, Vienna, Austria, September 28–30, 2009.

Van Damme, J., De Fraine, B., Van Landeghem, G., Opdenakker, M., & Onghena, P. (2002). A new study on educational effectiveness in secondary schools in Flanders. *School Effectiveness and School Improvement, 13*(4), 383–397.

Van Damme, J., Liu, H-Q., Vanhee, L., & Pustjens, H. (2010). Longitudinal studies at the country level as a new approach to educational effectiveness: Explaining change in reading achievement (PIRLS) by change in age, SES and class size. *Effective Education, 2*, 53–84

Van Damme, J., Opdenakker, M., Van Landeghem, G., De Fraine, B., Pustjens, H., & Van de gaer, E. (2006). *Educational effectiveness: An introduction to international and Flemish research on schools, teachers, and classes.* Leuven, Belgium: Acco.

Chapter 5
The Impact of PIRLS in England

Liz Twist

5.1   A Short Country Description

England is one of the four constituent nations of the United Kingdom of Great Britain and Northern Ireland. England, Northern Ireland, and Scotland participate in IEA studies as separate countries and have distinct education systems. Separated from mainland Europe by the English Channel and the North Sea, England borders Wales to the west and Scotland to the north. Northern Ireland and the Republic of Ireland are to the west, across the Irish Sea, and beyond that is the Atlantic Ocean.

England has a surface area of 130,422 square kilometers. The population of 52 million is growing as a result of migration and an increasing birth rate. The population density is 398 persons per square kilometer. A large proportion of the population (7.6 million) lives within the London area.

The GDP per capita in 2006 was US$44,000 (US$38,000 PPP Intl.). England's economy comprises mostly chemical and pharmaceutical sectors and technical industries such as aerospace, the arms industry, and the manufacturing side of the software industry.

Great Britain joined the European Union in 1973 but did not adopt the euro. It has retained the pound sterling as the official currency. Funding of schools is largely determined by the number and age of students on the school roll. Public expenditure on education in England in 2006 was six percent of GDP.

5.2   England's Education System

Approximately 93 percent of students in England attend publicly funded educational institutions. One percent of students attend special schools. The remaining seven percent attend privately funded institutions. Education at a national level is administered by the Department for Education (DfE). At municipal and county levels, local authorities are responsible for organizing state-funded education within their area, although a great deal of education policy is centrally determined and responsibility for day-to-day decisionmaking is with the schools. In January 2010, there were 16,971 primary schools in England, with 4,088,250 students enrolled, of whom 863,680 were under five years of age (DfE, 2010, p. 13).

In primary schools, the percentage of students (of compulsory school age and above) who were classified as being of minority ethnic origin had increased from 24.5 percent in 2009 to 25.5 percent in 2010 (DfE, 2010, p. 2). A similar trend is apparent in state-funded secondary schools, with 21.4 percent of students classified as being of minority ethnic origin in 2010, an increase from 20.6 percent in 2009. In terms of language spoken, in January 2010 the percentage of students (of compulsory school age and above) whose first language was known or believed to be other than English was 16.0 percent in primary schools (15.2% in 2009) and 11.6 percent in state-funded secondary schools (11.1% in 2009).

Compulsory schooling starts from the term after the child's fifth birthday and continues to age 16. Most primary schools include students from ages 4 or 5 to 11. Thereafter, students move on to secondary school. Most secondary schools include students up to the age of either 16 or 18. Publicly funded primary education is nonselective. Most secondary education is also nonselective, with students attending a local school based on parental choice. However, a minority of schools operate some form of selection based on ability or aptitude.

Since April 2004, all three- and four-year-olds have been entitled to free, part-time preschool education in a variety of provisions, including preschools and play groups. The preschool curriculum includes six areas of learning, covering children's development. These are personal, social, and emotional development; communication, language, and literacy; mathematical development; knowledge and understanding of the world; physical development; and creative development.

A revised secondary curriculum was implemented in a phased way from 2008 for students entering secondary school. The curriculum is being reviewed during 2011 to 2013.

Reading is one of three elements in the current National Curriculum for English, alongside speaking and listening, and writing. The knowledge, skills, and understanding to be taught at each stage are specified alongside the contexts, activities, areas of study, and ranges of experience through which the subject is to be taught. The proposed revised primary curriculum includes "understanding English, communication and languages" as one of six areas of learning. The intention is that the revised curriculum will facilitate cross-curricular learning, with opportunities for children to use and apply their knowledge and skills across subjects.

5.3   The Country's Current National Assessment System

The current national assessment system in primary and lower secondary education in England is undergoing review and reform. The previous system of formal assessments at age 11 (the end of the primary phase of education) and at age 14 (the end of the lower secondary stage) in English (reading and writing), mathematics, and science has been reformed. Since 2010, the only statutory whole-cohort testing is of 11-year-olds in English and mathematics. Consideration is being given to the introduction of a national (sampled) achievement survey at age 14, which may incorporate elements from IEA's Trends in Mathematics and Science (TIMSS) surveys. A reading test of six-year-olds, designed as a screening measure and focusing on children's phonic knowledge, is being piloted.

The remaining national assessments, in English and mathematics at age 11, continue to be controversial, and the system is currently being revised. Critics argue that the focus on these two subjects in the final year of primary education distorts the taught curriculum. Others argue that primary schools should be held accountable as publicly funded institutions and that formal testing of students in the final year is the most appropriate way of doing this. Probably the most controversial aspect is the publication of "league tables" of schools, compiled by the media from the published results.

5.4 The Country's Experience in International Large-Scale Assessments

England has been a regular participant in the various international surveys conducted by the IEA and, more recently, by the OECD. At the time that the international and national reports on PIRLS 2006 were published, an article appeared that cast doubt on the validity of PIRLS as an international comparison of literacy. In particular, the author (Hilton, 2006) identified concerns about what she termed "cultural bias" and "linguistic bias." She also raised the issue of sampling and claimed that the sample for England had been "advantageously organized." She argued that PIRLS 2001 was "often quoted and celebrated by government" (p. 818) as an indicator of a national rise in reading standards and a vindication of the National Literacy Strategy, a high-profile government initiative that has had a considerable influence on teaching strategies over the past decade.

In a response to Hilton's criticisms of international comparative surveys in general, and PIRLS in particular, Whetton, Twist, and Sainsbury (2007) showed how the complex methodological processes involved in the IEA surveys meant that issues concerned with the validity of the studies were considered at every stage of them. They argued that many of Hilton's criticisms were unfounded. Whetton and colleagues concluded that the criticisms were based on "partial understanding and some personal opinions rather than a robust examination of the sources" (p. 984) and were therefore misleading.

It is possible to see Hilton's article as a demonstration of the skepticism to be found in some quarters in England about the validity of international surveys and their findings, skepticism that is not new and that echoes the views of academics, such as Goldstein (2004). Nevertheless, the present government remains committed to participation in a range of studies, including IEA's PIRLS and TIMSS in 2011, and OECD's PISA in 2012. In its *Analysis and Evidence Strategy 2009–10*, England's education ministry, the Department for School, Children, and Families (DCSF), endorsed participation in the surveys:

These international studies … are an important complement to our own work. They encourage a different perspective on key features of our education system, ranging from accountability and funding frameworks through to pedagogy and pupil engagement. They also helpfully focus attention on gaps between high and low performers and on factors which may promote educational equity. (DCSF, 2009a, p. 45)

The prominence given to international surveys may actually increase if, as recommended by an advisory group, TIMSS is incorporated into a new national monitoring system at Grade 8 (DCSF, 2009b).

5.5   National Results, Impact, and (Expected) Long-Term Effects of PIRLS 2001 and 2006 Since the First Publication

The outcomes of PIRLS 2001 and 2006 were disseminated to various groups in England. The focus was largely on communicating findings to teaching professionals and various specialist literacy groups. The 2006 findings are occasionally referred to in the media, often in the context of a "bad news" story related to the nation's perceived growing illiteracy.

In 2008, the government commissioned the National Foundation for Educational Research (NFER) to undertake a review of selected primary core curricula worldwide (Ruddock & Sainsbury, 2008) with the aim of answering the following question: "How does the content of the primary curriculum in England at Key Stage 2 in literacy, maths, and science compare to the content of the same curricula in a range of high-performing countries?" The review provided one of the sources of evidence scrutinized by those reviewing the primary curriculum in England. The results of recent PIRLS and TIMSS surveys informed the selection of countries; the encyclopedia produced for the 2006 PIRLS survey also proved valuable. For literacy, the education systems reviewed included British Columbia (Canada), Chinese Taipei, Italy, Latvia, Ontario (Canada), the Netherlands, Singapore, and Sweden.

5.5.1   Standards over Time

It is important to understand the context in which the outcomes of national and international surveys are published in England. Since the election of a Labour (socialist) government in 1997, the country has seen an increasing emphasis on the accountability of public services, with schools and other public bodies expected to demonstrate success (as measured by outputs, such as improved national test results and shorter hospital waiting times). This development has had the inevitable effect of "raising the stakes" of the accountability measures: in education, these include the tests that all students take at the end of their primary education. Students take the test at ages 10 or 11 or Grade 5, which means they are generally a year older than the PIRLS' students. The outcomes are closely scrutinized as indicators of the impact of government policies.

The results of the reading tests that students in England take at the end of their primary education (the "Key Stage 2 tests") show that attainment has remained broadly stable since the first PIRLS survey. One of the most problematic aspects of the PIRLS 2006 results was their indication that attainment in England had fallen, not just relative to other countries but also in absolute terms, since 2001. This apparent anomaly, alongside the equally surprising finding that attainment in two other high-attaining countries in 2001—Sweden and the Netherlands—also appeared to have fallen, led to a preliminary further investigation. This suggested that the complexity of the measurement of trends had shrouded the findings in a degree of uncertainty and that further research was needed.

It is this very stability, or, in PIRLS' terms, fall in the standards achieved in primary reading that has contributed to another relatively recent (2009) policy announcement, namely that the organization that had overseen the implementation of the literacy and numeracy strategies (the "National Strategies") would be abolished in 2011. The introduction of the National Literacy Strategy in 1998 led to the adoption in almost all primary schools in England of a particular pedagogical approach to teaching literacy. In contrast to the National Curriculum, in which no specific pedagogical approaches are advocated, the teaching of reading and writing was organized by means of the "literacy hour" and included, for example, "group reading" and "guided writing."[1] Various commentators have suggested that this led to the adoption of what Soler (2007, p. 47) summarized as "technicist, prescriptive, less flexible pedagogical approaches, and ... a rejection of progressive, child-centred ideals and reflective practice." Others recognized more positive effects of this large-scale reform. The Office for Standards in Education (Ofsted), for example, claimed that "The National Literacy Strategy has had a significant improvement on the standards of attainment in English and on the quality of teaching over the last four years" (Ofsted, 2002, p. 2).

In recent years, the government has introduced a range of policies and initiatives designed to "narrow the gap" —to reduce inequalities in society. The narrowing-the-gap agenda goes well beyond inequalities in education, but it is in this area that the outcomes from PIRLS may have had some influence. The term "the long tail of underachievement" is used in many English-speaking countries to describe the phenomenon of a greater than expected proportion of students achieving fairly low standards despite what may be a relatively good performance on average.

Recognition of a long tail is not new. In 1996, researchers at NFER and the Open University looked at the reading literacy attainment of nine-year-olds (Grade 3) in England and Wales (Brooks, Pugh, & Schagen, 1996). One of the measures used came from IEA's 1991 Reading Literacy Survey. The overall performance of students in the 1996 study would have placed England and Wales at close to the overall international average in 1991. A significant feature of the 1996 study was the identification of the

---

1   For more information about the Literacy Strategy and framework, see http://nationalstrategies.standards.dcsf.gov.uk/primary/primaryframework/literacyframework.

long tail of students in England and Wales who achieved scores well below the average.

In both of the PIRLS surveys to date, data from England, along with data from a number of other English-speaking countries, and notably New Zealand, has shown a wide spread between the attainment of the best readers and that of the weakest readers. Combined with data from national assessments showing that improvements in reading achievement at the end of primary school had stalled, there has been a renewed emphasis on intervening to try to prevent early failure. This is illustrated by four recent initiatives, confidently named Every Child a Reader, Every Child a Writer, Every Child a Talker, and Every Child Counts. Focused on students from ages six to nine (Every Child a Talker is preschool), the programs are funded largely by central government. All four programs are being piloted but their future is currently uncertain.

5.5.2 Engagement in Reading

Another finding from PIRLS 2006 for England, and one highlighted in the national report, was students' comparatively poor attitudes toward reading and also the fact that quite a large proportion of students said that they barely read outside school, from choice. This finding echoed a key finding in PIRLS 2001, although the situation appeared somewhat worse in the later survey given the statistically significant increase in the proportion of students identified as having the most negative attitudes. When asked how often they read "for fun" outside school, 42 percent of students said they read once or twice a month or not even that much. This finding was picked up in the DCSF press release detailing the PIRLS 2006 results:

> This study shows that our highest achieving children are reading less, with children's busy days leaving less time for books at home. As parents we have to get the balance right and as a society we have to send the right messages about the value of reading to our children. (DCSF, 2007)

Not surprisingly, this finding and the amount of time that children were spending on computer games were the basis of an article about PIRLS in the press the day after release of the national and international reports.

The year 2008 in England was designated the National Year of Reading (NYR), the second such year in the country. At the official launch of the NYR in January 2008, attended by the prime minister, findings were cited from PIRLS 2006 concerning the (in)frequency with which children in England read novels and the fact that this type of reading appeared to be less frequent than in 2001. At another NYR launch event in April that year, the Secretary of State (Minister) for Education declared that:

> Reading opens doors to everything in life, from applying to jobs to enjoying your favourite hobbies. Getting your children—both boys and girls—to be passionate about reading is something all parents can do. Reading to your children for ten

minutes at bedtime is the best way of improving our kids' chances when they get to school.

The NYR's stated aim was "to create a reading culture in England and specifically to engage those people who need help with reading or think reading's not for them." The NYR applied a focused strategy in an attempt to reach and influence those people who would not come into contact with material distributed through libraries or book shops. The final evaluation of the NYR suggested it had achieved some successes with target groups but that much remained to be done to increase engagement with reading across the population (Thomson, 2009).

Another strategy to build children's engagement with reading is the continued development of "bookgifting" programs by Booktrust, a national charity promoting reading among children and young people. Books are given at no cost to the parents and caregivers of babies aged about eight months (this program is termed Booktime) and to children in their first year of schooling (Bookstart). All young people are able to choose a book from a selection in their first year of secondary school (Booked Up).

These initiatives, all of which began in the years after publication of the PIRLS 2001 findings, have the stated aim of engaging children, young people, and their parents in reading activities. In addition, the annual Reading Challenge runs over the long summer break from school. In a scheme organized by The Reading Agency, children, mostly of primary school age, record the books they borrow from their local library and achieve certificates for specific levels of reading, often presented at their schools when school starts again or by a local dignitary in the library.

Several other initiatives focus on engaging specific groups. Boys into Books is run by the School Library Association and is centrally funded. Lists are produced that offer specific suggestions of books that might prove engaging to reluctant male readers. Some work has been undertaken on the effectiveness of "reading champions" —well-known individuals (often sports stars) who identify a favorite book and explain why they particularly enjoy it.

Work by Shen and others (e.g., Shen, 2002; Shen & Pedulla, 2000) in relation to TIMSS highlights the relationship between attitudes to a subject and student attainment within and between countries. It is clear from the PIRLS data from England, in common with the data from all other participating countries, that the higher achieving students in PIRLS expressed more positive attitudes toward reading. Although some caution should be exercised when looking across countries at students' views about reading, due to different response tendencies (McGaw, 2008), students from England and Scotland still apparently feel less positive about reading when compared to their peers in countries where cultural differences can be considered relatively small (Canadian provinces, New Zealand).

One of the larger organizations offering professional development opportunities for teachers is the highly regarded Centre for Literacy in Primary Education (CLPE). Although the center continues to work predominantly with teachers in London schools, one of its projects, titled The Power of Reading, has involved teachers in nearly 1,200 schools from all around the country. This project was stimulated by the strong relationship, in both PIRLS 2001 and 2006, between reading attainment and positive attitudes to reading, and also by the fact that students in England were far less positive about reading than their peers in many other countries. The Power of Reading focuses on increasing teachers' knowledge of books and enjoyment of reading, as well as on extending the creative use of children's literature in the classroom.

5.6   Expected Future Activities

Interest in undertaking secondary analysis of international survey data in England is limited. The greater focus is on looking ahead to the next survey phase. NFER researchers will continue to disseminate PIRLS 2001 and 2006 findings and commentary to the community of literacy and education researchers in England. Work continues on drawing attention to the impact of the lack of engagement with reading demonstrated by many students.

The contract for the national research center for PIRLS 2011 has been again awarded to NFER, and the survey was administered alongside the TIMSS survey in summer 2011.

5.7   Concluding Remarks

The new government is taking a considerable interest in the outcomes of international surveys, focusing in particular on PISA 2009 and giving recognition to the unique contributions that international surveys make to our understanding of the health of England's education system. One of the ongoing challenges for the PIRLS national research center is to ensure the results are reported and interpreted accurately. During the first decade of the 21st century, we often heard the phrase "building the evidence base." Undoubtedly, the international surveys will continue to have a place in the evidence base in this new decade.

References

Brooks, G., Pugh, A. K., & Schagen, I. (1996). *Reading performance at nine*. Slough, UK: National Foundation for Educational Research.

Department for Children, Schools, and Families (DCSF). (2007, November 28). *National Year of Reading will instil a passion for reading in children of all ages— Ed Balls* (press release). Available online at http://www.gov-news. org/gov/uk/news/national_year_reading_instil_passion_reading/40084.html

Department for Children, Schools, and Families (DCSF). (2009a). *Analysis and Evidence Strategy 2009–10*. London, UK: Author. Retrieved from http:// publications.education. gov.ukeOrderingDownload/AES-2009.pdf

Department for Children, Schools, and Families (DCSF). (2009b). *Report of the Expert Group on Assessment*. London, UK: Author. Retrieved from http://www. edexcel.com/Policies/Linked%20to%20Documents/Expert-Group-Report.pdf

Department for Education (DfE). (2010). *Schools, pupils, and their characteristics: January 2010, statistical first release* (SFR 09/2010). London: Author. Retrieved from http://www.education.gov.uk/rsgateway/DB/SFR/s000925/ sfr09-2010.pdf

Goldstein, H. (2004). International comparisons of student attainment: Some issues arising from the PISA study. *Assessment in Education, 11*, 319–330.

Hilton, M. (2006). Measuring standards in primary English: Issues of validity and accountability with respect to PIRLS and National Curriculum test scores. *British Educational Research Journal, 32*(6), 817–837.

McGaw, B. (2008). The role of the OECD in international comparative studies of achievement. *Assessment in Education: Principles, Policy and Practice, 15*(3), 223–243.

Office for Standards in Education (Ofsted). (2002). *National Literacy Strategy: The first four years*. London, UK: Author.

Ruddock, G., & Sainsbury, M. (with Clausen-May, T., Vappula, H., Mason, K., Patterson, E. W., Pyle, K., Kispal, A., Siddiqui, R., & Rees, F.). (2008). *Comparison of the English Core Primary Curriculum to those of other high performing countries* (DCSF Research Report RW048). London, UK: Department for Children, Schools, and Families. Retrieved from http://www.uquebec.ca/ observgo/fichiers/48461_GSE-2.pdf

Shen, C. (2002). Revisiting the relationship between students' achievement and their self-perceptions: A cross-national analysis based on TIMSS 1999 data. *Assessment in Education, 9*(2), 161–184.

Shen, C., & Pedulla, J. J. (2000). The relationship between students' achievement and their self-perception of competence and rigour of mathematics and science: A cross-national analysis. *Assessment in Education, 7*(2), 237–253.

Soler, J. (2007). The Rose Report: One step further in a managerialist approach to the literacy curriculum in England. In R. Openshaw & J. Soler (Eds.), *Reading across international boundaries* (pp. 43–53). Charlotte, NC: Information Age Publishing.

Thomson, A. (2009). *Reading: The Future. Final report of the 2008 National Year of Reading*. London, UK: The National Literacy Trust. Retrieved from http://www.mla.gov.uk/what/programmes/library_action_plan/~/media/Files/pdf/2 009/Reading_The_Future

Whetton, C., Twist, L., & Sainsbury, M. (2007). Measuring standards in primary English: The validity of PIRLS—a response to Mary Hilton. *British Educational Research Journal, 33*(8), 977–986.

Chapter 6
The Impact of PIRLS in Germany

Jenny Lenkeit, Martin Goy, and Knut Schwippert

6.1   A Short Country Description: Germany at a Glance[1]

A central European country, Germany borders nine other countries of Europe as well as the North Sea and the Baltic Sea. From the northern borderline with Denmark to the southern end, where the country abuts the Alps, and with a length of 876 kilometers, the territory of Germany covers an area of about 357,000 square kilometers. Between the mountains of the Alps and the low-lying lands typically found in the north are the forested uplands in the middle of Germany. Together, these areas provide Germany with a variety of landscapes.

Germany's 82 million inhabitants make for an average population density of 229 persons per square kilometer. Only the three cities of Berlin, Hamburg, and Munich have more than a million inhabitants. Eighty-seven percent of the population lives in rural areas, most of them in communities with fewer than 100,000 inhabitants. In the last decade, however, some areas of Germany have experienced strong migration into the cities. This is especially the case in some regions of former East Germany, which were sparsely populated even before many young people began leaving for the cities due to a lack of apprenticeship-training positions and job offers in their home areas. After unification in 1999 of the two separated German states (East Germany and West Germany), Berlin again became the country's capital.

Germany is a parliamentary republic of 16 federal states. It is a member of the United Nations, NATO, the OECD, and the G8 Economic Group of countries. In 2009, the country's gross national product (GNP) per capita was estimated to be US$40,874 (US$34,212 PPP Intl.). The GNP comprises mainly manufacturing, industry, catering, financing, renting, and business services as well as public and private services. Germany is one of the world's biggest exporters (mainly in vehicles, machinery, and chemicals) and has developed a "high" standard of living[2] that includes a comprehensive system of social security.

In 2008, public expenditure on education amounted to €M155,000 (or 6.2%) of the GNP (Statistisches Bundesamt, 2010).

---

1   This introductory part is based on information drawn from the first edition of the *Impact of PIRLS*.

2   See the Human Development Index produced by the United Nations Development Program. The index condenses measures of life expectancy, literacy, education, and standards of living in one score.

6.2   Germany's Education System as a Context for PIRLS[3]

Germany's 16 federal states (*Länder*) have legislative and administrative power over policies within their respective geographical areas. Therefore, and although the school system is organized by the state, each federal state holds administrative control over its education system. Regulations and recommendations pertaining to education that are issued by the Standing Conference of Ministers of Education and Cultural Affairs of the Länder of the Federal Republic of Germany (Kultusministerkonferenz or KMK) do not become binding on the states until they are adopted as state laws.

In Germany, approximately seven percent[4] of school-age children attend private schools, which are state subsidized and controlled. With the exception of a few of these private schools, schooling is free for all children. Schoolbooks are usually issued to children free of charge. In those states where this is not the case, parents and caregivers receive reimbursement. The same system applies in instances where parents and caregivers have to pay for their children to attend school excursions or special programs.

Around three-quarters of children three years and older attend pre-primary education in the form of kindergarten. Attendance is usually voluntary, and the kindergartens have no direct link with the school system. In past decades, the curriculum of these institutions involved mostly play and social activities directed at developing children's physical, spoken, and creative skills. Today, however, there is an increased focus on developing children's language competencies, introducing them to basic scientific phenomena, and forging closer links between pre-primary and primary education.

Compulsory schooling starts when children enter primary school at the age of six and ends when they leave secondary school or an institution of the dual system at age 18. Parents can, however, elect to start their children at school when they reach age five or seven. Of the 12 years of compulsory schooling, 9 to 10 years have to be spent in full-time schooling.

With the exception of the provinces of Berlin and Brandenburg, primary school encompasses Grades 1 to 4 (ages 6 to 10). Most primary schools are half-day schools, although some of these do supervise students who stay on in the afternoon. Calls for implementation of all-day schooling are ongoing.

When students leave primary school, their teachers recommend the lower-secondary school track (or stream) they think these students should attend. However, across the states, the regulations governing this process of recommendation and parents' right to have a say in the matter tend to be inconsistent. Also, research shows

---

3   This section of the chapter is based on Germany's country profile in the *PIRLS 2006 Encyclopedia* (Hornberg, Bos, Lankes, & Valtin, 2007) and documents from the Standing Conference of Ministers of Education and Cultural Affairs of the Länder of the Federal Republic of Germany (KMK, 2006).

4   This percentage includes school-age children in general education.

strong links between the tracks that children enter and the socioeconomic status (SES) of their families. Contrary to the prevailing impression that teachers alone govern the selection process by favoring children from advantaged backgrounds, parents appear to have the greater say in which track their children should attend. Parental decisions, in turn, appear to be accentuating the SES link (Ditton & Krüsken, 2006; Ditton, Krüsken, & Schauenberg, 2005). Although the regulations governing tracking arose from the aim of forming an optimal alignment between institutional demands and individual ability (Cortina & Trommer, 2003; Ditton & Krüsken, 2006), tracking students early in their school career is one of the most controversial aspects of Germany's national education system.

The lower secondary level in Germany is traditionally trinomial, with the *Hauptschule* providing the academically least-demanding provision. Here, students receive a basic education, and those who leave this track after Grade 9 usually enter apprenticeships and trades-based employment. Students attending the *Realschule* receive a more extensive general education. At the end of Grade 10, they can acquire the qualification necessary for entry to vocational or higher education institutions and therefore more demanding occupations. The *Gymnasium* covers both the lower and upper secondary levels and imparts an in-depth general education directed toward a higher education entrance qualification procured at the end of Grades 12 or 13.[5] During the 1970s, more and more students began attending schools that integrate these traditional tracks in one institution (*Gesamtschule*) and offer all qualifications. Alongside these schools are several schools that offer alternative syllabi. There are also special schools for children with disabilities.

In Germany, the universities are responsible for teacher education programs. All training programs comprise two phases. During the first, students complete a mix of elective and specialized courses and study educational theory. During the second, they spend two years engaged in practical training at schools. They also attend in-depth courses on pedagogy related to specific school subjects as well as courses on education-related theory. Primary school teachers are expected to teach all major subjects even though they might not be especially trained for those. Across the country, nearly all primary school teachers (80% to over 90%) are female.

6.3   Experience with Large-Scale Assessments

6.3.1   International Perspectives

During the 1970s and 1980s, educational research in Germany (precisely West Germany) focused on reforms to the education system that were predicated on ideas such as "education for all" and "equal opportunity." The quality of instruction and the

---

5   Several years ago, almost all of the federal states began shortening the time students spend at the Gymnasium. This has meant that students in the academic track gain their school-leaving certificate after 12 years of schooling instead of 13.

value of different learning opportunities also came under scrutiny. The effects, whether intended or unintended, of these reforms were not empirically evaluated. Participation in large-scale assessments of educational achievement at this time thus received little attention from Germany's research community. Prior to a representative sample of West-German students participating in IEA's First International Science Study (FISS) in the early 1970s, only a few federal states had taken part in international surveys. Because students' achievement in FISS was not as good as had been expected or hoped for, Germany began to reform its education system, but took no further part in international system-monitoring studies for nearly 20 years, leaving the need for a formal evaluation tradition unfilled.

In 1991, the intervention of educational researcher Rainer Lehmann led to Germany taking part in IEA's International Reading Literacy Study (RLS), an event that prompted participation in international school surveys on a more regular basis. Although Germany's experience with large-scale-assessments is relatively short, it has nevertheless been intensive and in no way random. Today, Germany's participation in international surveys such as PIRLS and PISA indicates a sincere interest in using the results of these studies to evaluate the efficacy of the country's educational reforms.

6.3.2   National Perspectives

The period between the 1970s and the 1990s also saw Germany doing little with respect to conducting national or regional studies of educational achievement within its borders or across its states. This situation was mainly due to the predominantly humanistic approach to educational research at this time. The small number of comparative studies of education that were conducted within the country during this time period, such as SCHOLASTIK in the 1980s, covered only a few of the federal states, and they attracted little interest from either the research community or the public. However, during the mid 1990s, the number of regional studies began to increase markedly (see Table 6.2, p. 97, in Schwippert, 2007, for a listing of the studies up to 2001 and Table 6.1 below for a listing from 2002 on).

The increase in regional and cross-regional studies was prompted primarily by Germany's agreement to participate, in 1995, in IEA's Trends in International Mathematics and Science Study (TIMSS). The TIMSS results for Germany were deemed disappointing. At the same time commentators within the educational and research communities discussed the deficiencies in the structure and administration of large-scale cross-country comparative studies of achievement, such as TIMSS, resulting in major critiques of those studies.

Table 6.1: **Selected* regional and cross-regional large-scale surveys of educational achievement conducted in Germany, 2002–2005**

Year of data collection	Name of survey	Status of regional extension
2002	Study of Education Basics in Grade 11 (LAU 11)	Census of one federal state (Hamburg)—fourth "wave" (i.e., the measurement point of this longitudinal study)
2003	Competencies and Attitudes of Students in Grade 4 (KESS 4)	Census of one federal state (Hamburg)—follow-up study of LAU
2003	German–English Student Assessment (DESI)	Extension of German PISA study (Grade 9)
2003 2004 2005	Survey of Development in Reading and Mathematics Comprehension in Grades 4 to 6 in Berlin (ELEMENT)	Census of one federal state (Berlin)

Note: * For a comprehensive overview of educational large-scale assessments in Germany, see Schwippert and Goy (2008).

The increase in regional and cross-regional studies that followed Germany's participation in TIMSS can be seen as a two-fold reaction to the findings of the study and to the usefulness of large-scale assessments of this kind. First, the TIMSS findings indicated some major deficits in the German education system as a whole and across its different levels. Second, the perception that international assessments could cover only a core group of interests held in common by the participating countries meant that other aspects of interest relating to school level, class, and individual students would have to be explored separately. Studies such as LAU (Hamburg), QuaSUM (Brandenburg), MARKUS (Rhineland-Palatinate), and ELEMENT (Berlin) were a response to this thinking. These studies focused not only on students' competencies but also—and to a greater extent than international studies can—on the particular German-based processes and conditions of learning and teaching apparent across the different levels of Germany's education system.

Germany has also participated in the national extensions of the international PIRLS and PISA surveys. This ongoing participation, along with expansion of subject-related performance tests and background questionnaires, has enabled Germany to obtain in-depth information relating to the effectiveness of its education system overall and to student achievement across the regions of the country in particular. Today, the trend whereby participation in international studies drives the development of national evaluative studies has developed to the extent that this form of empirical research is now an intrinsic part of the work of educational institutes and universities. The establishment, in 2003, of a national institute called the Institute for Educational Progress or IQB solidified this trend. Founded by the KMK, the institute is responsible for developing and publishing national educational standards. Germany's ongoing desire to obtain deeper understanding of the reasons behind the country's performance in large-scale assessment studies will no doubt continue to encourage the country's engagement in national and regional large-scale surveys and mark its willingness to address pressing deficiencies in its education system.

6.3.3 Funding of Studies and Freedom of Expression

Participation in large-scale surveys in Germany is primarily funded by three major institutions: the Federal Ministry of Education and Research (Bundesministerium für Bildung und Forschung or BMBF), the aforementioned KMK, and the German Research Council (Deutsche Forschungsgemeinschaft). Regional studies are usually funded by provincial authorities.

While the three major institutions have no control over the direction and nature of the research, studies conducted by the provincial authorities are sometimes subject to political interests and therefore oversight. As a consequence, publications produced under the name of provincial ministries are typically revised and modified (usually to a limited degree only). In general, though, national funding institutions have no jurisdiction over the content of published research reports.

University academics in Germany have the right to conduct their research and teaching free of political interference. As such, research publications produced in universities are not constrained by political oversight. This freedom was granted as a reaction to the time during the Nazi regime in Germany when universities were used to propagate Nazi ideology.

6.3.4 Reporting of Survey Results

In Germany, the format used to disseminate survey results has been amended in recent years. Initially, the format used in publications suited the research community but not teachers and educational administrators, who struggled to understand the content. Lacking knowledge in research methodology and statistical reporting, teachers, in particular, had difficulty reading and interpreting the findings. However, amending the format in favor of teachers created new problems: journalists interpreted and publicized the simplified presentation of results in terms of "teachers not doing a good job", while school principals and teachers rightfully complained that the results were so generalized that they did not have recourse to information relevant to their particular schools and classes.

Renewed effort led to the results being presented in a format that served the needs of all readers, whether engaged in research, educational policymaking, teaching, or the media. Teachers and principals, for example, now receive information directly relevant to their school and classroom contexts while journalists are given press kits and encouraged to question the researchers involved. Teachers and principals can also attend courses and/or receive help when interpreting the results and/or remedying deficient pedagogical practices.

These efforts strongly contributed to the development of mutual trust between the research and pedagogical communities and thus to declining resistance against participation in large-scale surveys. Practitioners now see that the feedback they receive represents not a threat against their pedagogical practice but an opportunity to compare their students' performance with the performance of students in similar classes and schools. The feedback also enables them to discuss possible sources of underachievement and develop strategies to enhance and adjust practice (e.g., instructional methods).

Despite these positive steps forward, instances remain of researchers themselves disagreeing on interpretation of the results and subsequently "setting the cat among the pigeons" when presenting and discussing findings in the public arena. These differences generally reflect political beliefs, and they tend to have the unfortunate outcome of harming the credibility that educational research and those involved with it have been struggling to attain.

6.4 National Results and the Impact of PIRLS

6.4.1 National Results

German Grade 4 students' average achievement score on the PIRLS 2006 international literacy scale was 548 points. The international average score of 506 situated Germany in the upper-quarter level of scores for the participating countries. German students also performed significantly better than the students in two comparison groups—the European Union (EU) countries (average score on the literacy scale was 534) and the OECD countries (average score, 537). The German fourth graders who participated in PIRLS 2006 gained, on average, a score nine points higher than the score obtained by the students who participated in PIRLS 2001. However, the dispersion of achievement scores (an average standard deviation of 67 score points) remained unchanged between 2001 and 2006. The 2006 German students were, by an average of four score points, more competent in reading literary texts than informational texts. Just over 13 percent of students could be deemed functionally illiterate in 2006, although this percentage was a slight drop on the corresponding 2001 percentage.

On average, girls' achievement on the PIRLS 2006 reading literacy scale was seven points higher than boys' achievement; the international average was 13 points. More boys (19%) than girls (9%) said that they never read for fun outside of school. Although the relationship between family background characteristics and achievement was by no means as pronounced as in studies conducted at the secondary school level (e.g., PISA), distinct differences in achievement scores between students from more advantaged and more disadvantaged backgrounds as well as between students of different migration status were evident in PIRLS.

Germany reported the country's achievement results for the 2006 reading tests according to scaling set down in the PIRLS 2006 international report (Mullis, Martin,

Kennedy, & Foy, 2007) and technical report (Foy, Galia, & Li, 2007). Here, the model used was a three-parameter logistical model with conditioning.

In order to determine if scaling the international reading achievement data with a Rasch model would produce a different ranking of the countries according to their mean achievement scores, the German PIRLS research group rescaled the entire dataset using ConQuest software (Wu, Adams, & Wilson, 1998). The data were transformed in a way that made the 1-pl (one-parameter logistic model) international mean and standard deviation scores equivalent to the 3-pl (three-parameter logistic model) international mean and standard deviation scores. Comparison of the scores for the two models revealed only minor differences in country rankings. Where differences were apparent, they related to countries whose mean achievement scores did not differ significantly from one another (Bos, Valtin, Hornberg, Buddeberg, Goy, & Voss, 2007, p. 112 ff.).

The German PIRLS research group conducted the same analyses when reporting the reading achievement results for fourth graders from Belgium's German-speaking community. This community did not participate in PIRLS 2006 but decided to use the survey's test instruments (German translation) one year later (Bos, Sereni, & Stubbe, 2008). The scaling and conditioning of the data from the German-speaking Community of Belgium were executed according to the procedures used to prepare the international PIRLS 2006 data. These procedures thus employed the item parameters from the official international scaling (Martin, Mullis, & Kennedy, 2007, Appendix D), the software PARSCALE (Muraki & Bock, 1991), and the software DESI (Gladkova & Moran, 2005), a follow-up to the software MGROUP (Stubbe, Sereni, & Bos, 2008). In addition to rescaling the entire dataset with a Rasch model, using the ConQuest software, the research group also used PARSCALE to employ a three-parameter logistic model without conditioning to rescale the data. The comparison between the three models (international 3-pl model, Rasch model, and 3-pl model without conditioning) revealed that differences in ranking could only be found for those countries whose mean achievement scores did not differ significantly from one another (Bos & Stubbe, 2008, p. 70 ff.).

The national extension of the PIRLS 2006 survey sample allowed for intranational comparisons, which revealed differences as large as 42 points between the best- and worst-performing federal states. The lowest achievement scores emerged in the three major cities of Berlin, Hamburg, and Bremen, an outcome reflecting the high concentration of socially disadvantaged groups in these areas.

The PIRLS 2006 results also lent themselves to comparison with the outcomes of PISA 2006. Prior to the release of the PIRLS 2001 results, a strong debate arose over the apparently poor scholastic performance of 15-year-olds. Some commentators argued that the under-performance of secondary schools was a consequence of deficiencies in the primary education system. Others, however, claimed that because primary schools provide a comprehensive education and their students do not need to work toward attainment of formal qualifications, the schools were not to blame for the poor achievement of secondary school students. Release of the PIRLS results supported the latter view.

Although the PISA 2006 survey results overall showed a slight increase in the reading achievement scores of 15-year-old students, the average performance of the German students (495 points) still set the country within the group clustered around the international average. Germany was significantly behind Korea, Hong Kong, Canada, and Australia as well as Finland, Ireland, the Netherlands, Sweden, and Poland. However, as stated above, the German fourth graders who participated in PIRLS 2006 performed significantly above the international average as well as above the averages for the EU and OECD country groups.

6.4.2 Dissemination of the PIRLS 2006 Results

Since the release, in 2007, of the report detailing the PIRLS 2006 international results, Germany has published three books featuring the study. The first compares the reading competency of German students with the reading competency of the international population (Bos, Valtin et al., 2007). The second offers an in-depth analysis of the results of the extended sample of all German federal states (Bos et al., 2008). The third book comprises the results of advanced analyses of PIRLS 2006 data relative to selected areas of interest, such as the process directing decisions about students' transition from primary to secondary school, the relationship between ICT use and reading literacy achievement, and the low levels of achievement among "at-risk" students (Bos, Hornberg et al., 2010). Summaries of all three publications can be found on the official PIRLS German website (http://www.iglu.ifs-dortmund.de/).

In the hope of attracting a public response to the PIRLS data, the PIRLS research team accompanied the publications of the first two books with press conferences and press releases on the days of publication. Television news reports and print media, which included highly respected and/or popular outlets, gave a good account of the results. Although public interest in the results of the international comparisons was apparent, it was nowhere near the level of interest aroused by the PISA 2000 and PIRLS 2001 findings.

Other outreach initiatives have included numerous presentations at conferences, such as those conducted by the European Conference on Educational Research (ECER) and the Arbeitsgruppe Empirische Bildungsforschung (AEPF).[6] The PIRLS 2001 data, however, have continued to prompt a higher number of publications in educational research and administrative journals than have the PIRLS 2006 data. This has been especially the case since publication of the first *Impact of PIRLS* report (Schwippert, 2007).

---

6   English translation: The Working Group on Empirical Educational Research.

6.4.3 Impact of PIRLS 2001 and 2006

In Germany, the PISA studies of 2000 and 2003 attracted considerably more attention than the PIRLS studies of 2001 and 2006.[7] Because the PIRLS fourth graders performed far better than the PISA 15-year-olds, the media, and therefore the public, concluded that problems arising out of Germany's system of education were not to be found at the elementary level and accordingly "fell in" with the adage that "good news is not newsworthy."

Also, over the past decade, the German public seems to have held different attitudes toward evaluation of the education system. At first, the question of whether German students should be evaluated at all and what the assumed benefits of the various studies were dominated reporting of the results. However, as more and more national and international assessments were conducted and reported on, people became habituated to their presence in the educational landscape. This habituation, especially among educational researchers and policymakers, helped fuel well-informed, considered debates in various spheres, including the media and the public, about deficiencies in Germany's education system and what could be done to remedy these.

One of the major impacts of the discussion relating to the PIRLS achievement results and, through close association, to the PISA findings was opening up to scrutiny the teaching and learning conditions in Germany's schools—scrutiny that Germany had long avoided. This attention, in turn, saw the media and the public, but even more so the educational research community, parent associations, and teacher unions, substantially advancing the debate about the merits or otherwise of Germany's traditional trinomial school system. The highlighting in the two studies of the strong relationship between SES and achievement, the underperformance of students from migration backgrounds, and the substantial numbers of other students at risk of poor educational achievement also led to the need to develop and implement strategies and programs directed at improving educational provision being placed high on the educational agenda.

The increasing receptivity among teachers, parents, and educational researchers to evaluation of all areas of the education system has not only enhanced cooperation across these groups during implementation and evaluation of reforms but also tightened the links between the two processes. Although political agents and educational researchers do not always agree on the what and the how of the reforms, both groups acknowledge that reform initiatives need to take account of the fact that learning is a cumulative process. Research programs such as PIRLS and PISA that are conducted at specific stages of children's school career (e.g., at the end of primary school in the case of PIRLS) are necessary and useful but not sufficient for capturing the learning process

---

7   When reporting in this section on the impact of the two PIRLS cycles on public and published opinion in Germany, we need to make clear that no comprehensive media analysis or opinion survey on this topic has been conducted to date. The description of such an impact is therefore based on our personal perceptions.

from earliest childhood on. As such, there is a need for research (both "snapshot" and longitudinal) that traces this process from kindergarten and other types of pre-primary education through primary schooling and on to secondary schooling.

Despite the general agreement that change is needed, Germany's federally organized system of education tends to hamper reform to varying degrees. Nevertheless, educational administration and research institutes have pressed on with reform-related research projects, strategies, and programs. Initiatives by the KMK and BMBF are documented in two statements issued in March 2008 (KMK & BMBF, 2008) and in December 2008 (KMK, 2008c). Taken together, the content of these two documents highlights the following four courses of action.

1. *Provision of remedial programs focussed on low-performing students, especially those attending lower secondary education:* The two groups of students deemed most in need of these programs are those from low-SES families and those from migration backgrounds. (Students can, of course, belong to both groups.) A particular feature of these programs is that of advancing students' language competencies from pre-primary level on in order to address and prevent ongoing language-acquisition problems. Another strategy, designed to ameliorate the persistent relationship between low SES and poor reading performance, is to increase children's learning opportunities by implementing all-day schooling throughout the education system and offering supervised after-school care (KMK & BMBF, 2008).

2. *Easier movement across and between the different stages and tracks of the education system:* Children who do not perform well at school also tend to be the children most disadvantaged by this feature of Germany's education system. Children from low-SES families and/or with a migration background generally already have learning and knowledge deficits when they enter first grade. Educational initiatives designed to tackle this problem include, for example, increasing the number of daycare centers available for children up to age three by 35 percent by the year 2013 (KMK & BMBF, 2008) and fostering the quality of both child care[8] and preschool education and advancement.[9]

   Systematic and compulsory cooperation between preschools and primary schools and between primary schools and secondary schools is being enhanced so that teachers and parents can make more informed decisions about students' respective educational careers and choice of educational track. The BMBF and the KMK also want the alignment between educational qualifications and educational tracks uncoupled, so that no matter what track a student enters, he or she will have the option of procuring the qualification that best suits his or her course of action on leaving secondary school (tertiary education, direct entry into work). According

---

8   Qualitätsinitiative Kinderbetreuung.
9   Qualitätsoffensive zur frühkindlichen Bildung und Förderung in der Kita.

to the KMK and BMBF (2008), this development would particularly advantage low-SES students, who tend to enter the vocational track of secondary schooling.

3. *Improved instructional practices and teachers' qualifications:* The programs focussed on instructional practices involve a process whereby teachers are encouraged to exchange practices deemed outmoded and ineffective with practices deemed effective. This process is being facilitated through the building of databases containing examples of best practice and the development of instructional tools that educational administrators and practitioners throughout the country can access. One project directed at enhancing reading instruction and reading practice in all school subjects is *Pro.Lesen* (ProReading) (KMK, 2009).

Another project, which commenced in 2007 and is called *For.mat*, is a teacher-training initiative. It takes into account two relatively new aspects of the German education system—competency-based instruction, and instruction related to the recently implemented educational standards (KMK, 2008b). A third project, introduced to enhance teachers' diagnostic competencies, also focuses on teachers' ability to accommodate heterogeneity in their classrooms and students' individual learning (KMK, 2008a).

PIRLS 2001 and 2006 made obvious that teachers were generally not good at assessing students' achievement. Comparison of teacher-graded assessment and standardized assessment showed substantial differences and discrepancies in teachers' marking, highlighting the need for a closer look at how teachers are trained in general and how they are taught and develop assessment skills in particular (Arnold, Bos, Richert, & Stubbe, 2007; Bos, Voss, Lankes, Schwippert, Thiel, & Valtin, 2004).

4. *Initiatives to increase and secure the transparency and quality of the German education system:* These include strategies for systematic evaluation of Germany's education system accompanied by ongoing measures directed at determining how well the system is performing in terms of student achievement. Participation in future cycles of PIRLS and in other international large-scale surveys such as TIMSS and PISA is one means of doing this. System monitoring is also being served through comparative assessments of school performance (Levels 3 to 8) across the German federal states (KMK & IQB, 2006). The most ambitious action that has been taken to date with respect to quality management of the education system is the implementation in 2003 of national educational standards and the concomitant founding of the Institute for Educational Progress (IQB). In 2006, Germany introduced a binenial national report on education (Autorengruppe Bildungsberichterstattung, 2006, 2008). The report details, in line with a set of standardized indicators, the conditions and outcomes of the different stages of the country's education system.

Because development and implementation of educational reform ultimately depends on political will, and although reform initiatives have been particularized in the earlier mentioned strategy and recommendation papers of the KMK, there is uncertainty about whether the documented reforms will receive the full amount of government funding necessary for their realization. However, the various resolutions and strategies put forward justify the long-term implementation of a research program directed toward implementing regional, national, and international evaluations of the education system. Many aspects of such a program have already been accomplished or are about to be put in place.

The PIRLS surveys have also prompted various research institutes in Germany to carry out initiatives related to students' reading achievement. One of these is the project *IGLU Transfer* (PIRLS Transfer), conducted by Wilfried Bos, the national research coordinator for PIRLS Germany, and colleagues at the Institute for School Development Research at TU Dortmund University. The aim of this project is to make the competency levels indicated by the PIRLS benchmarks of reading comprehension part of the educational standards currently being developed for primary and secondary education in Germany. This work should also see the development of resources that teachers can use to teach reading comprehension and that draw on the PIRLS concept of reading literacy and the different levels of competency denoted by the study's proficiency scale (Bos, Nahberger, Dohe, & Schmitz, 2010).

A further initiative is the *Hamburger Leseförderprojekt* (the Hamburg Enhancement of Literacy Project or HELP). The project was prompted by two groups of findings from both the PIRLS and PISA surveys: (i) the reading achievement of students from socially deprived homes and/or from migration backgrounds tending to lag behind that of their fellow students from socially advantaged and nonmigration family backgrounds; and (ii) boys' reading achievement generally being not as good as girls' (Blatt, Müller, & Voss, 2007; Blatt, Voss, Gebauer, & Kowalski, 2008). HELP comprises a number of interventions designed to improve students' reading literacy and orthography skills. More specifically, it combines the use of read-aloud methods with fostering of reading comprehension processes. The students targeted by these interventions came from selected Grade 5 classes in Hamburg schools (Blatt, Müller, & Voss, 2010), and from selected Grade 6 classes in the city of Dortmund (Frahm, 2010). The classes selected all had a high proportion of students from socially deprived homes and/or a migration background. This intervention proved to be successful, with children from migrant or low-SES backgrounds increasing their reading fluency (Frahm, 2010). Interventions based on the same concepts as HELP that have been implemented in classrooms in Grades 1 to 3 have been found to have even better results with these student groups (Pagel & Blatt, 2010).

Another project, *Vertiefende Analysen zum Leseunterricht im internationalen und interkulturellen Vergleich* (Advanced Analyses in Reading Instruction in International and Intercultural Comparative Contexts or VAL), is assessing reading instruction methods and outcomes in two countries, Germany and the USA (Institute for School Development Research, 2008). The study involves advanced secondary comparative analyses of the PIRLS 2001 and 2006 data. The VAL research team also intends to collect additional data by videotaping reading instruction in Grade 4 reading lessons in regular classrooms in the two countries.

A fourth research project with close ties to PIRLS is the *Förändringar i läskompetens*/Trends in Reading Assessments over Time (FIL/TREAT) study.[10] FIL/TREAT, an international cooperative research project between the University of Gothenburg in Sweden and the Institute for School Development Research at Dortmund University in Germany, has been using data from a number of IEA studies[11] to assess changes and trends in the reading achievement of 9- to 10-year-old students over the period 1970 to 2006 (Rosén, 2006; Rosén & Strietholt, 2010a, 2010b).

The FIL/TREAT research team developed a means of linking the different tests in these studies so that the reading achievement of the Grade 4 students could be assessed according to a common reading literacy scale that stretches over five studies and more than three decades. This approach to employing large-scale assessment studies to measure trends in reading achievement within and across countries should be of considerable interest to the educational research community given that the effects of educational reforms and other societal changes generally only become apparent when they are relatively well established.

In addition to projects with close ties to PIRLS, there are numerous projects underway in Germany that have, as their aim, enhancing students' interest in reading and their reading achievement. Many of these interventions have been designed for use in primary schools. An overview of these studies can be found in Artelt et al. (2007, p. 81 ff.) as well as in Frauen et al. (2007, p. 90 ff.). Further initiatives are being undertaken by an expert council of German researchers in the field of education, the *Aktionsrat Bildung* (Council for Action in Education), which was founded in 2005 to bring informed debate to matters relating to the German education system. The council delivers annual recommendations for educational policy (and politicians) that are based largely on empirical data. Whenever the council issues reports and recommendations on primary education in Germany, it always includes, as two major sources of information, the results from PIRLS 2001 and PIRLS 2006 as well as secondary analyses of these data (see, for instance, Blossfeld et al., 2011).

6.5   Future Activities

As was the case with the results of PIRLS 2001, the findings of PIRLS 2006 gave researchers, politicians, teachers, and the public a rich source of information to draw on

---

10   For further information, see http://www.ifs-dortmund.de/1058.html

11   Since the 1970s, IEA has carried out five studies of the reading achievement of 9- to 10-year-old students. They are the Six Subject Study of the 1970s (Thorndike, 1973), the Reading Literacy Study of 1991 (Elley, 1994) and its repeat in 2001 (Martin, Mullis, Gonzalez, & Kennedy, 2003), and the Progress in International Reading Literacy Study (PIRLS) 2001 (Mullis, Martin, Gonzalez, & Kennedy, 2003) and 2006 (Mullis et al., 2007).

when thinking about and discussing the future of primary schooling as well as schooling within the national system in general.

Substantial changes to education systems need time to become embedded. As such, the following descriptions of future activities are very similar to the corresponding section in the chapter on Germany in the first publication on the impact of PIRLS (Schwippert, 2007). Although we cannot be certain that all of these ideas will come to fruition, we nevertheless include them here to mark their importance for educational researchers.

6.5.1   Research

Because of the KMK's commitment to monitoring Germany's education system, Germany confirmed its participation in the 2011 iteration of PIRLS. This involvement is allowing an even deeper comparison of the reading achievement of students across different nations as well as further intranational in-depth analyses of the different factors that appear to influence that achievement.

The PIRLS 2011 study is also of special interest to those involved or interested in international comparative research on student performance because it will align with an iteration of another large-scale assessment of student achievement conducted by the IEA—TIMSS.[12] This alignment has opened up opportunity to conduct one comprehensive, concerted assessment of three subjects—reading, mathematics, and science—at one point in time. As a participant in both these 2011 studies, Germany has exercised the option of administering the tests to the same students in all three achievement domains, thus allowing for in-depth analyses of the relative strengths and weaknesses of students across these core competencies.

6.5.2   Publications

The German PIRLS research team plans to produce one further PIRLS-related report. This publication will present the results of orthography tests that were administered in Germany as a national add-on study to PIRLS 2006 (Bos et al., in preparation).

6.5.3   Programs

One consequence of Germany's absence from international large-scale surveys during the 1970s and 1980s was that teachers received no tuition whatsoever in research methodology during their training, a situation that left most of them incapable of "reading" and interpreting the information contained in reports of the findings. These teachers instead relied on journalists' interpretations of the findings. With national and international assessments becoming more and more a part of school process, the need

---

12   PIRLS surveys follow a five-year cycle. TIMSS surveys follow a four-year cycle.

for teachers to receive systematic preservice and inservice training in research methodology is obvious.

In 2003, the University of Bielefeld became the first institution to provide preservice teachers with systematic training. Since then, more and more universities have established departments specifically focused on quantitative research methods in education. These departments not only offer courses for teachers but also provide faculty staff in the areas of pedagogy and education with requisite research methodology skills. This development marks a positive response to an area of competency that has been long neglected but much required in these traditionally hermeneutic fields.

6.6 Concluding Remarks

For Germany, participation in PIRLS 2001 and 2006 has been a successful venture that has gained the acceptance of researchers, politicians, and school staff. Germany's late participation in TIMSS (i.e., in 2007) contributed to the general long-term lack of information about learning conditions and competencies in elementary schools. This gap was particularly obvious when the results of the first PISA study (2001) revealed an unexpected unsatisfactory level of achievement among students in the lower level of German secondary schools. This situation saw the German federal states (seven in 2001, all in 2006) agreeing to finance participation in the national extension of PIRLS and to conduct research aimed at gathering pedagogical and achievement data relating to subjects and skills other than reading.

Prominent educational stakeholders initially attributed the poor achievement of Germany's 15-year-old students in PISA 2000 to deficiencies in primary school education. The PIRLS results allowed a confident refutation of this claim. Germany's participation in PIRLS has also proved valuable in two other respects: confirmation of the need to observe, evaluate, and address weaknesses in the German education system, and indication of other areas of needed research relating to and beyond primary education.

References

Arnold, K.-H., Bos, W., Richert, P. & Stubbe, T. C. (2007). Schullaufbahnpräferenzen am Ende der vierten Klassenstufe [Tracking recommendations at the end of fourth grade]. In W. Bos, S. Hornberg, K.-H. Arnold, G. Faust, L. Fried, E.-M. Lankes, K. Schwippert, & R. Valtin (Eds.), *IGLU 2006. Lesekompetenzen von Grundschulkindern in Deutschland im internationalen Vergleich* [PIRLS Germany 2006: Reading competencies of primary students in Germany in an innternational comparison] (pp. 271– 297). Münster, Germany: Waxmann.

Artelt, C., McElvany, N., Christmann, N., Richter, T. Groeben, N., Köster, J. et al. (2007). *Förderung von Lesekompetenz: Eine Expertise* [Fostering reading competency: Expert opinion]. Bonn, Germany: Bundesministerium für Bildung und Forschung. Retrieved from http://www.bmbf.de/pub/bildungsreform_band_ siebzehn.pdf

Autorengruppe Bildungsberichterstattung. (2006). *Bildung in Deutschland: Ein indikatorengestützter Bericht mit einer Analyse zu Bildung und Migration* [Education in Germany: An indicators-based report featuring an analysis of education and migration]. Gütersloh, Germany: wbv.

Autorengruppe Bildungsberichterstattung. (2008). *Bildung in Deutschland 2008: Ein indikatorengestützter Bericht mit einer Analyse zu Übergängen im Anschluss an den Sekundarbereich I* [Education in Germany, 2008: An indicators-based report featuring an analysis of educational transitions following lower secondary education]. Gütersloh, Germany: wbv.

Blatt, I., Müller, A., & Voss, A. (2007). Schulentwicklung auf Unterrichtsebene [School development at the classroom level]. *Schulmanagement, 3*, 22–25.

Blatt, I., Müller, A., & Voss, A. (2010). Schriftstruktur als Lesehilfe: Konzeption und Ergebnisse eines Hamburger Leseförderprojekts in Klasse 5 (HELP) [Script structure as a reading aid: Concepts and results of a project to foster reading in Grade 5 in Hamburg (HELP)]. In U. Bredel, A. Müller, & G. Hinney (Eds.), *Schriftkompetenz und Schriftsystem: Linguistisch, empirisch, didaktisch* [Writing competency and writing systems: Linguistic, empirical, and didactic] (pp. 171–202). Berlin, Germany: Walter de Gruyter.

Blatt, I., Voss, A., Gebauer, M., & Kowalski, K. (2008). Integratives Konzept zur Lese- und Sprachförderung [An integrated view of promoting reading and language learning]. In N. Berkemeyer, W. Bos, & K. Müthing (Eds.), *Unterrichts- entwicklung in Netzwerken: Konzeptionen, Befunde, Perspektiven* [Instructional development through networks: Concepts, results, and perspectives] (pp. 183–199). Münster, Germany: Waxmann.

Blossfeld, H.-P., Bos, W., Daniel, H.-D., Hannover, B., Lenzen, D., Prenzel, M., & Wößmann, L. (Eds.). (2011). *Bildungsreform 2000–2010–2020: Jahresgutachten 2011* [Educational reform: 2000–2010–2020: Annual report 2011]. Wiesbaden, Germany: VS Verlag für Sozialwissenschaften.

Bos, W., Hornberg, S., Arnold, K.-H., Faust, G., Fried, L., Lankes, E.-M. et al. (Eds.). (2007). *IGLU 2006: Lesekompetenzen von Grundschulkindern in Deutschland im internationalen Vergleich* [PIRLS Germany 2006: Reading competencies of primary students in Germany in an international comparison]. Münster, Germany: Waxmann.

Bos, W., Hornberg, S., Arnold, K.-H., Faust, G., Fried, L., Lankes, E.-M. et al. (Eds.). (2008). *IGLU-E 2006: Die Länder der Bundesrepublik Deutschland im nationalen und internationalen Vergleich* [PIRLS Germany extended 2006: Germany's federal states within the context of national and international comparison]. Münster, Germany: Waxmann.

Bos, W., Hornberg, S., Arnold, K.-H., Faust, G., Fried, L., Lankes, E.-M., et al. (Eds.). (2010). *IGLU 2006: Die Grundschule auf dem Prüfstand. Vertiefende Analysen zu Rahmenbedingungen schulischen Lernens* [PIRLS Germany 2006: Primary school under scrutiny. In-depth analyses of learning conditions at school]. Münster, Germany: Waxmann.

Bos, W., Nahberger, G., Dohe, C., & Schmitz, S. (2010). *IGLU Transfer*. Retrieved from http://www.ifs-dortmund.de/assets/files/IGLU-Transfer24_11.pdf

Bos, W., Sereni, S., & Stubbe, T. C. (Eds.). (2008). *IGLU Belgien: Lese- und Orthografiekompetenzen von Grundschulkindern in der Deutschsprachigen Gemeinschaft* [PIRLS Belgium: Reading and orthographical competencies of primary school students in the German-speaking community]. Münster, Germany: Waxmann.

Bos, W., & Stubbe, T. C. (2008). Lesekompetenzen von Viertklässlerinnen und Viertklässlern in der Deutschsprachigen Gemeinschaft im internationalen Vergleich [Reading competencies of fourth-grade students in the German-speaking community: An international comparison]. In W. Bos, S. Sereni, & T. C. Stubbe (Eds.), *IGLU Belgien: Lese- und Orthografiekompetenzen von Grundschulkindern in der Deutschsprachigen Gemeinschaft* [PIRLS Belgium: Reading and orthographical competencies of primary school students in the German-speaking community] (pp. 67–96). Münster, Germany: Waxmann.

Bos, W., Valtin, R., Hornberg, S., Buddeberg, I., Goy, M., & Voss, A. (2007). Internationaler Vergleich 2006: Lesekompetenzen von Schülerinnen und Schülern am Ende der vierten Jahrgangsstufe [International comparison 2006: Reading competencies of students at the end of fourth grade]. In W. Bos, S. Hornberg, K.-H. Arnold, G. Faust, L. Fried, E.-M. Lankes, et al. (Eds.), *IGLU 2006: Lesekompetenzen von Grundschulkindern in Deutschland im internationalen Vergleich* [PIRLS Germany 2006: Reading competencies of primary school students in Germany. An international comparison] (pp. 109–160). Münster, Germany: Waxmann.

Bos, W., Voss, A., Hornberg, S., Arnold, K.-H., Faust, G., Fried, L. et al. (Eds.). (in preparation). *IGLU 2006: Orthographiekompetenzen von Grundschulkindern in Deutschland* [PIRLS Germany 2006: Orthographical competencies of primary school students in Germany]. Münster, Germany: Waxmann.

Bos, W., Voss, A., Lankes, E.-M., Schwippert, K., Thiel, O., & Valtin, R. (2004). Schullaufbahnempfehlungen von Lehrkräften für Kinder am Ende der vierten Jahrgangsstufe [Teachers' track recommendations for students at the end of fourth grade]. In W. Bos, E.-M. Lankes, M. Prenzel, K. Schwippert, R. Valtin, & G. Walther (Eds.), *IGLU: Einige Länder der Bundesrepublik Deutschland im nationalen und internationalen Vergleich* [PIRLS Germany: Some of Germany's federal states within the context of national and international comparison] (pp. 191–228). Münster, Germany: Waxmann.

Cortina, K., & Trommer, L. (2003). Die Übergangsentscheidung als Passungsproblem [Difficulties associated with decisions about school transition]. In K. S. Cortina, J. Baumert, A. Leschinsky, K. U. Meyer, & L. Trommer (Eds.), *Das Bildungswesen in der Republik Deutschland: Strukturen und Entwicklungen im Überblick* [The education system in Germany: An overview of structures and developments] (pp. 342–391). Reinbek, Germany: Rohwohlt.

Ditton, H., & Krüsken, J. (2006). Der Übergang von der Grundschule in die Sekundarstufe I [Transition from primary to secondary school]. *Zeitschrift für Erziehungswissenschaft, 9*(3), 348–372.

Ditton, H., Krüsken, J., & Schauenberg, M. (2005). Bildungsungleichheit: der Beitrag von Familie und Schule [Educational inequality: The contribution of family and school]. *Zeitschrift für Erziehungswissenschaft, 8*(2), 285–304.

Elley, W. B. (1994). *The IEA Study of Reading Literacy: Achievement and instruction in thirty-two school systems.* Oxford, UK: Pergamon Press.

Foy, P., Galia, J., & Li, I. (2007). Scaling the PIRLS 2006 reading assessment data. In M. O. Martin, I. V. S. Mullis, & A. M. Kennedy (Eds.), *PIRLS 2006 technical report* (pp. 149–172). Chestnut Hill, MA: Boston College.

Frahm, S. (2010). Leseförderung in Klasse 6? [Fostering reading in Class 6?]. *Die Deutsche Schule, 102*(4), 360–372.

Frauen, C., Johannsen, D., Möller, J., Ramm, G., Riecke-Baulecke, T., Wack, A. et al. (2007). *Lesekompetenz: Schlüsselqualifikation und Querschnittsaufgabe* [Reading literacy: Key competency and cross-sectional challenge]. Munich, Germany: Oldenbourg.

Gladkova, L., & Moran, R. (2005). *DESI: Direct estimation software interactive* [Computer software and manual]. Princeton, NJ: Educational Testing Service.

Hornberg, S., Bos, W., Lankes, E.-M., & Valtin, R. (2007). Germany. In A. M. Kennedy, I. V. S. Mullis, M. O. Martin, & K. L. Trong (Eds.), *PIRLS 2006 encyclopedia* (pp. 143–152). Chestnut Hill, MA: Boston College.

Institute for School Development Research. (2008). *VAL: Vertiefende Analysen zum Leseunterricht im internationalen und interkulturellen Vergleich* [VAL: Advanced analyses in reading instruction. An international and intercultural comparison]. Retrieved from http://www.ifs-dortmund.de/val.html

KMK. (2006). *Basic structure of the educational system in the Federal Republic of Germany* [diagram]. Retrieved from http://www.kmk.org/dokumentation/das-bildungswesen-in-der-bundesrepublik-deutschland.html

KMK. (2008a). *Aus- und Fortbildung der Lehrkräfte im Hinblick auf Verbesserung der Diagnosefähigkeit, Umgang mit Heterogenität, individuelle Förderung* [Teacher education and training for increased skills in achievement diagnosis, enhanced approaches to heterogeneity, and better instruction at the individual level]. Retrieved from http://www.schulministerium.nrw.de/BP/Presse/Meldungen/PM_2008/pm_21_11_2008.html

KMK. (2008b). *For.mat. Bereitstellung von Fortbildungskonzeptionen und -materialien zur kompetenz- bzw. standardbasierten Unterrichtsentwicklung* [For.mat: Ideas and resources for teacher training directed at developing competency-oriented and standard-based instruction]. Retrieved from http://www.kmk-format.de/

KMK. (2008c). *Stellungnahme der Kultusministerkonferenz zu den Ergebnissen des Ländervergleichs von IGLU 2006* [Statement of the Standing Conference of Ministers of Education and Cultural Affairs of the Länder of the Federal Republic of Germany on the results of the comparison of the German federal states in PIRLS 2006]. Retrieved from http://www.kmk.org/presse-und-aktuelles/

meldung/stellungnahme-der-kultusministerkonferenz-zu-den-ergebnissen-des-laendervergleich-von-iglu-2006.html

KMK. (2009). *ProLesen: Auf dem Weg zur Leseschule. Konzepte und Materialien zur Leseförderung in allen Fächern* [ProReading: On the road to a reading school. Concepts and materials for fostering reading in all school subjects]. Retrieved from http://www.bildungsserver.de/innovationsportal/blk_set.html?Id=645

KMK & BMBF. (2008). *Ergebnisse von PIRLS/IGLU 2006-I und PISA 2006-I. Gemeinsame Empfehlungen der Kultusministerkonferenz und des Bundesministeriums für Bildung und Forschung* [Results from PIRLS 2006 and PISA 2006: Joint recommendations of the Standing Conference of Ministers of Education and Cultural Affairs and the Federal Ministry of Education and Research]. Retrieved fromhttp://www.kmk.org/fileadmin/veroeffentlichungen_bechluesse/2008/2008_0 3_06-PISA-PIRLS-IGLU-2006-1.pdf

KMK & IQB. (2006). *Gesamtstrategie der Kultusministerkonferenz zum Bildungsmonitoring* [Concerted strategy for monitoring education developed by the Standing Conference of Ministers of Education and Cultural Affairs]. Retrieved from http://www.kmk.org/fileadmin/veroeffentlichungen_beschluesse/ 2006/2006_ 08_01-Gesamtstrategie-Bildungsmonitoring.pdf

Martin, M. O., Mullis, I. V. S., Gonzalez, E. J., & Kennedy, A. M. (2003). *Trends in children's literacy achievement 1991–2001: IEA's repeat in nine countries of the 1991 Reading Literacy Study.* Chestnut Hill, MA: Boston College.

Martin, M. O., Mullis, I. V. S., & Kennedy, A. M. (Eds.). (2007). *PIRLS 2006 technical report.* Chestnut Hill, MA: Boston College.

Mullis, I. V. S., Martin, M. O., Gonzalez, E. J., & Kennedy, A. M. (2003). *PIRLS 2001 international report: IEA's study of reading literacy achievement in primary schools in 35 countries.* Chestnut Hill, MA: Boston College.

Mullis, I. V. S., Martin, M. O., Kennedy, A. M., & Foy, P. (2007). *PIRLS 2006 international report: IEA's Progress in International Reading Literacy Study in primary schools in 40 countries.* Chestnut Hill, MA: Boston College.

Muraki, E., & Bock, D. (1991). *PARSCALE: Parameter scaling of rating data* [computer software and manual]. Chicago, IL: Scientific Software Inc.

Pagel, B., & Blatt, I. (2010). *Schriftspracherwerb: Systematisch und kulturell* [Acquisition of written language: Systematic and cultural]. Hamburg, Germany: University of Hamburg, Department of Education.

Rosén, M. (2006). *Analysing trends in levels of reading literacy between 1970 and 2001 in Sweden.* Paper presented at the Second IEA International Research Conference. Washington DC, USA.

Rosén, M., & Strietholt, R. (2010a). *On the degree of comparability in trend studies as a function of differences in age and schooling.* Paper presented at the Fourth IEA International Research Conference, Gothenburg, Sweden.

Rosén, M., & Strietholt, R. (2010b). *Trends in reading literacy from 1970 to 2006: A comparison of 9- to 10-year-olds in Sweden, Hungary, Italy, and the USA.* Paper presented at the Fourth IEA International Research Conference, Gothenburg, Sweden.

Schwippert, K. (Ed.). (2007). *Progress in reading literacy: The Impact of PIRLS 2001 in 13 countries* (Studies in International Comparative and Multicultural Education). Münster, Germany: Waxmann.

Schwippert, K., & Goy, M. (2008). Leistungsvergleichs- und Schulqualitätsforschung [Research on achievement comparisons and school quality]. In W. Helsper & J. Böhme (Eds.), *Handbuch der Schulforschung* [Handbook of research on schools] (2nd ed., pp. 387–421). Wiesbaden, Germany: VS Verlag für Sozialwissenschaften.

Statistisches Bundesamt. (2010). Bildungsausgaben. Budget für Bildung, Forschung und Wissenschaft 2007/2008 [Education expenditure: Budget for education, research, and science 2007/2008]. Retrieved from http://www.destatis.de/jetspeed/portal/cms/Sites/destatis/Internet/DE/Content/Publikationen/Fachveroefentlichugen/BildungForschungKultur/Content75/AusgabenBudget__Pdf,property =file.pdf

Stubbe, T. C., Sereni, S., & Bos, W. (2008). Anlage und Durchführung der Internationalen Grundschul-Lese-Untersuchung in der Deutschsprachigen Gemeinschaft (IGLU Belgien) [Framework and realization of the Progress in International Reading Literacy Study in the German-speaking Community in Belgium (PIRLS Belgium)]. In W. Bos, S. Sereni, & T. C. Stubbe (Eds.), *IGLU Belgien: Lese- und Orthografiekompetenzen von Grundschulkindern in der Deutschsprachigen Gemeinschaft* [PIRLS Belgium: Reading and orthographical competencies of primary school students in the German-speaking Community] (pp. 19–39). Münster, Germany: Waxmann.

Thorndike, R. L. (1973). *Reading comprehension education in fifteen countries: An empirical study.* Stockholm, Sweden: Almquist & Wiksell.

Wu, M. L., Adams, R. J., & Wilson, M. R. (1998). *Acer ConQuest: Generalised item response modelling software* [computer software]. Melbourne, Victoria, Australia: ACER Press.

Chapter 7
The Impact of PIRLS in the Hong Kong Special Administrative Region of China

Shek Kam Tse and Elizabeth Ka Yee Loh

7.1 Hong Kong at a Glance

Hong Kong is one of the world's major commercial capitals. After the end of British rule in 1997, China regained sovereignty under the "one country, two systems" principle (Hong Kong SAR Government, 2009). The total area of Hong Kong is 1,104 square kilometers; less than 25 percent of the land has been developed. According to the 2008 census, Hong Kong's population is nearly seven million. Ninety-five percent of its residents are of Chinese descent; the remaining five percent come from various countries, including the Philippines (1.6%), Indonesia (1.3%), and Western nations (0.5%). Filipinos (112,000) comprise the largest ethnic subgroup. Hong Kong has a high degree of religious freedom. Although Buddhism and Taoism are the most widely practiced faiths, Confucianism, Christianity, Islam, Hinduism, Sikhism, and Judaism are also practiced (Census and Statistics Department, 2006, 2009).

Over the past two decades, the Hong Kong economy has almost tripled in size, with GDP growing at an average annual rate of 5.6 percent in real terms. Per capita GDP has more than doubled, making it equivalent to an average annual growth rate of 3.8 percent in real terms. In 2008, per capita GDP reached HK$215,355 at current market prices (World Bank, 2009).

Public expenditure on education has risen at a constant rate of 4.1 percent since 1998. In 2008/2009, the total expenditure on education was HK$M75,935, which accounted for 24.1 percent of total public expenditure and 4.5 percent of GDP. Of the recurrent expenditure on education, secondary education absorbed the highest proportion (37.9%), closely followed by tertiary education (25.9%). The primary education sector accounted for 21.9 percent, and all other categories accounted for 14.3 percent.

7.2 Hong Kong's Education System as a Context for PIRLS

Since 1979, Hong Kong has had in place nine years of free compulsory education for all children between the ages of 6 and 15 years. In 2008, the government extended free education to cover senior secondary education in public sector schools. This development means that children in these schools now receive 12 years of free education (Education Bureau, 2009).

The school year consists of 200 school days (Hong Kong SAR Government, 2001). Admission to primary schools, whether fully government funded or subsidized, is conducted through a centralized system, but parents can send their children to private primary schools if they wish. To diversify the school system and give parents more choice, the government authorized, in 1999, the development of Direct Subsidy Scheme schools and non-profit-making private independent schools (Hong Kong SAR Government, 2003).

After completing primary education, students participating in the Secondary School Places Allocation System are given secondary school places in the public sector; allocation is based on parental choice, internal school assessments, and students' performance on the Pre-Secondary One Hong Kong Attainment Test (Education Bureau, 2008a). To strengthen collaboration between the primary and secondary sectors, the government introduced a "through-train" mode in 2001. The more specific aims of this initiative are to enhance curriculum continuity, strengthen support for students, reduce school-transfer problems, and ensure that all children are provided for equally (Education Bureau, 2008b).

7.2.1   Language in Schools

English and Chinese enjoy equal status as official languages in Hong Kong. Although the Cantonese dialect of Chinese is the mother tongue of most residents, modern standard Chinese is the official written form. Chinese became the medium of instruction in most secondary schools and government-funded primary schools when Hong Kong became a special administrative region of China in 1997. The government, well aware of the need to maintain students' English-language competence, encourages "fine-tuning" of the medium of instruction in secondary schools in order to accommodate the learning capability and needs of children in each intake. Given that effective learning is the prime concern in schools, children are taught mostly in the mother tongue but may receive English-medium instruction in key learning areas up to a maximum of 25 percent of total lesson time (Suen, 2009).

7.2.2   Reading Standards

The government expects school-leavers to be able to read independently in both Chinese and English languages (for details, see Tse & Loh, 2007, p. 111). The government has identified promotion of a reading culture among students as a key means of encouraging lifelong learning (Curriculum Development Institute, 2002). Determined that school-leavers can read confidently and independently for learning and pleasure, the government made *reading to learn* one of four key targets of the educational reform implemented in Hong Kong in 2000 (Curriculum Development Council, 2001).

7.2.3 Reading Curriculum

The Curriculum Development Council specified clear reading goals for schools in 2000. All teachers, regardless of subject specialization, are expected to actively promote reading in general and building up a reading culture and ethos in schools in particular. The council published a curriculum guide to help schools realize these aims (Curriculum Development Council, 2001, 2002). The Education Bureau ensures that all schools receive support when endeavoring to promote a reading culture (Law, 2002). Although the government sets the general syllabus, schools are encouraged to devise their own school-based literacy curriculum in order to cater for the literacy needs of their student intake (Curriculum Development Council, 2000; for details, see Tse & Loh, 2007, p. 111).

7.2.4 Literacy Programs

With the aim of encouraging students' literacy acquisition and promoting reading for pleasure, the Education Bureau has, over time, recommended a number of literacy programs. These include the "reading aloud" and "shared reading with big books" schemes, both of which aim to improve the reading habits and skills of primary and secondary school students (Education Commission, 1996). Funding from the Quality Education Fund has been set aside to help schools carry out reading projects and action research. In 2008, the bureau also launched a reading website for students, called Book Works. In order to promote the importance of reading and to help parents foster good reading habits and attitudes in their young children (infants through to nine-year-olds), the bureau recently published three booklets and one leaflet for parents. These advise parents on the kinds of parent–child reading activities they can engage in with their children at different ages (Education Bureau, 2009).

7.2.5 Curriculum Reform and Monitoring Learning

The government has invested heavily in education so as to enhance school-leavers' ability to work and compete successfully in local and global marketplaces. Considering curriculum reform to be at the heart of educational development, the government encourages ongoing monitoring of and amendments to the curriculum. The major objectives of recent reforms have been to develop within students positive values and attitudes toward learning and to help them acquire a solid foundation for lifelong learning (Hong Kong SAR Government, 2003).

The government urges all primary school teachers to be teachers of literacy. Wishing to widen the focus beyond teaching subjects per se, the government asked schools to focus on the basic academic competence and profile of each student. It introduced the Basic Competency Assessment (BCA) to provide teachers with a means of assessing learning of Chinese, English, and mathematics. The BCA helps teachers monitor students' learning needs and areas requiring improvement so that timely assistance can be provided (Hong Kong SAR Government, 2003).

Another government measure designed to improve student learning is small class teaching (i.e., no more than 25 students per class). Implementation of this practice began in Hong Kong's public-sector primary schools in 2009 (Education Bureau, 2008c).

7.3   Experience with Large-Scale Assessments

7.3.1   International Perspectives

Hong Kong has participated in several large-scale international (IEA or OECD) assessment surveys of educational achievement. They include mathematics and science (TIMSS and PISA), reading literacy (PIRLS and PISA), information technology in education (SITES), and civic education (CIVED). Hong Kong's first participation in an international comparative study of reading standards was the Reading Literacy Study in 1991.

The government and other educational stakeholders in Hong Kong have found the results of these large-scale international assessments very useful, especially in terms of providing baselines for assessing the learning progress of students and permitting comparisons of the performance of students in Hong Kong against that of their counterparts in other countries. The results of these assessments are fed back as data to participating schools and individual teachers to inform curriculum reviews, teaching materials selection, and instructional methods.

7.3.2   Regional Perspectives

The two regional large-scale assessments described below followed the frameworks established for PIRLS 2001 and 2006 and were conducted in 2004 and 2007, respectively.

The 2004 researchers investigated the current state of Chinese and English reading literacy at Grade 4 in Hong Kong, and the approaches and strategies that schools were using to enhance the quality of the teaching and learning of reading. The study's researchers also reflected on and extended the Hong Kong component of PIRLS 2001, which addressed the Chinese and English reading proficiency of Grade 4 students as well as factors influencing literacy attainment. Sixty-six primary schools (randomly selected) took part in the study. The 4,300 students, 4,300 parents, 269 Chinese and English language teachers, and 66 school principals associated with these schools were thus also involved in the study. The study's researchers not only evaluated the bilingual reading performance of Grade 4 students (Tse, Lam, Lam, & Loh, 2005b) but also investigated the impact of factors such as the pedagogical characteristics of Chinese and English language teachers (Tse, Lam, Loh, & Lam, 2007) and the employment of

English-speaking domestic helpers on students' Chinese and English reading performance (Tse, Lam, Loh, Ip, Lam, & Chan, 2009).

The second study took place one year after PIRLS 2006. This follow-up to the 2004 Hong Kong study assessed the progress that Grade 4 students had made with respect to bilingual reading (English and Chinese). Forty randomly selected primary schools took part, as did the 1,283 Grade 4 students, 1,283 parents, 83 teachers, and 40 principals associated with those schools. Other facets of the study included strategies for enhancing the quality of teaching and learning reading, the relationship between motivation to read Chinese and English and bilingual reading performance (Loh & Tse, 2009), and the impact of students' blogging behavior on bilingual reading performance (Tse, Loh, Lam, & Lam, 2010; Tse, Yuen, Loh, Lam, & Ng, 2010).

Other relevant regionally based large-scale assessments in which Hong Kong has participated include the following:

1. *Territory-Wide System Assessment (TSA):* The TSA was first set out in policy form in a 2000 report from the Education Commission. It is not a public examination, and it is low-key/low-stakes in nature (Hong Kong Examination and Assessment Authority, 2009a). Students assessed include those in Grades 3, 6, and 9. The main purpose of the assessment, which is carried out on a territory-wide, individual school basis, is to provide government and school management with information on school standards in the key areas of Chinese, English, and mathematics. The assessment not only helps the government provide targeted support to schools in need of assistance, but also helps teachers use the information to improve teaching and learning.

2. *Hong Kong Diploma of Secondary Education Examination (HKDSE):* The HKDSE, which takes three years to complete, was implemented in 2009, under the auspices of the Hong Kong Education Bureau, in the senior level (Grades 10 to 12) of Hong Kong's secondary school system. Students who work toward the diploma must first complete three years of junior secondary education (from Grades 7 to 9) (Hong Kong Examination and Assessment Authority, 2009b).

3. *School-Based Assessment (SBA):* Schools carry out SBA as part of their teaching and learning process. Subject teachers are responsible for assessing their students, and the marks awarded count toward the results of public examinations (Hong Kong Examination and Assessment Authority, 2009c). The inclusion, from 2012 on, of the SBA component in HKDSE subjects will enable schools, students, and parents to gain a good understanding of the assessment's implementation and benefits (Hong Kong Examination and Assessment Authority, 2009c).

7.4   National Results and Impact of PIRLS

7.4.1   Results of PIRLS 2006 Compared with PIRLS 2001

Hong Kong students made substantial progress in their reading literacy acquisition between 2001 and 2006. In PIRLS 2001, Hong Kong students obtained a mean score of 528 for overall reading attainment and ranked 14th out of the 35 participating countries or regions. The overall mean reading score in PIRLS 2006 of 564 gave Hong Kong second-place ranking. The mean score for the top-performing country, Russia, was only one point higher than the mean score for Hong Kong. Singapore ranked 4th and Taiwan ranked 22nd: the scores for these four countries were significantly higher than the standardized international average score of 500.

When the mean scores for the subsections of the reading test were compared across countries, the Hong Kong students' average score for understanding informational text of 568 placed them at the top of the achievement scale. The students' understanding literary text mean score of 557 placed them fourth on the ranking scale. The increase in mean scores between 2001 and 2006 for the Hong Kong students was 31 for informational reading and 39 for literary reading (Lam, Cheung, & Lam, 2009; Tse, Lam, Lam, Loh, & Westwood, 2005).

The Hong Kong students also performed well with respect to both lower order comprehension skills (literal comprehension and simple inferences) and higher order comprehension skills (interpreting, making complex inferences, and evaluating). The mean scores for lower and higher order comprehension were 558 and 566, respectively. Performance at the higher level was better than at the lower level: the former score gave Hong Kong top ranking amongst the participating countries; the latter placed Hong Kong fourth. Comparison of the 2001 and 2006 scores showed an increase of 35 score points in the lower-level average, and an increase of 33 score points in the higher-level average (Lam et al., 2009; Tse, Lam, Loh, & Cheung, 2010).

The reading performance of girls in Hong Kong was markedly superior to the reading performance of boys. The mean score for overall reading for girls was 569 (second-place ranking amongst the participating countries). For boys, it was 559 (first-place ranking). The literary reading average for girls was 564 (giving them a ranking of fourth place), and for boys it was 551 (ranking them in sixth place). The average informational score for girls was 572; for boys, it was 564 (both ranked first). When we looked at the trends from 2001 to 2006, we found the boys apparently catching up with the girls. The difference in overall average reading scores between girls and boys was 18 points in 2001, but it was only 10 points in 2006. Rather disappointingly, only 15 percent of Hong Kong students achieved within the "top 10 percent" benchmark, whereas 19 percent of their Singaporean and Russian peers did so. The proportion of students internationally achieving at this level was 10 percent.

In terms of reading behavior, nearly 80 percent of the Hong Kong students said they read stories or novels outside school "more than once or twice a week." This proportion was 13 percent higher than the international average in 2006. When students were asked about reading for fun outside school, 35 percent of them said they read "every day or almost every day." In 2001, only 21 percent said they did so, making for an increase of 14 percent over the five years between the two assessments. Despite this substantial increase, the 2006 percentage was still five percent below the international average for that year.

Just over 80 percent of the Hong Kong students reported that they visited and borrowed books from the school or local library "at least once or twice a week." Although this proportion represented a significant increase on the 2001 percentage, Hong Kong students fell behind their counterparts in other countries in terms of being designated "motivated" readers. The Hong Kong students' overall reading self-concept was also relatively low. These characteristics negatively influence reading performance (Lam et al., 2009; Tse, Lam et al., 2010).

Home reading environment also had a statistically significant influence on Hong Kong students' reading attitudes, habits, and ability (Tse, Loh et al., 2010). However, home reading activities and parents' reading habits and attitudes toward reading changed little over the five years between the two PIRLS surveys. When parental data were examined against the Index of Early Home Literacy Activities (EHLA), it was evident that only 26 percent of the Hong Kong parents reached the "high level" in 2006. This proportion was a definite improvement over 2001, when 10 percent of parents reached the high level on the EHLA, but it was still 28 percent below the international average for 2006 (54%).

When we considered the 2006 PIRLS data for Hong Kong relating to home reading activities, we found that the number of parents engaging in "shared reading" and "going to the library" with their children was not as high as the 2001 number. There is clearly room for improvement here. Although there was a marked improvement between 2001 and 2006 with respect to parents reading for enjoyment "every day" (36.3% did so in 2006) and "once or twice a week" (39% in 2006), the percentages of parents reaching a high level and a medium level on the Parents' Attitudes toward Reading (PATR) scale were 29 percent and 65 percent, respectively. These proportions indicated no discernable improvement since 2001.

Comparison of the parents' responses in 2001 and 2006 revealed many parents still complaining that their children had too much homework, leaving them little time to read books for leisure. Paradoxically, teachers complained that the children's school timetable allowed insufficient time for them to teach reading for learning and for pleasure, and this was especially the case for students who needed to take the TSA. Although more of the 2006 than the 2001 teachers reported using novels and children's readers as supplementary teaching materials, most of the 2006 teachers were still using textbooks as the major teaching resource. The proportion of teachers who said they listened to students read aloud in class on a daily basis in 2006 was 49 percent, an increase of 10 percent over the 2001 figure, but this was still 14 percent below the 2006 international average. According to Lam et al. (2009) and Tse et al. (2007), Hong Kong teachers tend to find the notion of "reading across the curriculum" a vague one and so have difficulty putting it into practice.

7.4.2   Disseminating the PIRLS Results

In order to disseminate the findings of PIRLS 2006 in the community and in schools, we and colleagues from the University of Hong Kong are preparing a book setting out the background, theories, research methods, comparisons of the results of PIRLS 2006 and 2001, and the implications of the study for teaching and learning. We also submitted research articles featuring analyses and interpretation of PIRLS data to journals for publication (see, for example, Lam et al., 2009; Tse et al., 2009) and created a special website to disseminate the findings of PIRLS 2006. The wealth of valuable research data generated by PIRLS has meant that we are still writing and submitting related articles to research journals.

7.4.3   Teacher Training Programs

With the aim of adjusting the professional training of preservice and inservice teachers in Hong Kong, the University of Hong Kong now includes the outcomes and implications of the PIRLS 2001 and 2006 findings and of the bilingual reading 2004 and 2007 analyses in its teacher training programs.

7.4.4   Publications

These include a book introducing the PIRLS framework and the reading performance of Hong Kong students in PIRLS 2001 (Tse et al., 2005a) and a book chapter discussing the impact of PIRLS 2001 in Hong Kong (Tse & Loh, 2007). A number of articles have also been published in or submitted to international refereed journals. These include a discussion of the overall reading performance of Hong Kong students (Tse, Lam, Lam, & Loh, 2003), a comparison of the reading attitudes and reading self-concepts of students at different levels of reading ability (Tse et al., 2005c), and a comparison of the reading performance of students in Hong Kong, Singapore, and the United Kingdom (Tse, Lam, Lam, Chan, & Loh, 2006). These articles also include presentation and discussion of the outcomes of the following data analyses: the influence that the language Hong Kong primary school students habitually speak at home has on their Chinese reading ability in school (Tse et al., 2007); the influence of family resources on students' reading attainment (Tse, Lam, Ip, Lam, Loh, & Tso, in press); and the extent to which gender differences in teacher effectiveness affect students' reading attainment (Lam, Tse, Lam, & Loh, 2010).

IEA's Dick Wolf Award and the University of Hong Kong's Research Output Prize have both been given to the Hong Kong PIRLS research team in recognition of their contribution to the field of educational research in reading.

7.5   Impact of PIRLS 2006

7.5.1   Long-Term Effects

Although the findings of PIRLS 2006 are encouraging for educators in Hong Kong, there is no room for complacency. Since the launch in 2001 of a new round of educational reforms, the notion of *reading to learn* has been emphasized as a key learning objective for students. The promotion of a culture of literacy continues to be highlighted as a key component of lifelong learning, as does the role that the Education Bureau, schools, teachers, and parents play in supporting the reading environment of students.

Although the favorable PIRLS 2006 results are gratifying, issues relating to Hong Kong students' poor reading self-concept and poor reading habits along with the suboptimal quality of many home reading environments are a concern. Although schools have received plaudits for the way they now teach reading, they are being required to think more about the role of parents and the general public in boosting children's literacy skills.

7.5.2   Implications for the Government

Before the 2000 education reform, the predominant focus on teaching reading was close adherence to prescribed textbooks, such that students had no time to practice and use Chinese or English in class (Cheung, 1992; Wong, 1984). The PIRLS 2001 survey revealed that 97 percent of Hong Kong teachers relied on textbooks when teaching reading (Tse, Lam, Lam, Loh, & Westwood, 2005) and spent most reading lessons explaining text, vocabulary, and the author's style.

Recognizing the limits of this approach, the Curriculum Development Council, in collaboration with the Education Bureau and universities, prepared a series of professional training programs designed to update teachers' knowledge and their classroom skills, methods, and lesson planning. The ultimate aim of this initiative was to develop students' reading skills, attitudes, and habits. Teachers were also shown how to use a variety of high-quality teaching materials and resources. To introduce variety and a wealth of literacy attractions, the government provided each school with the resources it needed to establish class libraries and a central library (Education Bureau, 1997). The role of the teacher-librarian is "information specialist." His or her primary task is to provide students with attractive and challenging reading experiences.

The PIRLS findings were too important for a response to be left to schools and the public alone. A concerted effort was called for, and the Hong Kong PIRLS research team considered it prudent to turn first to the government. They therefore sent reports of the PIRLS findings to the Secretary of Education, the Permanent Secretary of the Education Bureau, government directors and senior officers, and members of the Reading Task Force. Reports were also sent to officers of the Quality Assurance Division, Curriculum Development Institute, Professional Development and Training

Division, School-Based Support Services Office, Education Commission and Planning Division, and regional education offices. When reporting these findings to the various bodies, the Hong Kong PIRLS team stressed that practice and policies would need to be modified if Hong Kong was to overcome the deficiencies apparent in the PIRLS results.

Because students had done so well in PIRLS 2006, many school principals and teachers relaxed their reading-based efforts, considering that they could now legitimately turn their attention to other subjects. Some schools immediately suspended school-based reading programs and used the time to drill students for the TSA. The Hong Kong PIRLS team not only had to deal with such reactions but also had to indicate to schools how they could further improve and refine the existing reading curriculum and seek ways to improve the quality of their own teaching and students' learning. Importantly, schools needed to devise ways of recruiting the cooperation of parents and then guiding them in setting up good home reading environments and fostering their children's reading attitudes and habits. A major task lay ahead in working with less well-educated parents and parents who spent long hours each week in the workplace.

Various government bodies found the PIRLS findings informative and agreed that large-scale international monitoring studies are important for identifying the areas of performance that Hong Kong schools, teachers, parents, and students need to improve. The competitive nature of Hong Kong students, it is thought, will help them meet the challenge, and the Hong Kong research team is sufficiently encouraged to participate in future PIRLS studies.

The Education Bureau, having recognized the success of previous education reforms, especially in the key learning area of *reading to learn*, agreed that this area needed to be kept to the fore so that improving the quality of teaching and learning of reading in schools would continue. Decisions were taken to place more resources in primary schools to facilitate reading across the curriculum and taking a whole-school approach to fostering students' reading ability. The government invited the national research coordinator (NRC) of the Hong Kong PIRLS study to be the consultant for a government-developed reading website. At the same time, the Hong Kong PIRLS 2006 team members were invited to give a series of talks to Chinese language teachers and parents (dissemination and interpretation of the PIRLS findings), school curriculum development officers and school-librarians (how to enhance the quality of teaching and learning of reading), and school principals and teachers (how to promote reading across the curriculum).

The Hong Kong NRC also raised the issue of the inferior reading performance of boys, pointing out that existing reading materials tend to cater mainly for girls' reading interests. In order to help address this problem, the library section of the Education Bureau published a booklist especially for boys in the hope that this list would stimulate boys' interest in reading. It is worth noting that Mainland China currently has

16 websites debating whether passages in textbooks used in Hong Kong and China favor girls' reading interests rather than those of boys.

One of the strongest submissions that the Hong Kong PIRLS team made to the government was the need for parents to be encouraged to play a more participative role in teaching children to read, both for learning and for leisure. They stressed that such encouragement should commence well before children enter the kindergarten/school system. In response, the government invited the Hong Kong PIRLS team to write a guidebook for parents of children up to nine years of age, explaining the role of parents in fostering children's reading habits, attitudes, and interests. The guidebook stresses that reading to children is a vital activity, and it provides information about schools' reading objectives and target levels for reading attainment. The guidebook also tells parents how they can help children make good progress in school by encouraging them to read, how to develop children's reading habits, and what they need to provide in the way of a good home reading environment.

7.5.3 Implications for the General Public

To capture the interest of the general public and make them aware of the issue of students' reading competence, the PIRLS results were swiftly brought to the attention of the wider community. A press release was issued setting out the results for Hong Kong against the results of counterpart schools internationally. The press release resulted in 19 web reports, articles in 22 Chinese and English newspapers, and interviews about PIRLS on five television channels and four radio programs. Three newspapers ran special features, as did two radio stations. Important newspapers presented editorials on the topic, and the findings were widely reported in 23 newspapers in Mainland China, Taiwan, Singapore, and Macau.

The findings excited the general public. They found it hard to believe that the Hong Kong students had outperformed their Taiwan peers and that their achievement had placed Hong Kong second among the countries that participated in PIRLS 2006. Members of the press were keen to identify factors affecting students' reading ability and habits and their attitudes toward reading as a tool for gaining information, as a means of widening personal horizons, and as a leisure activity. The public seemed to attribute the success to the positive impact of the education reform, to innovative school-based reading curricula, and to hard-working Chinese language teachers. Attention also focused on the contribution of the general public in promoting a reading culture, and on the development of students' reading habits and attitudes.

The PIRLS 2006 findings underscored the fact that many parents in Hong Kong are not well educated and thus feel unable to contribute much to the development of their children's literacy. Such parents are reluctant to involve themselves actively in their offspring's education, preferring to leave matters exclusively in the hands of schools.

7.5.4   Implications for Schools and Teachers

Schools and teachers nervously awaited the PIRLS 2006 results after several years of hard work trying to improve the reading curriculum and to build up a positive reading atmosphere and culture in schools. Although teachers realized the improvement among Hong Kong students was impressive, they knew that their classroom practice and use of reading materials had shortcomings. Many also worried that responding to TSA preparation demands by allocating space on the timetable to it reduced the instructional time available for the teaching of reading. They complained that they were uncertain about how to help students with reading difficulties and said that they had inadequate support from reading specialists in the Education Bureau.

The PIRLS research team was concerned that schools, teachers, parents, and the general public would become complacent about the good reading performance of Hong Kong students in PIRLS 2006. They feared, for example, that teachers might consider it unnecessary to try to improve students' reading any further or to increase the time allocation for developing new teaching skills and methods. There was, indeed, a cool response from some teachers to seminars and workshops provided by the PIRLS research team about the implications of PIRLS 2006.

After expressing their concerns to the Education Bureau, the team's members agreed jointly to organize talks and workshops for primary school teachers about how to organize classroom reading activities of high quality, and about how to promote reading across the curriculum not only for Chinese language teachers but also for curriculum development officers and school-librarians in Hong Kong primary schools. The response from those who attended the workshops was positive. They agreed that school-based reading curricula should focus on developing existing effective reading programs and classroom activities, and they favored efforts to promote high-quality reading in all subject areas of the curriculum.

The materials and resources habitually used by teachers also came in for criticism. Primary school curriculum development officers were encouraged to expand the range of textual material that school-based reading curricula require for effective Chinese language teaching, and to include popular fiction, storybooks, and newspapers for children and a wider variety of reading materials. Schools were encouraged to build up good reading environments and, where possible, to continue having a "reading for pleasure" session every morning.

Each school that participated in the PIRLS survey received an in-depth individual school report containing a detailed analysis of its students' reading performance, reading attitudes and behavior, and home reading environments. The Hong Kong PIRLS team hoped that schools would use this information to tailor programs in ways that would extend the reading strategies and capabilities of their own students.

Although, in PIRLS 2006, the discrepancy between boys and girls in Hong Kong narrowed, the Hong Kong PIRLS team considered that this was another matter that did not warrant complacency. The NRC of the team maintained that, in addition to possible differences in the literacy learning curves of boys and girls, existing reading materials favor girls' interests rather than boys'. This matter was therefore considered to be an issue that should not be ignored. The subsequent reading list catering specifically for boys prepared by the Education Bureau was welcomed as was as its distribution to all primary schools and its posting on internet in the summer of 2009. It is hoped that this arrangement is stimulating boys' interest and motivation in reading and further narrowing the attainment discrepancy between the genders.

The strong emphasis on securing parental involvement in the development of children's literacy led to schools being encouraged to invite more parents to act as reading-aide volunteers within schools. This development also necessitated providing relevant training for parents.

7.5.5 Implications for Parents

Chinese parents are strong in their conviction that education is very important for the life-chances of their children. They vigorously seek entrance for their children to prestigious schools and pay for extra tuition should they consider it necessary. They insist that their child completes homework meticulously and complain to the school if their child is not making good progress. After the release of the PIRLS 2006 results and the knowledge that students had performed well in terms of attainment in Chinese reading, parents were anxious to know how they could further improve their children's reading skills. Parents also knew that many experts were stressing reading as a key influence on students' present and subsequent academic achievement.

Although parents were quite keen for their child to acquire those reading habits that, in theory, affect reading ability, few knew what they themselves could do to help. Parents (and their parents) had been brought up with the attitude that their part in the parent–teacher unwritten contract is to ensure that the child goes to school, completes homework on time, and works hard to revise for examinations. Passing examinations well is, in the eyes of many parents, the chief purpose for going to school. Some parents, especially those from low socioeconomic backgrounds and with a history of poor academic achievement, still do not regard their children reading silently or for leisure as productive or purposeful. Thus, they seldom buy reading books for children (other than textbooks) or encourage their children to use libraries. There are few books in the home for their children to read, and parents are loath to discuss with their children any books the children are reading (Tse, Lam, Lam, Loh, & Westwood, 2005).

In short, although there has been some improvement in the home reading environment, parents' own reading attitudes and habits still need to be addressed. In addition, many parents remain unconvinced about the importance of early home reading activities for the development of children's literacy. It did not seem to come as a surprise to parents that girls are more "bookish" than boys. Nor did this seem to worry parents, since boys seem easily able to make up the deficit in secondary school.

The Hong Kong PIRLS team organized around 25 talks and workshops in primary schools. Nearly 1,600 principals, teachers, and school librarians attended them. The focus during these sessions was on careful explanation of theories of reading, reading process and strategies, and assessment of reading. Teachers also received information about conceptual changes in approaches to teaching reading, the place of decoding of words, student-based approaches, and self-directed learning.

Some of the schools sought assistance from the Faculty of Education at the University of Hong Kong about how to change parental perceptions and involvement. The PIRLS research team collaborated with the Education Bureau and primary and secondary schools to organize five large-scale workshops for parents. Over 2,800 parents attended. They were shown how to set up a good home reading environment, how to develop children's reading ability, how to instill positive attitudes toward reading in children, and how to ensure children acquire good reading habits. As we noted earlier in this chapter, the Education Bureau published a leaflet and a series of booklets (Education Bureau, 2009) for parents of infants and children up to nine years of age. These provide parents with advice on how to develop children's reading habits and literacy and how to provide suitable home reading activities for children of different ages.

7.5.6   Promoting Reading Competence with the Help of Non-Government Organizations

Members of the Hong Kong PIRLS team were convinced that students' literacy weaknesses were not a recent phenomenon. Nor did they believe that the task of rectifying any deficiency should be left solely to schools and the Education Bureau. Confident that research was needed into the reading and writing process and that the results of this research should be communicated to an audience wider than that of the education sector, the team took their views to the Education Bureau and voiced their concerns to various sections of the government. They argued that a number of non-government organizations could be productively involved in research into ways of improving standards of reading in the community and helping students to use reading as a vehicle for learning and as a source of pleasure.

The Hong Kong PIRLS team also launched a number of research initiatives in an effort to identify the most effective ways of teaching how to read and learning how to read in Hong Kong. The team furthermore conducted research aimed at clarifying the processes involved in the teaching and learning of reading. Another venture was "Developing Students' Independent Learning Capabilities in Primary and Secondary Chinese Language Curriculum." The aim of this project, which involved members of the PIRLS research team, five primary schools, and two secondary schools, was to help students to master, monitor, and evaluate their own reading progress and strategies. The PIRLS team also introduced information about independent learning strategies to teachers, parents, and the students themselves (Tse, Marton, Loh, & Chik, 2010).

Another branch of the Education Bureau that the research team contacted was Hong Kong Education City, a government-owned corporation. The corporation's main duties are fourfold: (i) to strengthen connections between educators, the business sector, industrial organizations, and government and non-government organizations; (ii) to provide information about educational provision for the public; (iii) to develop a quality platform for web-based learning and living; and (iv) to promote reading habits in the community. Joint projects with organizations such as Caritas Hong Kong and the Boys and Girls Club Association (BGCA) were arranged, along with a series of reading activities for the public. These included the following:

- Hong Kong Reading City website, *Reading Summer 2003 and 2004*
- Let's Read in the Morning: Thousand People's Campaign;
- Reading Ambassadors Program (for primary and secondary students and parents);
- Reading Contract;
- Reading Schools Program;
- Online Reading Club;
- Boundless Reading Campus;
- Chinese Classics Recitation Contest: Hong Kong 2009; and
- The Children's Reading Festival.

Hong Kong Education City invited the Hong Kong NRC of the research team to serve as consultant and to evaluate the effectiveness of the Reading Ambassadors Program and the Reading Contract.

The NRC was also invited by Caritas Hong Kong to serve as consultant on a reading program organized by the Youth and Community Services section and directed at training parents as "reading mothers and fathers." The aim was to help parents help teachers by promoting reading in schools and at home. The BGCA invited the research team to report the PIRLS 2006 results to some 50 senior officers and to share with them strategies to promote reading among the public in general and children from socially and economically deprived backgrounds in particular. The BGCA trained thousands of volunteer parents to read stories to students.

The thrust of these collaborations with non-government organizations has been that of educating parents about ways to help their children to read via channels quite unconnected with the schools that their children attend. The burgeoning and promising interest in ways to promote reading prompted the NRC to collaborate with a special school for students with intellectual disabilities and students who are autistic that is run by the Salvation Army in Hong Kong. This project seeks to enhance the reading ability of children with disabilities by using modern methods to help them learn Chinese characters so that eventually they can learn how to read text and online reading material on their own.

7.5.7 Impact on School Administration in Hong Kong

The PIRLS 2006 results reminded school principals and administrators that learning to read is one of the most important achievements affecting school performance. The results increased the momentum for change and prompted many school managers to look critically at their school curriculum. The PIRLS evidence reminded planners that *learning how to learn through reading* is a very important objective in the primary school. It also reminded schools that *learning to read* and *reading to learn* are equally important facets of students' education.

The success of many of the above region-wide initiatives rests on how well students can eventually read and employ reading skills to draw meaning from text. This emphasis on skills and strategies is very different from the stress on content-based assessment in the conventional curriculum. Principals have been reminded publicly of the need to emphasize the teaching and learning of reading strategies, to build up a supportive reading environment in schools, to persuade students to read more extracurricular books, and to organize workshops and information packs for parents. Parent-volunteers need to continue being recruited and sensitively trained to join in shared-reading activities with their children.

7.5.8   Impact at Administrative and School Levels outside Hong Kong

As a consequence of the outstanding performance of Hong Kong students in PIRLS 2006, the Hong Kong research team has been visited by officers from ministries of education in different countries and asked to share their experience of promoting the teaching and learning of reading to schools and the general public. Visiting dignitaries have included the Assistant Director and colleagues of the Office for Standards in Education, Children's Services, and Skills (Ofsted), the United Kingdom; the Director General of Education, Singapore, and her colleagues; the Minister for Education and the Secretary of the Department of Education and Early Childhood Development of the state government of Victoria, Australia, and their colleagues; and officers of the Taiwan Ministry of Education. The NRC has been invited by several countries and cities to talk about factors leading to Hong Kong students' reading success in PIRLS 2006. These places include Beijing, Chengdu, Shenzhen, Guangzhou, Hangzhou, Macao, Singapore, and Taiwan. The NRC also gave a presentation about the reading performance of these students to the General Assembly of IEA.

In December 2006, the Common Wealth Educational Foundation of Taiwan invited the PIRLS research team to provide three talks for all Chinese-language teachers in Taipei, Taiwan. More than 3,000 teachers attended. During the talks, the team shared Hong Kong's experiences of educational reform and the teaching and learning of reading. In May 2008, financial support from the Common Wealth Educational Foundation enabled 30 selected primary school teachers from Taipei to visit Hong Kong. They participated in workshops provided by the Hong Kong PIRLS team. They also visited partnership schools. Inspired by the work being done by the primary school teachers and the excellent performance of students in Hong Kong, the Taiwan teachers, on returning home, shared their impressions and experiences with fellow teachers and conducted "seed projects" in their own schools, which included trying out various innovative strategies observed in classrooms in Hong Kong.

7.6 Anticipated Future Activities

7.6.1 Research

To obtain objective evidence for monitoring the bilingual reading (BR) attainment of students in Hong Kong, the "Progress in Chinese and English Reading Literacy Study at Grade 4 in Hong Kong and Approaches to and Strategies for Enhancing the Quality of the Teaching and Learning of Reading" (BR2010) was conducted in 2010. This is the third study, after the bilingual reading studies in 2004 (BR04) and 2007 (BR07), in a three-year cycle of assessment that measures trends in children's Chinese and English reading-literacy attainment, the reading habits and attitudes of students, and policy and practices relating to literacy.

Other areas considered during the study were English reading curricula, English reading teaching strategies, students' English reading habits and attitudes toward English reading, and the home English reading environment in countries where English is a first, second, or additional language. The results will be very important for highlighting the strengths and weaknesses of reading pedagogy in Hong Kong.

The findings of the study, which has kept to the framework guiding the PIRLS 2001 and 2006 surveys and employed similar research instruments to those used in these studies, will permit comparisons with language-attainment standards in English-speaking countries around the world.

7.6.2 Teacher Training Programs

In order to advance the reading-based professional development of preservice and inservice teachers in Hong Kong, the outcomes and implications of the PIRLS 2001 and 2006 findings and of the Bilingual Reading 2004 and 2007 analyses are now included in the University of Hong Kong's teacher training programs.

7.7 Concluding Remarks

Participation in the PIRLS exercise has been a very valuable experience for Hong Kong. The PIRLS findings presented a comprehensive picture of the reading performance, habits, and attitudes of students in Hong Kong schools. They also highlighted the interface between home and school and its influence on students' reading performance. It is hoped that the efficacy of the measures taken in response to PIRLS 2001 and 2006 will be shown to be successful when put to the test in the latest iteration of the PIRLS surveys, that is, PIRLS 2011.

The release of the PIRLS 2006 findings certainly had an impact in Hong Kong. The outstanding reading performance of Grade 4 students excited everyone throughout the region. There has been widespread recognition of the hard work of the students, the positive impact of the education reform, and the contributions of schools, teachers, and the general public.

Ongoing attention needs to be given to helping parents, especially those with low academic achievement and of low socioeconomic status, to help their children acquire literacy. The interest shown by parents in the PIRLS findings is evidence of their desire to help their children do well at school. Many parents accept that it is their responsibility to create a good reading environment in the home and to encourage children to read for pleasure. However, very few parents feel that they possess the relevant expertise to help their child use reading as a study aid for learning the various subjects in the curriculum. Quite understandably, these parents believe that such expertise resides in the schools to which they send their children. They also expect that teachers and schools will respond positively to the PIRLS evidence, and that they will reshape practice in order to attend to any weaknesses identified.

Learning how to read and promoting independent learning through reading are emphases that should not be neglected in the coming years. In today's ever changing technological society, students are communicating via text messages, blogs, and web pages on a scale previously undreamt of. Youngsters wear computerized timepieces on their wrists and carry mobile phones capable of web surfing and instant exchange of verbal and written messages. It will be interesting to see, from the findings of future studies, the extent to which the presence of such activities can be detected in children's reading and writing.

It is vital that research of this type is communicated to interested parties in appropriate ways. For this reason, the Hong Kong PIRLS research team has prepared separate publications for the public and for teachers and academics. In addition, materials handed out in PIRLS seminars have been posted on the Chinese Education Web (Hong Kong) for the public to access and download. As we stated in the introduction to this chapter, there is a strong case for using research into literacy as a catalyst for alerting schools, parents, and society to how they can pool their efforts, given that a combined response to problems tends to be more effective than effort carried out by just one person or agency.

Mindful of the interests of academics, the Hong Kong PIRLS research team has published the findings and implications of the PIRLS study in Hong Kong and other countries (Lam et al., 2010; Tse et al., 2003, 2005a, 2006, 2007, 2010, in press; Tse, Lam, Lam, Loh, & Westwood, 2005; Tse & Loh, 2007). It is hoped that these publications will serve as a reference for students of literacy and for the teaching of research methodology in universities. Educators, teachers, and parents who are interested in the PIRLS study may also obtain information from the books and international journal articles in which reports are posted.

As is always the case, each research exercise gives rise to further questions and issues that need to be addressed. We need to take into account the influence of ongoing innovations in educational provision and region-wide assessments. These include changes to the medium of instruction used in schools, as well as changes to educational practice introduced to accommodate advances in information technology.

References

Census and Statistics Department. (2006). *Hong Kong in figures 2006*. Hong Kong: Hong Kong SAR Government.

Census and Statistics Department. (2009). *Hong Kong in figures 2009*. Hong Kong: Hong Kong SAR Government.

Cheung, I. S. (1992). A preliminary report on the Chinese reading ability of Hong Kong pupils. *International Language Education Journal, 9*, 35–47.

Curriculum Development Council. (2000). *Learning to learn: The way forward in curriculum development*. Hong Kong: Author.

Curriculum Development Council. (2001). *"Learning to learn—the way forward in the curriculum." Basic education curriculum guide: Building on strengths (Primary 1 to Secondary 3)*. Hong Kong: Author.

Curriculum Development Council. (2002). *Chinese language education: Key learning area curriculum guide (Primary 1 to Secondary 3)*. Hong Kong: Author.

Curriculum Development Institute. (2002). *Reading to learn: The promotion of a reading culture at school*. Hong Kong: Author.

Education Bureau. (1997). *Extensive reading scheme*. Hong Kong: Hong Kong SAR Government.

Education Bureau. (2008a). *Pre-Secondary One Hong Kong Attainment Test*. Hong Kong: Hong Kong SAR Government.

Education Bureau. (2008b). *"Through-train" mode*. Hong Kong: Hong Kong SAR Government.

Education Bureau. (2008c). *Education Bureau Circular No. 19/2008: Small class teaching in public sector primary schools*. Hong Kong: Hong Kong SAR Government.

Education Bureau. (2009). *Reading with your kids is fun: To the parents of children 0 to 9 years old*. Hong Kong: Hong Kong SAR Government.

Education Commission. (1996). *Education Commission Report No. 6*. Hong Kong: Hong Kong SAR Government.

Hong Kong Examination and Assessment Authority. (2009a). *Assessment for learning resource bank: Basic competency assessment—student assessment*. Hong Kong: Author. Retrieved from http://www.hkbca.edu.hk/index_eng.htm

Hong Kong Examination and Assessment Authority. (2009b). *About Hong Kong: Certificate of Education Examination (Hong Kong CEE)*. Hong Kong: Author. Retrieved from http://www.hkeaa.edu.hk/tc/hkcee/

Hong Kong Examination and Assessment Authority. (2009c). *School-based assessment (SBA)*. Hong Kong: Author. Retrieved from http://www.hkeaa.edu. hk/en/sba/

Hong Kong SAR Government. (2001). *Hong Kong 2000*. Hong Kong: Author.

Hong Kong SAR Government. (2003). *Hong Kong 2003*. Hong Kong: Author.

Hong Kong SAR Government. (2009). *Hong Kong 2009*. Hong Kong: Author.

Lam, J. W. I., Cheung, W. M., & Lam, R. Y. H. (2009). Learning to read: The reading performance of Hong Kong primary students compared with that in developed countries around the world in PIRLS 2001 and 2006. *China Education and Society, 42*(3), 6–32.

Lam, R. Y. H., Tse, S. K., Lam, J. W. I., & Loh, E. K. Y. (2010). Gender differences in teacher effectiveness and their impact on pupils' reading attainment in Hong Kong primary schools. *Teaching and Teacher Education, 26*(4), 754–759.

Law, F. (2002). *Letter from the Permanent Secretary for Education Bureau on "Promotion of a Reading Culture in School."* Hong Kong: Education Bureau, Hong Kong SAR Government.

Loh, E. K. Y., & Tse, S. K. (2009). The relationship between motivation to read Chinese and English and the impact on the Chinese and English reading performance of Chinese students. *Chinese Education and Society, 42*(3), 66–90.

Suen, M. Y. M. (2009). *Speeches by Secretary for Education on the forum on "Fine-Tuning the Medium of Instruction for Secondary Schools between the Secretary for Education and Heads of Secondary Schools."* Hong Kong: Hong Kong SAR Government.

Tse, S. K., Lam, R. Y. H., Ip., O. K. M., Lam, J. W. I., Loh, E. K. Y., & Tso, A. S. F. (in press). Family resources and students' reading attainment: Capitalizing on home factors. *Educational Studies in Language and Literature Journal.*

Tse, S. K., Lam, R. Y. H., Lam, J. W. I., Chan, Y. M., & Loh, E. K. Y. (2006). Attitudes and attainment: A comparison of Hong Kong, Singaporean, and English students' reading. *Research in Education, 76*, 74–87.

Tse, S. K., Lam, J. W. I., Lam, R. Y. H., & Loh, E. K. Y. (2003). PIRLS 2001: Hong Kong component. *Chinese Language Testing, 4,* 1–9.

Tse, S. K., Lam, J. W. I., Lam, R. Y. H., & Loh, E. K. Y. (2005a). *PIRLS: Comparison of Hong Kong and other countries.* Hong Kong: Hong Kong University Press.

Tse, S. K., Lam, J. W. I., Lam, R .Y. H., & Loh, E. K. Y. (2005b). Follow up study of PIRLS. *CERCular, 10*(1), 7.

Tse, S. K., Lam, J. W. I., Lam, R. Y. H., Loh, E. K. Y., & Westwood, P. (2005). Students' test performance in PIRLS, attitude to reading, and reading self-concept across three ability groups: Data from Hong Kong. *Australian Journal of Learning Disabilities, 10*(1), 9–18.

Tse, S. K., Lam, J. W. I., Loh, E. K. Y., & Cheung, W. M. (2010). *PIRLS 2006: Hong Kong report.* Hong Kong: Centre for Advancement of Chinese Language Education and Research, Faculty of Education, University of Hong Kong.

Tse, S. K., Lam, R. Y. H., Loh, E. K. Y., Ip, O. K. M., Lam, J. W. I., & Chan, Y. M. (2009). English-speaking foreign domestic helpers and students' English reading attainment in Hong Kong. *Chinese Education and Society, 42*(3), 49–65.

Tse, S. K., Lam, J. W. I., Loh, E. K. Y., & Lam, R. Y. H. (2007). The influence of the language that Hong Kong primary school students habitually speak at home on their Chinese reading ability in school. *Journal of Multilingual and Multicultural Development, 28*(5), 1–18.

Tse, S. K., & Loh, E. K. Y. (2007). The impact of PIRLS in Hong Kong SAR. In K. Schwippert (Ed.), *Progress in reading literacy: The impact of PIRLS 2001 in 13 countries* (pp. 109–126). Munster, Germany: Waxmann Verlag GmbH.

Tse, S. K., Loh, E. K. Y., Lam, R. Y. H., & Lam, J. W. I. (2010). A comparison of the English and Chinese reading proficiency of primary school Chinese students. *Journal of Multilingual and Multicultural Development, 31*(2), 181–199.

Tse, S. K., Marton, F., Loh, E. K. Y., & Chik, P. P. M. (2010). Learning to read and write better. In F. Marton, S. K. Tse, & W. M. Cheung (Eds.), *On the learning of Chinese* (pp. 123–146). Rotterdam, the Netherlands: Sense Publishers.

Tse, S. K., Yuen, A. H. K., Loh, E. K. Y., Lam, J. W. I., & Ng, R. H. W. (2010). Impact of blogging on Hong Kong Primary 4 students' bilingual reading literacy. *Australian Journal of Educational Technology, 26*(2), 164–179.

Wong, P. K. (1984). *Collected essays in Chinese language teaching.* Hong Kong: Chinese Language Society of Hong Kong.

World Bank. (2009). *World development indicators database: Key development data and statistics.* Washington, DC: Author. Retrieved from http://data.worldbank.org/products/data-books/ WDI-2009

Websites

Census and Statistics Department, Hong Kong SAR Government:
http://www.info.gov.hk/censtatd/home.html
Chinese Education Web (Hong Kong): http://www.chineseedu.hku.hk
Education Bureau: http://www.edb.gov.hk/
Hong Kong Education City: http://www.hkedcity.net

Further Reading

Curriculum Development Council. (2000). *Learning to learn: Chinese key learning area.* Hong Kong: Hong Kong SAR Government.

Education Commission. (2000). *Life-long learning, whole person development: Education reform.* Hong Kong: Hong Kong SAR Government.

Tse, S. K., & Lai, F. K. (2001). *A study on the promotion and implementation of extensive reading in schools: Report submitted to the Education Bureau, Hong Kong SAR Government.* Hong Kong: Faculty of Education, the University of Hong Kong.

Chapter 8
The Impact of PIRLS in Hungary

Péter Balkányi

8.1   Hungary at a Glance

Hungary, or its official designation, the Hungarian Republic, is an independent, democratic nation situated in Central Eastern Europe, within the Carpathian Basin. It borders Slovakia in the north, Ukraine in the north-east, Romania in the east and south-east, Serbia in the south, Croatia and Slovenia in the south-west, and Austria in the west. The country, which is landlocked, covers 93,036 square kilometers. The lowest point geographically is 78 meters above sea level and the highest—Kékes Peak in the Mátra Mountains—is 1,014 meters above sea level.

The country has 10,020,000 inhabitants, with a population density of 108 persons per square kilometer. Hungary's capital and its biggest city is Budapest. There are 19 counties in the seven regions of the country. Hungary's bigger cities (100,000 inhabitants or more) are, in order of decreasing population size, Debrecen, Miskolc, Szeged, Pécs, Győr, Nyíregyháza, Kecskemét, and Székesfehérvár.

Unlike other countries in the region, Hungary is relatively homogenous ethnically. In addition to the overall Hungarian majority, Hungary is home to Roma, Germans, Slovaks, Croatians, Romanians, Ukrainians, Serbians, and Slovenians, along with smaller ethnic groupings. Ninety-nine percent of the country's population speaks Hungarian as their first language.

Hungary has been a republic since 1989, a member of the OECD since 1996, NATO since 1999, the European Union since 2004, and the Schengen Agreement since December 21, 2007. Hungary is also one of the founding members of the Visegrád Group. Hungary's economic output positions it as an OECD member and therefore a developed country. The gross domestic product (GDP) was US$M198,100 in 2008, and the GDP per capita was US$19,732.

According to OECD analyses, Hungary's educational expenditure of 4.9 percent of GDP in 2007 was below the average OECD expenditure (5.7% of GDP). However, the estimated average expenditure per student from the first grade of elementary to the end of secondary schooling was US$52,433, just 55 percent of the OECD average.

8.2   Hungary's Education System as a Context for PIRLS[1]

Hungarian is Hungary's only official language. Not surprisingly, the language of instruction in the public education system is also Hungarian. Under the auspices of the

---

1   The information in this section is drawn from Felvégi and Ostorics (2007).

Public Education Act, institutions providing public education can be founded and operated by the state, local governing bodies, regional and national minority governments, registered religious legal persons, and nationally founded economic organizations, as well as foundations, associations, and private citizens. The state, however, has oversight of all public education provision and is responsible for financing it. The Hungarian compulsory education system consists of three levels: kindergarten, elementary, and secondary. Tertiary education conforms to the Bologna Process (European Commission, 2011).

Elementary and secondary education is compulsory for children 6 to 18 years of age. Children can be enrolled in kindergarten at the age of three; enrollment is mandatory from age five. Children at this level engage in learning directed toward character development, inclusiveness (i.e., integration into the community), social and emotional wellbeing, adoption of a healthy lifestyle, and overall development of skills and competencies. Targeted educational provision is available for children from socially disadvantaged backgrounds.

Elementary education consists of eight grades, which, in line with Public Education Act regulations, are divided into four two-year sections: Grades 1 to 2 (introductory), Grades 3 to 4 (beginner), Grades 5 to 6 (basic), and Grades 7 to 8 (developmental). Although children are not required to sit examinations at the end of their elementary schooling, they may have to sit written examinations, covering mathematics and literacy, if the vocational school or the secondary grammar school that they elect to attend has passing examinations as an entrance requirement. The examination booklets are prepared by the centrally based Education Authority and cover content mandated by sets of national standards.

Schooling at the secondary level features three types of school—vocational, grammar, and secondary vocational. In vocational schools, the ratio of vocationally oriented tuition to general studies for students in Grades 9 and 10 is generally 40 percent to 60 percent respectively. Students attending vocational schools do not have to sit the school-leaving examination, the Matura, before leaving school, but they do have to sit an examination related to the studied trade.

Grammar schools (generally referred to as gymnasiums) teach general studies and conventional academic subjects, which are included in the Matura. Students in these schools typically work toward tertiary study or entering the workforce. About two thirds of the grammar schools operate four grade levels (9 to 12). However, the number of grammar schools able to enroll students for six or eight years (i.e., students can enter these schools after the fourth or sixth grade of elementary school) is increasing. The secondary grammar level ends with the school-leaving examination; entrance to tertiary education depends on the results of this examination.

Secondary vocational schools feature characteristics of both the grammar and the vocational schools. During their first four years in these schools, students learn the same subjects as in the gymnasiums and attend classes that prepare them for their later vocational training. At the end of the fourth year, students take the school-leaving examination and then spend the next one to three years preparing for a technical examination.

Reading instruction is regulated by the national core curriculum and the curriculum framework: the former includes the goals and tasks; the latter the actual educational content. According to these documents, the primary goal of reading instruction in the first four grades is to establish reading as a basic skill so that students can silently read and comprehend the content in their school books. Students also are expected to learn to retrieve information and to use it to accomplish learning tasks, to read aloud expressively, and to form a basis for analytical, critical, and creative reading.

Because the first two grades are regarded as one whole developmental phase within the elementary school curriculum, there are no set goals for the end of the first year. However, by the end of the second year of this introductory phase, students are expected to be able to fluently read a known text aloud. By the end of Grade 3, students should be able to read and understand a literary or expository text comprising around half a page, and on reaching the end of Grade 4, they should be able to read aloud, after some preparation, an unknown text featuring a familiar subject. They should also, at this time, be able to read age-appropriate texts silently, and to comprehend and communicate their central ideas.

In Hungarian elementary schools, students stay with the one teacher, who teaches all subjects, until the end of Grade 4. The overwhelming majority (92%) of primary school classroom teachers are women. Teachers are required to prepare a written report of each student's progress during his or her time in Grades 1 to 4. This grading system uses a four-level scale: exemplary, good, acceptable, needs remediation. More specifically, teachers are expected to describe, in considerable detail, in these reports, students' oral communication skills, performance with respect to general subjects, and attitudes toward school and learning. If the school determines that a child needs remedial tuition, it discusses this course of action with the child's parents, outlining the areas of concern and suggesting what should be done next. There is no formal provision for students in the lower grades to repeat a year, but parents can request that their children be held back if they think it is necessary.

8.3   Hungary's Experience of Large-Scale Assessments

Since the 2001/2002 academic year, Hungary has annually administered its National Assessment of Basic Competencies (NABC) in order to determine student proficiency in mathematics and reading. All students in Grades 6, 8, and 10 have been assessed since 2004 (see Table 8.1). Although the Ministry of Education has overall responsibility for the NABC, which is mandated by the Public Education Act, the Educational Authority's Department of Assessment and Evaluation is the agency that conducts it.

Table 8.1:   National reading assessment studies conducted in Hungary

Year of data collection	Name of survey	Target population	Assessment domain
1986	Monitor 1986	Grades 4, 8, 10, 12	R, M, IT
1991	Monitor 1991	Grades 4, 8	R, M, IT
1993	Monitor 1993	Grade 10	R, M, IT, S
1995	Monitor 1995	Grades 3, 4, 7, 8, 10, 12	R, M, IT
1997	Monitor 1997	Grades 4, 6, 8, 10, 12	R, M, IT, S
1999	Monitor 1999	Grade 8	R, M, IT, S
2001	Monitor 2001	Grades 4, 8	R, M, S
2003	National Assessment of Basic Competencies (NABC)	Grades 5, 9	R, M
	Monitor 2003	Grades 4, 8	R, M, S
	NABC	Grades 6, 10	
2004	NABC	Grades 6, 8, 10	R, M
2005	Monitor 2005	Grade 8	R, M, S
2006	NABC	Grades 4, 6, 8, 10	R, M
2007	NABC	Grades 4, 6, 8, 10	R, M
2008	NABC	Grades 4, 6, 8, 10	R, M
2009	NABC	Grades 4, 6, 8,10	R, M
2010	NABC	Grades 4, 6, 8,10	R, M

Key: M = mathematics, R = reading; S = science, IT = information technology.

The assessment ascertains whether students can use their skills and knowledge to solve everyday situations; it does not focus on textbook knowledge, and it benchmarks this performance along four levels of competency. Schools and the organizations responsible for them receive a report and data analysis software that enables them to determine students' performance against these benchmarks. This information, in turn, provides schools with the information they need to identify areas for improvement and to develop future educational goals. Participating students and their parents can also use a unique student ID code to access student performance data. During academic year 2005/2006, Hungary began another assessment that parallels the NABC. It assesses Grade 4 students' basic reading, mathematics, problem-solving, and writing skills. In addition to guaranteeing the annual administration of the NABC, the Public Education Act requires all schools to conduct, as part of their quality-control programs, ongoing assessment of their students' performance.

The Educational Authority's Department of Assessment and Evaluation has oversight not only of the NABC and what are known as national monitor studies, but also of the IEA assessments PIRLS and TIMSS and OECD's PISA. The department is responsible for the national implementation and scoring of these assessments and for analyzing the data produced. With respect to literacy, Hungary has participated in other IEA studies in this area, including the Reading Literacy Study and PIRLS 2001.

Hungary has participated in PISA since its inception. PISA has a greater influence than PIRLS on Hungarian educational policy, in part because the results of that study are more widely known due to the perceived relative importance of the population surveyed (15-year-olds) and the consequently more critical reception of the student performance results. As noted in more detail later in this chapter, publication of the PISA 2000 results led not only to the development of educational materials focused on developing key competencies throughout the education system but also to the creation of the NABC.

8.4   National Results[2]

Hungary's average achievement on the PIRLS reading scale in 2006 was 551 score points, which was considered a good result given that only four other countries had significantly higher average scores. Hungarian students' average score of 543 points in PIRLS 2001 meant that their achievement in PIRLS 2006 was slightly but significantly better (by eight score points). The other countries that showed an increase in performance over the six years between the two surveys were Hong Kong, Germany, Russia, Singapore, and Slovakia.

Because Hungary lies in the Central-European region, it generally measures itself against the countries of that region when considering the results of international comparative student assessments. Compared to the other countries of the Central-European region,[3] Hungary performed significantly above the regional average of 525 points (SE: 1.3). And because similar historical roots suggest similar educational backgrounds, we considered it useful to compare Hungary's performance with that of other former socialist countries.[4] The average for this group of countries in PIRLS 2006 was 524 score points (SE: 1.0), which means that Hungary again performed significantly better.

A broader comparison can also be made with respect to the countries of the European Union,[5] given that Hungary is a member. Once again, Hungary's performance was significantly better than the group (EU) average of 536 score points

2   This section draws on information contained in Balázsi, Balkányi, Felvégi, and Szabó (2007) and Mullis, Martin, Kennedy, and Foy (2007).
3   Calculations for the Central-European region drew on PIRLS data for Austria, Hungary, Poland, Romana, Slovakia, and Slovenia.
4   Calculations for the former socialist countries drew on PIRLS data for Bulgaria, Hungary, Latvia, Lithuania, Macedonia, Moldova, Poland, Romania, Slovakia, and Russia.
5   Calculations for the European Union countries drew on PIRLS data for Austria, Belgium, Denmark, England, France, Germany, Hungary, Italy, Latvia, Lithuania, Luxembourg, the Netherlands, Poland, Spain, Scotland, Slovakia, Slovenia, and Sweden.

(SE: 0.5). The same pattern of better performance was evident when we compared Hungary's average score against the average score of 537 points (SE: 0.3) for the OECD countries[6] that participated in PIRLS.

Having presented these general results, we would now like to highlight two interesting sets of data from PIRLS 2006. The first is the considerable difference in the national results relative to the international results for purpose of reading (this difference was one of the biggest to emerge from the international data set). The second is the generally low use of information technology in Hungarian schools.

The PIRLS assessment framework differentiates between reading for literary experience and reading for information, and has separate achievement scales for each type. Compared to the results pattern for students in the other countries participating in PIRLS, Hungarian students were considerably better at reading texts for pleasure than for procuring information; they also had one of the highest scores on the reading for literary experience scale. The difference in the Hungarian averages for the two scales was 16 points in favor of reading for pleasure. Nevertheless, Hungarian students' average score for reading informational texts was still very good at 541.

One of the reasons for this gap may be because Hungarian students primarily read literary passages to learn and practice reading and so encounter considerably fewer informational texts when reading in class. They generally do not encounter informational texts until they reach Grades 5 to 7, when subject-based education requires their use. The difference in achievement between the two scales is one of the main reasons why reading experts in Hungary have encouraged the use of more informational materials in the lower grades. The experts' particular aim here is to limit the likelihood of students experiencing difficulty when reading this type of text later in their schooling.

In Hungary, use of personal computers has become more widespread in education and in facilitating children's reading development. As a consequence, there was particular interest in gaining some understanding from the PIRLS survey about how information technology is being used in our schools. Responses on the teacher questionnaire told us about the opportunities students were having at the time of the survey to use computers at school, whether these computers had internet access, and the frequency with which information technology was being used to develop reading literacy skills. International data show that, on average, 65 percent of students attend schools equipped with computers that are available to fourth graders, and that (on average internationally) the majority of Grade 4 students (57%) attend schools that have computers with internet access. Across countries, 39 percent, on average, of Grade 4 students were reported as being asked at least once a month to read stories or

---

6   Calculations for the OECD countries drew on PIRLS data for Austria, Belgium, Canada (by provinces), Denmark, England, France, Germany, Hungary, Iceland, Italy, Luxembourg, the Netherlands, New Zealand, Norway, Poland, Scotland, Slovakia, Spain, Sweden, and the USA.

materials on the computer, while 30 percent, on average, were said to be using educational software. The corresponding percentages for Hungary were 22 and 12.

Except for Russia, all countries that performed better than Hungary on PIRLS had greater student access to and use of computers and the internet in general, and for reading literacy tasks in particular. Luxembourg was twice as likely as Hungary to have these provisions. Closer inspection of the data for Hungary led us to believe that the information technology resources available in schools at the time of PIRLS 2006 were not being used to their full potential with respect to developing children's reading skills.

Viewed from a school-resourcing perspective, the PIRLS results showed that, on average, Hungarian schools were on a par with those in the other PIRLS countries. Hungarian school principals noted in the PIRLS school questionnaire that funding is generally not an issue for teachers. Despite this, the PIRLS reading literacy data show Hungarian students' achievement lagging behind that of their counterparts in Hungary's more developed Western neighbors, as well as behind those in other Central-European countries. However, overall, Hungarian students' reading achievement improved during the period between the 2001 and 2006 PIRLS assessments.

8.5   Impact of PIRLS

When mentioned in the Hungarian press, PIRLS results are generally reported with reference to PISA because the latter is more widely known. One reason why this is so may be that Hungary began participating in PISA some time before it began taking part in PIRLS. Another may be that Hungarian secondary school students' relatively weak performance on PISA has attracted more attention and publicity from both the press and educational professionals.[7]

While the PISA results have typically led to calls for school improvement, the generally good PIRLS results have been greeted with equanimity. In consequence, little has been published about PIRLS in Hungary. What has been produced generally comprises brief reports summing up the press release from the PIRLS national research center. None of these reports has gone beyond a mere introduction to the results and mention of the good performance of Hungary's 10-year-olds (fourth graders).

Researchers in the Education Authority's Department of Assessment and Evaluation have published articles in Hungarian pedagogical journals about the results of PIRLS 2006 (e.g., Balázsi & Balkányi, 2008) and about the probable causes of the differences in student performance on PISA and PIRLS. The national report on the Hungarian PIRLS results prepared by the department's officials is also available in English.

In general, we consider that the main focus of the Hungarian press and interested members of the public with regard to the PIRLS results is the question of why fourth

---

7   Hungary's results in PISA 2006 are summarized in Balázsi, Ostorics, & Szalay (2007).

graders do so well in international assessments yet, only five years on, when in Grade 9, students perform only at the international average or below. The concern is, we believe, a valid one. What is it that works well in the lower grades? And what needs to be changed in the upper grades in order for students to lift their reading achievement once they are in secondary school? These questions might explain why so much of the reporting of PIRLS results is accompanied by consideration of PISA findings, and why academics and policymakers strive to determine connections between educational policies and practices and the outcomes of the two assessments.

Although PIRLS on its own perhaps does not receive the amount of particular attention hoped for in the media and among the general public, it and the other international comparative assessments in which Hungary participates are having an increasing influence on the Hungarian education system. The results of the PIRLS and PISA studies were a strong factor in the Ministry of Education's decision to extend official teaching of reading into Grades 5 and 6. Until school year 2008/2009, students received formal tuition in reading only until the end of Grade 4.

This development has been one of the most significant educational policy changes of the past few years. It has not only changed the basics of Hungarian education but also highlighted the potential that enhancing the quality of educational provision has for students' achievement. The Ministry of Education hopes that by bringing reading practice in elementary schools into line with practice in many of the countries with which Hungary compares itself, it will provide the means of improving the reading performance of its secondary school students.

The change has met with some opposition. Critics argue, for example, that extending teaching of developmental reading penalizes better readers because it holds them back and limits their opportunities to receive teaching commensurate with their abilities. Some experts suggest that the change has produced a 6 + 6 system (i.e., six grades of elementary and six grades of secondary tuition), but this has not been the ministry's intent.

Another influence of the international assessments in Hungary has been the development of educational policy focused on skills development, namely, the competency-based programs mentioned earlier in this chapter. The introduction of the NABC, which annually assesses the performance of around 400,000 students, has helped shape public thinking about the importance of children attaining a high standard of reading literacy. In essence, Hungary's response to the deficiencies in the teaching of reading brought to light by the country's participation in national and international comparative student assessments has been that of implementing various skills-based remediation programs throughout Hungary's schooling system.

8.6   Future Activities

Partly because of information obtained during PIRLS 2006, the Hungarian Government recently announced its intention to enhance the implementation and use of information technology in schools so that students can develop the computer literacy and related skills necessary for work and life in the 21st century. PIRLS has also served as the basis of a longitudinal research project that began in 2010 at the University of Szeged. The project involves development of a web-based formative assessment for students in Grades 1 to 6 that will give teachers immediate information about their students' reading literacy, mathematical and science literacy, and social skills. The assessment items being developed are based on the PIRLS test items and are informed by PIRLS data.

A conference involving the seven regions of Hungary and focused on the results of national and international large-scale assessments is being organized. The aim of the conference is to identify and establish further educational policy goals derived from the data obtained in the PIRLS school questionnaire. Workshops for important stakeholders of assessments, notably teachers, parents, school principals, and researchers, are also being mooted. One such recent workshop was a two-day event attended by educational researchers, sociologists, and school principals. All of these people had opportunity to familiarize themselves with the PIRLS and TIMSS background questionnaires and results databases, to learn about the design of international assessments, and to use the IEA IDB Analyzer, a software package specifically designed for analysis of IEA database content.

An anticipated outcome of these conferences and workshops is a stream of articles published in pedagogical journals and covering a range of considerations such as the association between the home reading activities of students and their ability to read and comprehend different types of text. Finally, Hungary intends to continue its participation in international research projects such as PIRLS, TIMSS, and PISA.

8.7 Concluding Remarks

Because Hungary has participated in PIRLS and TIMSS since they were first implemented, the country has gathered extensive data on and formed a generally favorable image of the reading literacy and mathematics performance and skills of its students in the lower grades of Hungary's education system.

The results of PISA 2000, however, shed a different light on the performance of Hungary's education system. It signaled serious problems with the reading literacy of the country's 15-year-old students. As a response, Hungary implemented its National Assessment of Basic Competencies (NABC), which now serves as the means of annually assessing every student in Grades 4, 6, 8, and 10. The NABC also allows those students and their parents, teachers, school principals, and administrators to track the performance of each student and the performance of each school.

The generally good performance of Hungarian students on the PIRLS assessments continues to show that the pedagogical work relating to reading literacy accomplished in the lower grades of Hungarian schools is of a high standard internationally. This outcome has prompted educational policymakers to theorize on how to close the performance gap between students in the lower and higher grades and thereby raise the overall performance of Hungary's education system.

References

Balázsi, I., & Balkányi, P. (2008). PIRLS 2006: A negyedik osztályosok szövegértése [PIRLS 2006: Reading comprehension of fourth graders]. *Pedagógiai Szemle, 1*, 3–11.

Balázsi, I., Balkányi, P., Felvégi, E., & Szabó, V. (2007). *PIRLS 2006: Összefoglaló jelentés a 10 éves tanulók szövegértési képességeiről* [PIRLS 2006: Summary report of the reading skills of 10-year-old students]. Budapest, Hungary: Educational Authority.

Balázsi, I., Ostorics, L., & Szalay, B. (2007). *PISA 2006: Összefoglaló jelentés. A ma oktatása és a jövő társadalma* [PISA 2006: Executive summary: Today's education and tomorrow's society]. Budapest, Hungary: Educational Authority.

European Commission. (2011). *The Bologna process: Towards the European Higher Education Area.* Retrieved from http://ec.europa.eu/education/higher-education/doc1290_en.htm

Felvégi, E., & Ostorics, L. (2007). *PIRLS 2006 encyclopedia: Hungary.* Chestnut Hill, MA: Boston College.

Mullis, I. V. S., Martin, M. O., Kennedy, A. M., & Foy, P. (2007). *PIRLS 2006 international report: IEA's Progress in International Reading Literacy Study in primary schools in 40 countries.* Chestnut Hill, MA: Boston College.

Chapter 9
The Impact of PIRLS in Latvia

Antra Ozola

9.1 Latvia at a Glance[1]

Latvia, one of the three states of the Baltic region of north-east Europe, is located on the shore of the Baltic Sea. It borders Lithuania, Estonia, Russia, and Belarus and covers approximately 64,600 square kilometers. Topographically, it is a relatively flat country, with 57 percent of its land mass less than 100 meters above sea level. The highest point is 312 meters above sea level. Forests cover 45 percent of the country. Latvia's main exports are food and agricultural products and wood and wooden articles.

The Republic of Latvia was founded on November 18, 1918. It has been occupied and ruled by the Soviet Union (1940–1941), Nazi Germany (1941–1945), and again by the Soviet Union (1944–1991). Latvia regained its independence in 1991.

The population of Latvia in 2009 was 2.25 million. Population density averages 35 people per square kilometer. Thirty-two percent of the population lives in the capital city, Riga, which has a population density of 2,353 people per square kilometer. Latvia has 77 towns; in 2009, 68 percent of the population was living in urban and 32 percent in rural areas. The migration data available for the period between 1995 and 2008 showed a negative migration balance of approximately 34,000 people in Latvia, which means that more people emigrated than immigrated at this time. The most popular destinations were Russia and Germany, although Great Britain and Ireland tended to be the countries attracting Latvia's skilled workers.

The infant mortality rate (i.e., the rate for children under one year of age) in 2009 was 7.8 per 1,000 live births. The average life expectancy for men in Latvia is 68; for women, it is 78. In 2009, six percent of Latvia's population comprised students in various higher education institutions.

Latvia is a unitary parliamentary republic. It has been a member of the United Nations since 1991, and a member of both the European Union and NATO since 2004. In 2008, the country's GDP per capita was approximately US$14,000.

The official state language of Latvia is Latvian. This language belongs to the Indo-European family of languages, and it is one of the two Baltic languages still spoken (the other is Lithuanian). In 2009, the ethnic make-up of Latvia was approximately 59 percent Latvian, 28 percent Russian, 4 percent Byelorussian, 3 percent Ukrainian, 2 percent Polish, and 1 percent Lithuanian. The remaining 3 percent comprises other

---

1   All statistical data are taken from the Central Statistical Bureau of Latvia's website: http://www.csb.gov.lv

nationalities. The main religions in Latvia are Evangelic Lutheran, Roman Catholic, and Russian Orthodox.

9.2   Latvia's Education System[2]

Latvia's education system is relatively centralized, and it is has three levels of administration—national, municipal, and institutional. The Latvian Parliament (Saeima), the Cabinet of Ministers, and the Ministry of Education and Science are the main decisionmaking bodies at the national level. The Ministry of Education and Science is responsible for developing and implementing educational policy and for setting national standards of education. Education policy is also shaped by regulations and standards issued by the Latvian Cabinet of Ministers.

The major levels of education are preprimary education (compulsory for five- and six-year-olds), compulsory general basic education (Grades 1 to 9), general secondary education (Grades 10 to 12), and tertiary education. Children currently enter Grade 1 in the calendar year when they turn seven, but serious consideration is being given to requiring children to enter Grade 1 at age six.

Legislation requires that state or local governments finance all basic and secondary schools that they establish. Schools set up by private agents charge fees, the amount of which is determined by each school. In general, though, education in Latvia is free of charge until the tertiary level. The state pays the salaries of teachers working in compulsory preprimary, general basic, and general secondary schools.

Latvia's General Education Law states that the purpose of preprimary education is to develop not only children's individuality and intellectual, physical, and social skills but also their initiative, inquisitiveness, independence, and creativity. It is also meant to enhance their general health and prepare them psychologically for entry to basic education, and to ensure that they have sufficient skill in speaking Latvian. These provisions apply whether the preprimary education is provided in preschools (including those for children with special needs), in preparatory schools attached to basic schools, or within the family home.

Table 9.1 sets out all school types in Latvia. According to statistical data provided by the Ministry of Education and Science, there were 948 general education schools in Latvia in the 2008/2009 school year. Of these, 45 were elementary schools, 463 were basic schools, 377 were secondary schools, and 63 were special education schools.

---

2   This description is based on information about Latvia's education system provided in Ozola (2007).

Table 9.1: **Types of schools offering general education in Latvia**

School type	Grades	Level of general education
Elementary school	1–4 or 1–6	Part of general basic education
Primary school	1–9	General basic education
Secondary school	1–12	General basic and secondary education
Gymnasium and state gymnasium	7–12 or 10–12	Part of general basic education and general secondary education
Vocational school	8–9 and/or 10–13	Part of general basic education and/or general secondary education
Evening (part-time) schools	7–12	Part of general basic education and general secondary education
Special education schools	1–9, 1–10, 1–11 for general basic and three years for general secondary education	General basic and/or secondary education

Students in the Latvian education system are not tracked from one level of the system to the next. Students, along with their parents or caregivers, choose the type of school that they consider most appropriate for their individual needs. Students can thus move freely among all types of schools, with the exception of special schools. Students (let us say Grade 3 students) can expect to receive the same standards of education whether they are attending an elementary, a primary, or a secondary school.

Gymnasiums and state gymnasiums are usually considered to produce, on average, a higher level of student achievement. Although vocational schools work to the same standards of education as schools within the general education system, they provide students with the particular knowledge and skills they will need to enter their chosen part of the labor market. Gymnasiums, however, tend to direct students toward tertiary education.

Students are eligible to progress to the next school grade (year) if their end-of-year assessment grade is no lower than 4 (on a scale of 10, with 10 being the highest grade) in all of the subjects they studied in Grades 10 to 12, in all of the subjects they studied (with the possible exception of not more than two subjects) in Grades 5 to 9, and in all of the subjects they studied (with the possible exception of one subject) in Grades 1 to 4. If students do not fulfill these requirements, they may have to repeat the year. Special education schools are exempted from this ruling.

Universities are responsible for all teacher education in Latvia. The program a prospective teacher chooses depends on the subject or subjects he or she wants to teach and on what level of the education system (elementary or secondary) he or she wants to teach at. Preservice teachers complete a teacher training course in parallel with their work toward a Bachelor's degree, or they complete a one- to two-year professional teacher education program after completing their Bachelor's.

Information provided by the Ministry of Education and Science in the 2008/2009 school year shows that the gender composition of teachers in all general education schools in Latvia at that time was 88 percent female. Ninety-seven percent of teachers in Grades 1 to 4 were female. In Grades 5 to 6, 87 percent were female, in Grades 7 to 9, 84 percent, and in Grades 10 to 12, 83 percent.

9.3   Participation in Large-Scale Assessments

9.3.1   International Perspectives

Latvia began its participation in international large-scale assessments after the Soviet Union collapsed and Latvia regained its independence in 1991. This period also marked the time when Latvia began comparative educational research. It has been extremely interesting to finally have the opportunity to compare Latvian students' achievement nationally as well as internationally, especially given the lack of objective measurement of or information about students' achievement until this time. Latvia's early participation in IEA studies provided the country with impetus to gain ongoing experience in large-scale assessments and to establish a tradition of comparative studies in education.

Since 1991, Latvia has taken part in 17 international comparative studies in education. They include IEA's Reading Literacy Study, Computers in Education Study, Languages Education Study, Trends in International Mathematics and Science Study 1995 to 2007, Second Information Technology in Education Study, Progress in Reading Literacy Study 2001 and 2006, the Civic Education Study, and the International Civic and Citizenship Education Study, as well as OECD's PISA 2000 to 2012. Various organizations have funded implementation of these studies in Latvia. They include IEA and the World Bank, Latvia's Ministry of Education and Science, the University of Latvia, and the Soros Foundation-Latvia. These organizations have differentially covered the expenses associated with each study, and not every study has received support from all the institutions mentioned here.

The people initially responsible for conducting the large-scale international assessments in Latvia were a group of researchers headed by Professor Andris Kangro of the University of Latvia. In 1996, the Faculty of Education and Psychology at the University of Latvia established its Institute of Educational Research, which has been responsible from that time for conducting all large-scale international studies of educational achievement.

9.3.2 National Perspectives

National tests at the end of Grades 3, 6, 9, and 12, national examinations at the end of Grades 9 and 12, and centralized national examinations at the end of Grade 12 carried out by the Ministry of Education and Science comprise Latvia's national assessments of educational achievement. The tests are differentiated according to the respective subjects or fields of the national curriculum, while the examinations are used to determine students' progression from one level to the next in the education system. Because the centralized national examinations are scaled each year according to a normal distribution, they cannot be compared in quantitative terms over time.

9.4 National Results and the Impact of PIRLS

9.4.1 National Results

The average reading achievement score of the Latvian students who participated in PIRLS 2006 was 541 scale points. This score was significantly above both the international average and the PIRLS scale average, and it was similar to (i.e., not significantly different from) the average scores for Austria, Bulgaria, Chinese Taipei, England, Denmark, Lithuania, and the United States. There was no significant change in students' average achievement scores between PIRLS 2001 and PIRLS 2006.

The gender gap in the reading achievement of Latvian students was the sixth largest internationally. The difference, which favored girls, was 23 scale points, and it was significantly higher than the international average gender difference. This gender gap was just as large in 2006 as it was in 2001. When we analyzed gender differences across the two PIRLS assessments with respect to urbanization, we found a rise in the average score of girls and a fall in the average score of boys in rural areas, which means that the gender gap in these places grew across the six-year period.

There was no difference in Latvian students' average achievement scores on the two text-type scales—literary and informational. When we compared the average scores on these scales for PIRLS 2001 and PIRLS 2006, we found a significant decline in students' ability to read informational texts over the six years but no change in students' ability to read literary texts.

Comparison of the Latvian students' average achievement scores on PIRLS in terms of the cognitive processes associated with reading showed the students were significantly better at interpreting, integrating, and evaluating texts than they were at retrieving information/meaning or drawing inferences from them. The PIRLS 2001 Latvian students were significantly better than their 2006 counterparts at retrieval and inference.

When we looked at the index of students' attitudes toward reading, we were interested to find that, internationally, Latvian students had the smallest percentage of students within the high range of scores. We also found that the proportion of Latvian students in this index declined between PIRLS 2001 and 2006, while the proportion in the low index increased across the six years. In short, Latvian students' attitudes toward reading had become significantly worse across time.

We also observed a significant decrease in the average achievement scores of students in the large cities of Latvia (capital not included) between PIRLS 2001 and 2006. In both surveys, the highest average reading achievement scores among the participating students were evident in the capital city, Riga, and the lowest were observed in rural areas. Comparison of Latvian students for whom Latvian was the language of instruction with students for whom Russian was the language of instruction showed the latter group performing 10 points higher than the former group on the PIRLS 2006 achievement scale.

As another point of comparison, the average reading achievement score for Latvian 15-year-old students in PISA 2009 was 484 scale points, an outcome that was not significantly different from the average PISA scores for Portugal, Macao-China, Italy, Slovenia, Greece, Spain, the Czech Republic, and the Slovak Republic. The Latvian average achievement score was significantly higher than the average achievement score for one of the usual countries with which Latvia is compared, Lithuania. Another reference point is the third Baltic country, Estonia. PISA showed this country's students to be significantly better readers than their Latvian and Lithuanian peers. Since PISA 2000, the average reading achievement (as measured by PISA) of Latvian students has risen significantly. The gender gap, however, has remained large. In PISA 2009, the difference, which favored girls, was 47 scale score points.

In summary, the PIRLS trend data (i.e., data for PIRLS 2001 and that for PIRLS 2006) show that the average reading performance of 11-year-old Latvian students and the gender gap remained the same over time. The performance of Latvian 15-year-olds on the PISA reading assessment improved between 2000 and 2009, but the same cannot be said of the gender gap for this cohort of Latvian students.

9.4.2   Publication of the PIRLS Results

The PIRLS 2006 and PISA 2006 results were released in tandem at a press conference. This dual presentation was done in order to attract the maximum attention possible. Each study was presented separately at the time, and journalists received press kits specific to each study.

The presentation was attended by very different people, ranging from television and newspaper journalists through teachers, university academics, and people from the Dyslexia Association to politicians from the various national and municipal levels. The PIRLS national and international results received attention on Latvia's main (most highly rated) television evening news program and were twice featured on the Latvian National News Agency website. Articles on the results also appeared in Latvian newspapers. One of these was prepared by the national research coordinators of both studies (Kangro & Ozola, 2007) and four were written by professional journalists (Nagle, 2007a, 2007b, 2008; Rozentāle, 2007; Viduleja, 2006).

The day on which the PIRLS 2006 results were released also saw publication in Latvia of a monograph (Geske & Ozola, 2007a) providing detailed national and international analyses of the results. Everyone present at the press release event received a copy of this publication free of charge, as did every school that participated in the study. The Ministry of Education and Science also received copies. Remaining copies continue to be given gratis to anybody interested in PIRLS 2006.

Since the press release, articles featuring the PIRLS results and information about reading literacy have been published in *Teacher* magazine, a publication which, as its name implies, is directed primarily at practitioners. The articles were written by Geske and Ozola (2007b, 2008a). Academics and students in the field of education have also been targeted through publications produced by the University of Latvia (see Geske & Ozola, 2006, 2009a; Johansone & Preuschoff, 2009). Several publications have also been published in English with the aim of spurring international discussion (see Geske & Ozola, 2007c, 2008b, 2009b). At the time of writing, one doctoral dissertation featuring analyses of the PIRLS 2001 and PIRLS 2006 data has been completed (Johansone, 2009), and another is in progress.

In order to personally discuss and clarify aspects of the findings, the Latvian PIRLS 2006 national research coordinator attended six different seminars devoted to reading literacy in primary schools in general and the PIRLS 2006 results in particular. The Ministry of Education and Science organized three of these seminars (one for politicians responsible for education, one for school leaders, and one for Grades 1 to 4 teachers). The other three, each of which was organized by a different agency, catered for elementary school teachers in Riga, education specialists in the Latvian town of Bauska, and teachers of bilingual education and the Latvian language in Latvia.

The PIRLS 2006 result that attracted the most media attention was the Latvian Grade 4 students' comparatively poor attitude toward reading. Lesser attention was given to Latvian students' placement on the international ranking scale, probably because it was deemed satisfactory. At the time of writing, some attention was still being paid to the PIRLS results in the media, but typically only in relation to discussion of the decline in reading achievement between elementary school and secondary school, evidenced by the overall poorer performance of Latvian 15-year-olds on PISA.

A particular positive is that the educationalists and researchers who conduct the large-scale international comparative studies in education in Latvia have gained prominence and credibility among journalists, who now tend to seek their opinion when reporting matters relating to educational achievement. Unfortunately, this expertise appears to have rarely influenced political decisions, even though it seems imperative for the wellbeing of the educational system that policymakers and decisionmakers heed the studies' findings.

9.4.3   Impact of PIRLS 2001 and 2006

A very straightforward impact of the PIRLS 2006 survey has been the development of guidelines (Curriculum Development and Examination Center, 2008) directed at helping Grades 1 to 4 teachers bring a unified pedagogical approach to their teaching of both oral and written language skills. The center (working under the auspices of the Ministry of Education and Science) that developed the guidelines cited the PIRLS 2006 results (particularly students' negative attitude toward reading) as a strong reason for bringing in changes to teachers' methods of teaching reading and other language-related skills.

The PIRLS results have not, however, been the only reason for these changes. Financial considerations brought about by the worldwide economic crisis have also been an influence, as have the growing urbanization of Latvian society and developments in state policy relating to agriculture. In order to optimize school resources, very small schools (usually found in rural areas) are being closed and their students moved to the nearest bigger schools. As Ieva Johansone states in her doctoral thesis, "Improving the quality of community composition (peer effects) has an important effect on improving the achievement of individual students. To minimize the negative effect, student segregation should be minimized to the greatest possible extent. The revealed interactions of the most influential factors and student achievement support the idea of organizing bigger schools in centers of the rural communities" (Johansone, 2009, p. 149).

As Johansone (2009) implies, the process of merging schools has both positives and negatives. The PIRLS results showed students in larger (generally urban) schools tending to perform better than students in smaller (typically rural) schools. Also, school integration cuts down costs. However, these benefits are typically undermined if students from the previously small schools do not have good transportation to their new schools and if integration is not carefully planned within and across regions. A compromise would probably be to retain Grades 1 to 4 in schools that offer schooling up to Grade 9 and then to eliminate Grades 5 to 9 by having these older children move to the bigger school.

Another reform in education concerns compulsory school entry age. Latvian students have, for a long period, not been required to attend school until age seven, although many, as noted above, do attend preprimary school from ages five or six. The compulsory school entry age of seven led to the Latvian students being one of the oldest national cohorts participating in PIRLS. If, as seems to be the government's intention, the age at which children must begin attending school is lowered to six, and if there is a commensurate effort to improve standards of early years education, especially for disadvantaged children and their communities, this development should have a positive impact on overall student achievement in Latvia (Johansone, 2009).

It is not easy to determine how much the results of the large-scale international assessments influence decisions about education in Latvia, in part because no explicit mention is made of them doing so, even if they do. In likelihood, the results tend to serve as justification for reforms that have already been planned. We would like to see a situation in which policymakers and decisionmakers confer (with an open mind) with the researchers and educationalists who are involved with these studies and/or have other relevant knowledge before they begin developing and implementing changes. This dialogue would help ensure that reforms are informed by sound understandings procured from research and would thus maximize the likelihood of the changes being successful. Such information also makes economic sense because it would help reduce the chance of costly "mistakes".

9.5   Future Activities

Because of a lack of funding and political will, Latvia will not be participating in the next rounds of TIMSS and PIRLS for the first time in its history of international assessment of education. Regardless of this development, we are still analyzing data from the earlier studies and publishing our findings in reports. Also, a doctoral dissertation seeking reasons for the large gender gap in reading literacy is nearing completion.

9.6   Concluding Remarks

Latvia's participation in both PIRLS 2001 and 2006 has provided the country with important and rich information about the reading proficiency of Latvian students in an international context, brought greater understanding of the different factors that influence educational outcomes, and provided knowledge of how to carry out detailed, ongoing national monitoring of student performance.

The satisfactory performance of Latvian fourth graders on the PIRLS assessment indicates that the quality of education in the first years of elementary school is relatively high. However, the generally poor performance of 15-year-old Latvian students on PISA shows that something changes for students during their last years of elementary schooling. Given that the patterns of achievement for both groups of students have remained static since approximately 2001, it seems that changes— whether large or small—to the Latvian system of education since that time are not having the desired effect on achievement levels. Another reason may be that these developments have not had sufficient time to bed in and produce the hoped for results.

References

Geske A., & Ozola A. (2006). Skolēnu lasītprasmi ietekmējošie faktori sākumskolā [Factors influencing reading literacy at the primary school level]. In *Latvijas Universitātes raksti, Izglītības vadība* [Research from the University of Latvia: Educational management] (Vol. 709, pp. 61–68). Rīga, Latvia: University of Latvia.

Geske A., & Ozola A. (2007a). Sasniegumi lasītprasmē Latvijā un pasaulē [Reading achievement in Latvia and worldwide]. *Monogrāfiju sērija Izglītības pētniecība Latvijā, monogrāfija, 5*. Rīga, Latvia: University of Latvia Academic Publishers.

Geske A., & Ozola A. (2007b). Pētījumi sākumskolā: Skolēnu sasniegumi lasītprasmē [Primary school studies: Students' reading achievement]. *Skolotājs, 5*(65), 13–22.

Geske A., & Ozola A. (2007c). Analyses of factors associated with a high level of reading literacy: The IEA PIRLS perspective. *Humanities and Social Sciences, 3*(52), 58–74.

Geske A., & Ozola A. (2008a). Sarptautiskā lasītprasmes novērtēšanas pētījuma rezultāti Latvijā [Results of the International Reading Literacy Study in Latvia]. *Skolotājs, 3*(69), 33–37.

Geske A., & Ozola A. (2008b). Factors influencing reading literacy at the primary school level. *Problems of Education in the 21st Century, 6*, 71–77.

Geske A., & Ozola A. (2009a). Kontekstuālo izglītības faktoru ietekme uz meiteņu un zēnu literāro izpratību [Contextual educational factors influencing boys' and girls' reading literacy]. In *Latvijas Universitātes raksti, Izglītības vadība* [Research from the University of Latvia: Educational management] (Vol. 749, pp. 7–15). Rīga, Latvia: University of Latvia.

Geske A., & Ozola A. (2009b). Different influences of contextual educational factors on boys' and girls' reading achievement. *US–China Education Review, 6*(4), 38–44.

Johansone. I. (2009). *Managing primary education in Latvia to ensure quality and achievement equity: Discussion paper*. Riga, Latvia: University of Latvia.

Johansone, I., & Preuschoff, A. C. (2009). Izglītības kvalitāte Latvijas laukos un pilsētās ar ieskatu IEA PIRLS 2006 pētījuma rezultātos [Quality of education in rural versus urban areas of Latvia and insight into the IEA PIRLS 2006 results]. In *Latvijas Universitātes raksti: Izglītības vadība* [Research from the University of Latvia: Educational management] (Vol. 749, pp. 23–35). Rīga, Latvia: University of Latvia (in Latvian).

Kangro A., & Ozola A. (2007, December 11). Mūsu bērni lasīt prot, bet negrib [Our children can read, but do not want to]. *Diena*.

Nagle, I. (2007a, November 30). Izglītībai Eiropā kaitē sociālās krīzes [Social crises harm education in Europe]. *Latvijas Avīze*.

Nagle, I. (2007b, December 6). Viduvēji biologi un slinki lasītāji [Average biologists and lazy readers]. *Latvijas Avīze*.

Nagle, I. (2008, February 12). Lasīs pieaugušie, lasīs arī bērni [If adults read, so will children]. *Latvijas Avīze*.

Ozola, A. (2007). Latvia. In A. M. Kennedy, I. V. S. Mullis, M. O. Martin, & K. L. Trong (Eds.), *PIRLS 2006 encyclopedia: A guide to reading education in the forty PIRLS 2006 countries* (pp. 227–235). College Park, MA: Boston College.

Rozentāle, L. (2007, December 7). Mūsu bērni lasa reti, ķīmija nepatīk [Our children rarely read, do not like chemistry]. *Diena.lv*. Retrieved from http://www.diena.lv/lat/politics/focus/muusu_beerni_lasa_reti_kjiimija_nepatiik.

Viduleja, A. (2006, December 1). Pētījums: Pamatskolas jāuztver kā zemas lasītprasmes riska zonas [Study: Primary schools seen as low-risk areas for reading literacy]. *Izglītība un Kultūra*. Retrieved from http://www.izglitiba-kultura.lv/raksti/petijums-pamatskolas-jauztver-ka-zemas-lasitprasmes-riska-zonas

Chapter 10
The Impact of PIRLS in the Netherlands

Andrea Netten

10.1 The Netherlands at a Glance

The Netherlands is located in Western Europe, with neighboring countries Belgium to the south and Germany to the east. The country covers a total area of 41,526 square kilometers, of which 33,889 square kilometers comprise land and 7,643 square kilometers comprise water. Water is an important matter for the Dutch people, not only because the northern and western parts of the Netherlands abut the North Sea but also because the country is geographically low lying, with about 27 percent of its area and 60 percent of its population located below sea level.

The Netherlands has approximately 16 million inhabitants and is a country with a high population density (486 people per square kilometer). The ethnic composition of people in the Netherlands is diverse, but the majority of the population is Dutch. In 2009, ethnic minorities formed 20 percent of the total population. They included people from Turkey, Morocco, Suriname, the Netherlands Antilles, Indonesia, Africa, Asia, and the 26 countries of the European Union (Central Bureau of Statistics, 2009).

The Netherlands is a parliamentary democratic constitutional monarchy. The queen is the head of state and the prime minister is the head of government. The capital of the Netherlands is Amsterdam, but the seat of government lies in The Hague. The Netherlands is divided into 12 provinces, all of which are responsible for issues at the regional level. The Netherlands is a member of the European Union (EU), NATO, the OECD, and the United Nations. Gross national product per capita in 2008 was estimated to be US$50,150. The Dutch economy is internationally oriented; imports and exports are an important source of income. In 2004, national spending on education amounted to 4.9 percent of GDP, which is lower than the OECD and EU averages of 6.2 percent and 5.4 percent, respectively (Ministry of Education, Culture, and Science, 2008).

10.2 The Netherlands' Education System as a Context for PIRLS[1]

An important principle underlying the Dutch education system is freedom of education, which is guaranteed by Article 23 of the Dutch Constitution. Different agencies therefore have freedom to establish schools, organize the teaching in those schools, and

---

1   This introduction draws on information from the Dutch Eurydice Unit, Ministry of Education, Culture, and Science (2007) and Netten and Verhoeven (2007b).

determine the principles on which they are based (Ministry of Education, Culture, and Science, 2007).

10.2.1 System Structure

The Dutch education system comprises several levels of responsibility: national government, provincial and municipal authorities, school boards, and school principals. The government, working through the Ministry of Education, Culture, and Science, sets the regulatory and legislative framework for educational provision. It also has primary responsibility for structuring and funding the system. The Education Inspectorate monitors the quality of education and schools. It periodically visits schools in order to observe compliance with statutory regulations, and reports its findings to the Ministry of Education and the individual schools.

Provincial and municipal authorities have jurisdiction over the education provided in their province or town. Public schools are run by the municipal authorities or by a governing committee appointed by the municipality for this purpose. However, most children attend private schools that are founded on specific religious or pedagogical beliefs. All schools have a legally recognized competent authority—the school board. Each school board administers and manages the school(s) for which it is responsible. School boards have autonomy with regard to the curriculum, budget allocations, teacher inservice education, and school policies (such as disciplinary actions and parental involvement). The day-to-day management of a school lies with the principal.

The Netherlands' formal education system encompasses three levels—primary, secondary, and tertiary. Most children start primary school at four years old, although compulsory schooling does not start until age five (and ends at age 16). Primary school, both public and private, is free of charge. Kindergarten is embedded in the primary school and is thus part of the education system. Formal reading and writing instruction begins at Grade 3 when children are six years old (ISCED Level 1). Students whose progress lags behind that of their classmates can be held back a grade. There are no statutory rules to determine when a student should repeat a grade, but grade repetition is avoided to the greatest extent possible.

Primary education consists of eight grades, so most children are 12 years old when they enter secondary education. Secondary education in the Netherlands encompasses schools catering to different age groups and is tracked. The secondary school track that students enter depends on a recommendation from their primary school. These recommendations are based on teachers' observations and a test that children take at the end of their primary schooling in order to determine their scholastic proficiency.

Tertiary or higher education is divided into two programs—*Hoger Beroeps-onderwijs* or HBO and *Wetenschappelijk Onderwijs* or WO. HBO offers higher professional education leading to a four-year Bachelor's degree. WO offers university education leading to a three-year Bachelor's degree, after which a Master's degree can be earned in another one or two years.

The Netherlands has no provision for formal education for children under the age of four, but the government does regulate, under the auspices of the Childcare Act 2005, the funding and quality of childcare. Parents of children under four years of age can access various childcare facilities, such as playgroups, registered child-minders, and day nurseries. Parents receive a childcare benefit when they place their child in a government-approved childcare facility, thus helping them to combine work and family.

Early childhood education (in Dutch, VVE) is provided by playgroups and day nurseries and caters for two- to five-year-olds. Since 2002, municipal authorities have funded VVE. The VVE programs target children whose parents have a low level of educational attainment as well as children from ethnic minority groups who are at risk of educational or language disadvantage. Between 2006 and 2010, the government endeavored to reach 70 percent of the target group before the children reached age five. The objective of the VVE programs is to prepare children for entry to primary school by expanding their vocabulary and improving their social, cognitive, and emotional development.

10.2.2 Core Objectives

To ensure a high quality of education in primary schools, the Ministry of Education prescribes a number of core objectives that students are expected to master before they enter secondary education at age 12. These core objectives were established in 1993 and revised in 2006. Accompanied by standards, the objectives describe in detail what students should be able to accomplish at various stages in their school career. The core objectives cover the areas of Dutch language, English language, Frisian language, arithmetic and mathematics, social studies, art education, and physical education. The freedom of education principle guaranteed by the Dutch Constitution means that schools can determine which curriculum subjects they will teach, the content of those subjects, and how much time students will spend on each of them. Thus the core objectives describe attainment targets only; they do not describe how these targets should be reached and how they should be taught.

10.2.3 Teacher Education (Primary School)

Primary-school teacher-education colleges provide preservice courses for students who have successfully finished secondary education. Since 2006, students starting at a teacher-education college have been tested on their Dutch language and mathematics skills in order to guarantee standards of competence. Teacher education takes a total of four years. Most of the training program consists of practical work experience in primary or special education. After completing the four years of education, students receive a Bachelor's degree and are qualified to teach all subjects (except physical education) across the primary school curriculum.

10.3 Experience with Large-Scale Assessments

10.3.1 National Assessments

Schools are free to choose the tests that monitor their students' progress. Schools often use "curriculum-embedded" tests that match the subject matter provided in the textbooks for various subjects. Most primary education schools also use the monitoring tool called the *Student Tracking System* to assess the competence of students in Grades 1 to 8. This system, which was developed by CITO, the National Institute for Educational Measurement, is also used by the Dutch Education Inspectorate to assess whether the quality of education in each school is sufficient or needs to be improved. Tests also help teachers provide parents and school boards with more accurate reports of students' ability. Parents receive (usually three times a year) a report detailing their children's progress.

Primary schools are not obligated to participate in national standardized tests, although most schools administer an attainment test at the end of primary school. The percentage of schools that do not administer such a test is small. Eighty percent of schools use tests developed by CITO; the remaining percentage use other tests. The CITO tests measure academic skills in four areas: language, arithmetic and mathematics, study skills (different sources of information, schedules, tables, etc.), and world orientation (history, science, and geography). It is the results of these (or similar) tests, along with the recommendations from classroom teachers, that are used to determine the most appropriate secondary school track for each student.

In 1987, CITO began a longitudinal study called PPON (Periodic Assessment of Education). The study's aim was to evaluate how well children were achieving scholastically by the end of their primary schooling. CITO reviewed, according to a system of five-year cycles, all educational subjects being taught at the end of primary education. CITO also tested Grade 5 students' abilities in the Dutch language and in science and mathematics.

Since 1994, the Institute for Applied Social Sciences (ITS) and the SCO-Kohnstamm Institute have been conducting cohort studies designed to measure student and school performance in the Netherlands. The earliest such study, the PRIMA cohort study (successor to the LEO study that began in 1986), assessed developments in primary education against government educational policies in order to obtain an overall view of how well this sector of the education system was performing. Since 1994, six PRIMA assessments have taken place. Each has involved 600 schools and about 60,000 Grades 2, 4, 6, and 8 students. In both 1997 and 2001, the study researchers followed Grade 8 students as they left primary education and worked through their secondary education.

The aim of another cohort study, the VOCL (Secondary Education Cohort Students), was to gain insight into relationships between background variables (e.g., ethnicity) of students in secondary education, the courses of study they follow, and how well they do in them. Three cohorts were followed: 1989, 1993, and 1999. The approximately 20,000 students in each cohort were tracked from their first year in secondary school until they left the education system.

The year 2007 saw the start of the COOL cohort study. This study, which is monitoring, until 2015, student achievement in primary and secondary education, is the successor to PRIMA and VOCL. COOL tests students in Grades 2, 5, and 8 (primary school) and Year 3 of secondary school. It is conducted every three years.

10.3.2 International Large-Scale Assessments

The government has funded the Netherlands' participation in international studies since the 1960s. Most national and international educational research is funded directly by the Ministry of Education or by the Dutch Program Council for Educational Research (NWO-PROO). NWO-PROO conducts research studies of primary, secondary, and (pre)-vocational education, and teacher-education institutions. The Ministry of Education funded PIRLS 2001 and 2006. NWO-PROO is financing, at the government's behest, PIRLS 2011.

International surveys have long attracted the attention of Dutch policymakers, particularly with respect to how well Dutch students' educational achievement compares with the achievement of their peers in other countries. The Netherlands typically benchmarks its students' performance against the performance of students in neighboring countries—Belgium (Flanders), England, and Germany.

In 1991, IEA conducted its first international study specifically aimed at reading achievement, the Reading Literacy Study. The study showed Dutch students lagging behind students in most of the other participating countries (27 in all). Their performance gave the Netherlands a ranking of 21 on the international reading achievement scale, just six places above the lowest-ranked (i.e., 27th) country. The average achievement score of the Dutch students was 485, below the international mean of 500 (de Glopper & Otter, 1993). This outcome led to the Ministry of Education establishing a National Center for Language Education.

The Netherlands' long participation in large-scale international studies of educational achievement means that it has a considerable amount of longitudinal data on its students' scholastic performance. However, there has been ongoing debate about the usefulness (validity) of these data, especially in terms of comparability over time, given that the frames of reference, test instruments, and cohorts of participating countries vary from study to study, and even within the same areas of achievement, such as reading literacy.

10.4 PIRLS 2006: National Results

The Dutch PIRLS 2006 results showed Dutch students performing well internationally. Only three Canadian provinces, Hong Kong SAR, Luxembourg, Singapore, and the Russian Federation scored significantly higher on the overall achievement scale. The

Dutch students performed at the same level or better than their peers in the other European countries that participated in PIRLS 2006. However, the Dutch students' overall performance declined between 2001 (average scale score, 554) and 2006 (average scale score, 547).

The gap between the achievement scores of the most able and the weakest readers in the Netherlands was, in both PIRLS 2001 and 2006, small compared to the gap in most other PIRLS countries. The difference in scale scores between the 5th and 95th percentile was 174 points, whereas the majority of the countries had a 250-point difference. The PIRLS benchmarks confirmed that, as was the case in 2001, most of the PIRLS 2006 Dutch students were reading at (at least) a basic level; 91 percent reached the intermediate benchmark. However, the benchmarks also showed that the number of high-achieving students in the Netherlands declined between 2001 and 2006, and that the percentage of 2006 Dutch students reading at an advanced level was smaller than the percentages of advanced readers in the other countries that did well in the 2006 iteration of PIRLS.

As was the case in most of the participating 2006 countries, girls outperformed boys in the Netherlands. However, the gap between the genders decreased between 2001 and 2006 because of a drop in achievement by the girls in 2006. Their overall achievement score at this time was 11 scale points lower than in 2001, which was a significant decline.

A look at students' average scores on the two reading purposes scales—reading for literary enjoyment and reading for information—makes evident the significant decline in achievement on the literary texts between 2001 and 2006 (average scores of 552 and 545, respectively). A closer look, however, reveals that the decline on the literary texts was significant for the girls only. This poorer performance by the girls in 2006 seems to explain the overall decline in reading achievement scores in the Netherlands.

Dutch students' attitudes toward reading were poor compared to the attitudes of their peers in surrounding countries. In 2006, only 39 percent of the Dutch students reported feeling positive about reading. This result was a significant decline on the percentage (44%) reporting positivity about reading in 2001 and was below the 2006 international mean of 49 percent. Although 60 percent of the Dutch students viewed themselves as good readers, almost the same percentage was either lukewarm about reading or did not like reading. Of this group, 16 percent said they did not like reading at all. The Dutch students also spent less time reading than did their peers in other countries. A big group of the 2006 Dutch students said they read every day for fun (36%), but an even bigger group said they never read at all at home (42%).

PIRLS analyses show strong associations between reading attitudes, the amount of time that students spend reading for enjoyment, and reading literacy achievement scores. Other studies support these apparent connections. Current models of reading comprehension consider reading abilities, reading attitudes, and motivation as key factors related to reading proficiency (see, for example, Diepen, 2007; Kamil, Mosenthal, Pearson, & Barr, 2000).

These findings indicate that reading needs to be stimulated in the schools as well as in the home. There is also a clear need to improve students' motivation to read. The focus should be on giving all students a chance to expand their vocabulary and to learn more reading strategies simply by reading more. Giving Dutch students opportunities to gain additional "reading miles" would hopefully lead to them lifting their level of reading achievement above the average.

10.5 Impact of PIRLS 2006

In 2007, the same day the international PIRLS 2006 report was released in Boston, USA, the Dutch Ministry of Education and the National Center for Language Education scheduled a joint press conference in The Hague to release the Dutch national report (Netten & Verhoeven, 2007a). The national report, which was also made freely available on the web, presented, without any secondary analysis, the results for the Dutch students and compared these with the results for the international population. During the press conference, journalists received a press release, as did media representatives not attending the presentation. Although PIRLS did not attract television attention, most daily newspapers published a summary of the results.

The Ministry of Education and various educational institutes have an obvious commitment to PIRLS and appreciate the usefulness of its findings for informing not only educational policy and practice but also teachers, principals, and the general public about the reading achievement of Dutch primary school children. However, beyond this "official" interest, PIRLS remains relatively unknown. When international assessments are mentioned in reports or when an educational reform is discussed, the study that tends to be mentioned is the Programme for International Student Assessment (PISA), conducted by the Organisation for Economic Co-operation and Development (see, for example, OECD, 2007). This occurs not only when a broader educational picture is necessary, but also when the topic is the reading proficiency of Dutch students. An exception is evident in most ministerial reports, which usually mention both PIRLS and PISA.

In addition to their presentation in the Dutch national report (Netten & Verhoeven, 2007b), the Dutch PIRLS 2006 results along with findings from secondary analyses of these data have been presented at several national and international conferences. These include the European Conference on Educational Research 2006 and 2009, the International Reading Conference 2008, and the Dutch Education Research Days (ORD) 2008. They have also been the key topic of symposia for the Ministry of Education and the Education Inspectorate. Articles featuring in-depth analyses of the PIRLS 2006 data have either been published (Netten, Droop, & Verhoeven, 2011) or are still under preparation. Many articles based on the 2001 data have also been published (e.g., Diepen, 2007).

In the Netherlands, policymakers tend to use the results of international comparative research as confirmation of trends that are already apparent. For instance, the CPB (Dutch Bureau for Economic Policy Analysis) reports on the "health" of the Dutch education system by combining performance indicators from various international reports and surveys. The Netherlands has a long history of conducting national longitudinal studies that monitor students' achievement. Because Dutch policymakers have ready access to reports and results from these surveys, the added value or impact of an international comparative study such as PIRLS can be seen as limited. This "thinking" also influences the direct impact of PIRLS on schools and the general public. Essentially, international benchmarks are seen as a starting point for formulating new or modifying existing policies; they are not seen as indicators of whether or not an implemented policy is performing satisfactorily (Antenbrink, Burger, Cornet, Rensman, & Webbink, 2005). However, policymakers are becoming increasingly interested in developing educational policies and reforms that are based on sound research evidence (Borghans, 2007). PIRLS has a distinct function in this regard because it provides international comparative evidence of what tends to work and not work with respect to enhancing educational quality and, from there, students' scholastic achievement.

As we noted earlier, PISA is viewed as the most influential international comparative study in the Netherlands. In 2006, researchers compared the performance of Dutch students on PISA and PIRLS. Dutch students' average score of 507 scale points on PISA set them above the international average (491 points) for this study. The students in Finland and Ireland were the only national cohorts to perform significantly better than the Dutch students, while the performance of the Polish and Swedish students was on a par with that of the Dutch students. The percentage of Dutch students performing at a low reading level was small compared to the international mean, a trend paralleled in PIRLS.

In 2008, the Commissie Dijsselbloem (a parliamentary research committee) published a report about educational innovation. Although the committee's main focus was on presenting the results of its own research into reforms made to Dutch secondary education between 1990 and 2008, its members did refer to findings from other national studies, as well as international studies such as PIRLS and PISA. The committee stated in their report that although international studies showed Dutch students performing well compared to students in the reference countries, these results needed to be interpreted with caution. The committee's main concern was that the PISA test was constructed by CITO. Maintaining that the results of a country on any one test are influenced by the nature of the items in that test, they argued that PISA probably favored Dutch students because CITO would have constructed a test that had a strong connection to the content of the Dutch Curriculum. The committee also commented that it is difficult to draw valid conclusions when endeavoring to interpret the results (whether within a national or an international context) of the different studies (TIMSS, PIRLS, PISA). Different countries, the committee explained, participate in the different studies and in the iterations of each one. Moreover, the number of participating countries is too small to provide an overview of all the factors likely to be contributing to students' achievement scores. The committee also observed that the participating countries, the composition of their populations, and the structure and ethos of their education systems are very different.

The many national and international publications prompted by PIRLS and PISA during 2007 and 2008, along with reports ancillary to these studies, such as the report just discussed (Commissie Dijsselbloem, 2008) and the Dutch PISA report published by CITO (2008), all report the overall satisfactory performance internationally of Dutch students. However, all of them also emphasize, as their main message, the ongoing decline in student performance across time. As the Dutch Education Inspectorate wrote in its annual report for 2008, "... the Inspectorate has concerns about: the growing number of students whose basic skills (language and maths) are insufficient to be able to function properly in our society" (p. 4).

To tackle the problem of declining student performance in language and mathematics, the Ministry of Education launched what it termed its Quality Agenda in 2008, a reform program directed at primary education. The drop in average achievement between PIRLS 2001 and 2006 was used as one justification for the agenda. The Quality Agenda outlines steps being taken to reinforce the Netherlands' commitment to ensuring that literacy and numeracy remain as core focuses at all levels of the education system. The ultimate aim, of course, is to improve students' achievement in these two subjects.

The agenda also provides descriptions of what students should know and be able to achieve at the various stages of their school career. In 2010, clear standards were established with regard to what knowledge students should have and what they should be capable of by the end of their primary education (Expertgroep Doorlopende Leerlijnen Taal en Rekenen, 2008). Student performance on mathematics and reading is now being monitored annually, although the Ministry of Education decided not to make the testing program compulsory for primary schools.

The Quality Agenda is complemented by several policy initiatives with respect to such matters as special education, teachers, and school leadership. Students reading at an advanced level receive special attention in the agenda. This emphasis is a direct outcome of the PIRLS results, which showed, as noted earlier, that the percentage of Dutch students able to read at a level well beyond the national mean is small compared to the corresponding percentages in nearly all other PIRLS countries. Students appear to reach a basic level of reading competency but are not given the chance to excel. The Quality Agenda policy initiative has, as its aim, identifying students who are in the top percentages of educational achievement and then giving them opportunities to fully develop their talents and potential (Fullan, Levin, & Watson, 2008).

10.6 Future Activities

The Dutch government is committed to participating in PIRLS 2011 so that it can assess changes in achievement results between 2001 and 2011 and provide opportunity for further in-depth analyses of factors influencing Dutch students' reading skills. The Netherlands will also take part in the next cycles of TIMSS and PISA, maintaining its trend of participation in international comparative research. At the time of writing, the programs and reforms signaled in the Quality Agenda launched by the Dutch Government were expected to be well established by the end of 2011. The PIRLS 2011 results in association with data obtained from the various educational monitoring programs that have been put in place since 2008 should thus provide information on the efficacy of these agenda-related reforms.

Currently, several studies drawing on the information contained in the PIRLS database are underway. Secondary analyses are being conducted to identify factors that affect students' performance, and the National Center for Language Education is investigating differences in reading achievement between various subgroups of students in the Netherlands.

10.7 Concluding Remarks

For the Netherlands, international comparative studies in general and PIRLS in particular are viewed as tools that provide policymakers with additional information about the status of the Dutch education system. The results provide an extra incentive to launch reforms of or other initiatives relating to education. The results of PIRLS 2011 will also provide an answer to the all-important question of whether or not the level of student reading achievement in the Netherlands has risen or fallen over the last 10 years.

References

Antenbrink, P., Burger, K., Cornet, M., Rensman, M., & Webbink, D. (2005). *Nederlands onderwijs en onderzoek in internationaal perspectief* [The Dutch system of education: Performance, research, and innovation from an international perspective] (CPB Document 88). Utrecht, the Netherlands: CPB Netherlands Bureau for Economic Policy Analysis.

Borghans, L. (2007). *De betekenis van internationale indicatoren voor de verbetering van het onderwijs* [The meaning of international indicators for improving the education system]. Maastricht, the Netherlands: University of Maastricht.

Central Bureau of Statistics. (CBS). (2009). *Bevolkingstrends* [Trends in population]. The Hague/Heerlen, the Netherlands: Author.

CITO. (2008). *Samenvatting Resultaten PISA-2006* [Summary results of PISA-2006]. Arnhem, the Netherlands: Author.

Commissie Dijsselbloem. (2008). *Parlementair onderzoek onderwijsvernieuwingen* [Parliamentary research into educational innovation]. The Hague, the Netherlands: Author.

de Glopper, K., & Otter, M. E. (1993). *Nederlandse leesprestaties in international perspectief* [Dutch reading performance in an international perspective]. Amsterdam, the Netherlands: SCO.

Diepen, M. (2007). *Reading literacy development from an international perspective.* Unpublished doctoral dissertation, Expertisecentrum Nederlands, Radboud University, Nijmegen, the Netherlands.

Dutch Eurydice Unit, Ministry of Education, Culture, and Science. (2007). *The education system in the Netherlands 2007.* The Hague, the Netherlands: Author.

Education Inspectorate. (2008). *The state of education in the Netherlands 2006/2007.* Utrecht, the Netherlands: Author.

Expertgroep Doorlopende Leerlijnen Taal en Rekenen. (2008). *Over de drempels met taal en rekenen* [Crossing the thresholds of reading and mathematics]. Enschede, the Netherlands: Author.

Fullan, B., Levin, B., & Watson, N. (2008). *Report/advice to the Ministry of Education on the Quality Agenda.* The Hague, the Netherlands: Ministry of Education.

Kamil, M. L., Mosenthal, P. B., Pearson, P. D., & Barr, R. (Eds.). (2000). *Handbook of reading research* (Vol. 3). Mahwah, NJ: Lawrence Erlbaum Associates.

Ministry of Education, Culture, and Science. (2007). *Scholen voor morgen: Kwaliteitsagenda primair onderwijs* [Schools for tomorrow: Quality Agenda for primary education]. The Hague, the Netherlands: Author.

Ministry of Education, Culture, and Science. (2008). *Key figures 2003–2007: Education, culture, and science in the Netherlands.* The Hague, the Netherlands: Author.

Netten, A. R., Droop, M., & Verhoeven, L. (2011). Predictors of reading literacy for first and second language learners. *Reading and Writing: An Interdisciplinary Journal, 24*(4), 413–425.

Netten, A. R., & Verhoeven, L. (2007a). The Netherlands. In A. M. Kennedy, I. V. S. Mullis, M. O. Martin, & K. L. Trong (Eds.), *PIRLS 2006 encyclopedia: A guide to reading education in the forty PIRLS 2006 countries* (pp. 269–278). Chestnut Hill, MA: Boston College.

Netten, A. R., & Verhoeven, L. (2007b). *PIRLS 2006: De Nederlandse resultaten* [PIRLS 2006: The Dutch results]. Nijmegen, the Netherlands: Expertisecentrum Nederlands.

Organisation for Economic Co-operation and Development (OECD). (2007). *PISA 2006.* Paris, France: Author.

Chapter 11
The Impact of PIRLS in New Zealand

Megan Chamberlain[1]

11.1 New Zealand at a Glance

New Zealand is an island nation comprising two main islands, commonly known as the North Island and the South Island, as well as Stewart Island, the Chatham Islands, and several uninhabited island groups. Situated in the southwest region of the Pacific Ocean and about 1,600 kilometers from Australia, the islands cover an area of 271,000 square kilometers, with over 18,000 kilometers of coastline. The country's capital, Wellington, is on the southern coast of the North Island. The geographical features of the country are diverse, and the nature of them means that there are many small isolated communities throughout the country (Walrond, 2008).

According to the last official census in March 2006, there were 4.1 million people living in New Zealand.[2] The population density is relatively low at 15 people per square kilometer.[3] Approximately 75 percent of the country's total population lives in the North Island, and about 70 percent of New Zealanders live in urban areas consisting of 30,000 people or more. Over a quarter of the country's population lives in New Zealand's largest city, Auckland, located in the North Island. About 23 percent of people in New Zealand were born in another country; the most common birthplace was England (Statistics New Zealand, 2007).

New Zealand is a culturally diverse country. A key social attribute that is used along with other features to summarize the diversity of its population is ethnicity.[4] Five main ethnic categories are commonly used to summarize the ethnic identity of the New Zealand population. *Māori* comprise approximately 15 percent of the population. They are the indigenous people of New Zealand, having arrived from Polynesia around the 10th century. *Asian* people, mostly of Chinese or Indian heritage, comprise about nine per cent of the population. *Pasifika* (or Pacific Islands peoples), mostly of Samoan or Cook Islands Māori heritage, comprise about seven per cent of the population.

---

1   Opinions expressed in this article are those of the author and do not necessarily reflect those of the New Zealand Ministry of Education.

2   As at December 2010, New Zealand's estimated resident population was 4.4 million people (Statistics New Zealand, 2011).

3   By comparison, the population density is considerably less than that of the United Kingdom, which is of similar land area but has about 243 people per square kilometer (Statistics New Zealand, 2005a).

4   Ethnicity refers to the ethnic group or groups with which people identify, or to which they feel they belong. It is a measure of cultural affiliation as opposed to race, nationality, ancestry, or citizenship (Statistics New Zealand, 2005b).

Approximately one per cent of New Zealanders identify with being either of Middle-Eastern, Latin American, or African heritage; they are included in the grouping referred to as *Other ethnic groups*. The largest grouping, forming about 68 percent of the population and often referred to as *Pākehā/European*, includes people of British Isles or European heritage.

English, Māori (the indigenous language), and New Zealand Sign Language are the official languages of New Zealand, but English is the language used most commonly.[5] Other languages spoken, particularly in urban areas, include the various languages of the South Pacific and those of eastern and western Asia.

New Zealand is a parliamentary democracy and a constitutional monarchy. A former colony of England, it became effectively self-governing in 1856. In 1947, New Zealand adopted the Statute of Westminster, which confirmed that only New Zealand's Parliament has the power to make laws for the country. Queen Elizabeth II is the head of state; her representative in New Zealand is the Governor General, who has a ceremonial role rather than any involvement in the governing of the country (Wilson, 2008).

New Zealand is a member of the Commonwealth of Nations and the United Nations. It participates in the World Trade Organization (WTO), Asia Pacific Economic Cooperation Forum (APEC), and the Organization for Economic Co-operation and Development (OECD). In 2006, the gross national product per capita, using current purchasing power parity (PPP), was estimated to be US$27,431, which is 82 percent of the OECD average. Use of PPP rates gives expenditure per student in New Zealand primary schools of US$4,952 and in secondary schools of US$6,043. Both rates are just under the OECD averages (OECD, 2009).

11.2 New Zealand's Education System

11.2.1 System Governance

Education in New Zealand is delivered by early childhood services, schools, and tertiary institutions via a decentralized system involving four key government agencies. The *Ministry of Education*, the lead agency, provides policy advice, has responsibility for education property, develops national education guidelines and the curriculum, and allocates funding. The *Education Review Office* is responsible for reviewing schools' operations to ensure that they are meeting the educational objectives set out in their charters. The *New Zealand Qualifications Authority* oversees and coordinates secondary school, academic, professional, and trades qualifications, certificates, and awards. The *Tertiary Education Commission* (TEC) manages government funding for,

---

5   English is a de facto official language by virtue of its widespread use. Both Māori and New Zealand Sign Language were given official status under acts of parliament, namely, the Māori Language Act 1987 and the New Zealand Sign Language Act 2006 respectively.

and relationships with, the tertiary education sector. The commission also provides policy advice (Ministry of Education, 1999, 2002, 2009a).

11.2.2 School Governance and Funding

Schools in New Zealand are self-governing, with state or state-integrated[6] primary and secondary schools each having its own board of trustees. Boards of trustees employ staff, manage school property, control school finances, and set their schools' governing policies. They are accountable to both their school community and to government.

Schools are funded directly from central government for basic operations, relief-teaching, special education, and property work. The funding for each school is determined by the number of students enrolled, the year (grade) level of the students, the socioeconomic status of the school community, and the school's location. Teachers' salaries are paid directly by the Ministry of Education. Schools can also access various pools of contestable or discretionary funding for programs such as second language learning and alternative education, as well as being able to access a range of resources such as software licenses, laptops for principals, ICT support, and professional development. Locally-raised funds are a second source of income for schools.

Independent or private schools (4% of all schools) are run by religious or philosophical organizations or by private individuals. Fully registered independent schools receive partial funding from government (Ministry of Education, 2009b).

11.2.3 Structure of the Education System

Early childhood education (ECE) is available to children under the age of six. Although ECE is not compulsory, the majority of children attend one of a number of early education services, either teacher-led (kindergartens, education and care services, and home-based services) or parent-led (*kōhanga reo, playcenters,* and *playgroups*),[7] before starting primary school. From July 2010, all three-, four- and five-year-olds were able to attend an ECE service for six hours a day, up to a maximum of 20 hours per week at no charge (referred to as *20 Hours ECE*) (Ministry of Education, 2010a).

Compulsory schooling is from age 6 through to age 16; however, in practice, nearly all New Zealand children enter primary school on or just after their fifth

---

6   State-integrated schools are schools that were registered private schools but have voluntarily integrated into the state education system. Proprietors are responsible for capital works while the state assumes responsibility for all recurrent costs. Schools are required to comply with curricular and syllabus requirements.

7   The programs in *kōhanga reo* are based on total immersion of children from birth to school age in Māori language, culture, and values. Playcenters are based on the philosophy of ideas of child-initiated play and parents as first educators.

birthday. Children attend either a full primary school until the end of Year 8,[8] or a contributing primary school until the end of Year 6, at which point they progress either to an intermediate school (Years 7 and 8) or to a composite Years 7 to 13 secondary school. The majority of primary schools are co-educational. Primary school teachers typically teach all curriculum areas.

Secondary education begins at Year 9, with most children, by now about 13 years of age, attending the secondary school that is nearest to where they reside. The schools are usually Years 9 to 13 or Years 7 to 13 comprehensive secondary schools. Some composite schools, most often in rural locations, provide for students from Years 1 to 13. More recently, middle/junior high schools have been established for students in Years 7 to 10. Most secondary school students receive instruction from subject-specialists. Single-sex education is more prevalent at the secondary level than at the primary level, although most secondary school students receive their education in co-educational schools. The majority of learners in independent schools are at the secondary level.

The school year usually runs from late January through to mid December. The Ministry of Education specifies the number of half-days state and state-integrated primary and secondary schools are to be open for instruction; boards of trustees are responsible for determining the actual dates. In 2010, primary schools were required to be open for 388 half-days and secondary schools for 380 half-days.[9] Typically, a primary school day spans the morning and afternoon (e.g., 8:45 a.m. to 3 p.m., including instructional time and breaks) (Ministry of Education, 2009c).

Tertiary education programs, including teacher education programs, are offered by a range of institutions, including universities, polytechnics, institutes of technology, *wānanga* (Māori-based tertiary institutions), and private training establishments. Entry requirements into tertiary programs vary, but in general relate to students' success in high-stakes secondary school qualifications. Initial teacher education qualifications for primary school teaching are three or four years in duration and lead to a Bachelor's degree in teaching or, for those already with university degrees, a graduate diploma of teaching. Prospective secondary school teachers complete a three- or four-year university degree, followed by a one-year postgraduate teacher education program (Ministry of Education, 2009d).

11.2.4 Māori-Medium Education

Māori-medium education involves delivering the curriculum in the Māori language for either all or some of the time, in early childhood settings (e.g., *kōhanga reo*) through to tertiary education settings (e.g., *wānanga*). In an international context, Māori-medium education can be viewed as a form of *bilingual* education, specifically *immersion*

---

8   The official nomenclature refers to *Year*. The majority of Year 8 students are in a class level equivalent to Grade 7; Year 6 students are in a class level equivalent to Grade 5.

9   The number of half-days in 2011 was 390 and 380 respectively.

education, because the majority of students are learning in their "second" language to become bilingual and biliterate (May, Hill, & Tiakiwai, 2004, 2006). Māori-medium education is a very complex area, not only because it plays a critical role in preserving and revitalizing an indigenous language and culture, but also because it attempts to provide an education program in which students can experience academic success, as in the mainstream education system (Hohepa, 2008).

Māori-medium education in primary and secondary schools is provided in a number of ways, including through full immersion (curriculum delivery is for 81–100% of instructional time) and bilingual programs (12–80% of instructional time). Full immersion education is provided in *kura kaupapa Māori* (primary) and *wharekura* (secondary),[10] and in designated-character schools, including *kura-a-iwi* (schools with tribal affiliations). Bilingual schools also provide opportunities for students to learn in the Māori language. Some English-medium schools offer curriculum delivery in the Māori language, in either full immersion (*rumaki*) or bilingual (*reorua*) classes or units.

11.2.5 Special Education

A range of support is available to early childhood education services and schools to ensure all New Zealand children can take part in education. While a small group of students with special education needs are enrolled in special schools, most special education students learn in a regular ("mainstream") school setting. All state and state-integrated schools receive a special education grant (SEG) to fund programs in their schools. Students with high or very high needs and those who have hearing or vision impairments receive additional and individualized funding and support for their education in either a regular school setting with specialist teaching or a special education school setting (Ministry of Education, 2010b).

11.2.6 New Zealand Curricula

Te Whāriki is New Zealand's early childhood education curriculum. It sets out a framework for the early childhood education sector, integrating both care and education goals for young infants to children of school-entry age. The official policy for teaching and learning in English-medium schools is described in *The New Zealand Curriculum* (NZC), released at the end of 2007 and fully implemented at the beginning of 2010. The document for Māori-medium education, *Te Marautanga o Aotearoa* (TMoA),[11] released at the end of 2008, was fully implemented during 2011 (Ministry

---

10 *Kura kaupapa Māori* (primary) and *wharekura* (secondary) are schools that adhere to a particular philosophy known as *Te Aho Matua*. Māori pedagogy and Māori worldview are integral to the delivery of the philosophy.

11 TMoA and NZC are not direct translations of each other. While both are underpinned by the same valued educational outcomes, TMoA outlines the role Māori language has to play in accessing Māori culture.

of Education, 1996, 2007a, 2008a). The NZC and TMoA articulate broad objectives for the eight, and in the case of TMoA, nine learning areas for both primary and secondary schooling. Both are characterized as being less prescriptive than previous curricula.[12]

11.2.7 The Policy Context for PIRLS [13]

Over the last decade, *literacy* (reading and writing) has been a focus area for both education policymakers and practitioners. The strategy has been to *align* literacy policies, programs, and projects across the education sector and to develop resources and initiatives for schools to access. However, most of the initiatives were not in place prior to 2001, the year in which the first cycle of PIRLS was administered in New Zealand. One example of a very effective program in terms of outcomes for students was the Literacy Professional Development Project (LPDP). This whole-school, two-year intervention program aimed to raise student achievement in literacy by improving teacher content knowledge in literacy, pedagogy, and practice. However, because LPDP began in 2004 and had only reached approximately 300 (out of about 2,100) primary schools by the end of 2007 when a second cohort of schools had completed the program, it is unlikely that the project's influence would have been reflected in a large-scale assessment such as PIRLS 2006.[14] *Te Reo Matatini*, the literacy strategy for the Māori-medium education sector, released in 2007, has also sought to align existing literacy-related initiatives with other initiatives specific to Māori-medium education (Ministry of Education, 2007b).

11.3 Experience in Large-Scale Assessments

11.3.1 International Studies

New Zealand's involvement in international surveys first began in the early 1970s with its participation in IEA's Six Subject Survey, followed by the Second International Mathematics Study (SIMS), for which New Zealand was the international center. Since the mid 1990s, New Zealand has participated, in addition to PIRLS, in successive cycles of IEA's Trends in International Mathematics and Science Study (TIMSS) and the OECD's Programme for International Student Assessment (PISA).

---

12 At the time PIRLS 2006 was being implemented, the curriculum for reading in English-medium settings was outlined in a substrand of written language in *English in the New Zealand Curriculum* and as a substrand of receptive language (Reo Torohu) in *Te Reo Māori i roto i te Marautanga o Aotearoa*.

13 For more detail on the policy context for reading at the time PIRLS was administered in late 2005 (i.e., the time for PIRLS Southern Hemisphere countries), refer to "New Zealand" in the *PIRLS 2006 Encyclopedia* (Chamberlain, 2007a).

14 For details, see McDowall, Cameron, Dingle, Gilmore, and MacGibbon (2007). LPDP finished at the end of 2009, with a further 100 schools completing the 2008/09 cycle.

The agency with responsibility for funding, managing, implementing, and reporting on the IEA and OECD studies is New Zealand's Ministry of Education; this function is undertaken by the Comparative Education Research Unit, which is part of the ministry's Research Division.[15] For a number of years, the over-arching vision statement for the Ministry of Education articulated in its annual *Statement of Intent*[16] has been to build "a world-leading education system that equips all New Zealanders with the knowledge, skills and values to be successful citizens in the 21st century" (Ministry of Education, 2009a, p. 6; 2011, p. 12). The ministry draws on information from the international studies to develop system-level indicators that are used to monitor how well New Zealand is on track to achieving this outcome. Research evidence from these studies is also used in conjunction with evidence from national research activities to determine how best to achieve this outcome.

11.3.2 National Studies

Until 1995, New Zealand had no regular collection of system-level information on students' progress in primary school. Interestingly, the need for system-level information had first been advocated more than 30 years earlier in the *Report of the Commission on Education in New Zealand* (released in 1962).[17] The commission recommended a system of national assessment in core subjects every five years alongside a system of regular classroom assessment.[18] The optional use of standardized tests as part of classroom assessment practice was endorsed by the educator sector, and for some years the need for a national assessment was "obviated or at least lessened" (Ewing, 1972, p. 28).

The call for regular collection of system-level information continued, however, during the 1970s and 1980s, with three more working parties recommending some form of national assessment. But it was not until implementation of major reforms in the late 1980s to the administration of the New Zealand education system, known as "Tomorrow's Schools", along with changes in curricula and requirements for assessment that, a national assessment program, known as the National Education Monitoring Project (NEMP), came to fruition (Ministry of Education, 1991). The Educational Assessment Research Unit of the University of Otago was contracted to

---

15 New Zealand's Ministry of Education is the member institution of the IEA; the senior manager of the Research Division is the IEA General Assembly representative.

16 The *Statement of Intent* is a document that sets out what the ministry wants to achieve and how it will deliver key (ministerial) priorities for education.

17 The commission comprised 11 members and was chaired by Sir George Currie. The resulting report is thus also known as the *Currie Report*.

18 Up to the end of 1936, children at the end of their primary schooling were required to sit the *proficiency examination*. An outcome of its discontinuation was that the majority of children were able to progress from one class to another with their peers (i.e., "social promotion") (Department of Education, 1978; Ewing, 1972).

run all aspects related to NEMP on behalf of the Ministry of Education from 1995 until the end of 2009.

The purpose of NEMP was to provide a broad picture of achievement at two points in primary schooling: Year 4 and Year 8, with the latter is the final year of primary schooling. Reading, writing, mathematics, science, technology, social studies, physical education and health, art, and music were assessed. Three of these learning areas were assessed each year, with the cycle such that each area was assessed every four years. NEMP involved a representative sample of schools and a random sample of students from each sampled school. It also employed a range of techniques to assess students' skills and competencies: pencil and paper tests, interviews, performance-based tasks, and cooperative work.

In 2010, a modified form of NEMP was run whereby reading, writing, and mathematics were the focus, with the aim of aligning NEMP tasks with commonly used classroom assessment tools, and with the new National Standards (see 11.4.4.2). A new national monitoring project, which will report on student outcomes, is scheduled to be implemented in 2012.

While no formal system-level monitoring akin to NEMP has operated at the secondary level, information from the high-stakes assessments for the National Certificates of Educational Achievement (NCEAs)—national qualifications undertaken by students in Years 11 to 13—provide aggregated information that is used to monitor the achievements of subpopulations of interest to policymakers.

11.4 PIRLS 2006: New Zealand Results and the Impact of PIRLS

11.4.1 The Results in International and National Contexts[19]

As was the case in PIRLS 2001, nearly all (98%) of the New Zealand students who participated in PIRLS 2006 were assessed in English, with just a small percentage (2%) assessed in the Māori language. New Zealand students were, on average, 10 years of age.[20]

In PIRLS 2006, the overall reading literacy score for New Zealand students was 532 scale score points, which was significantly higher than the PIRLS scale mean of 500. However, it was significantly lower than the means for 17 countries, including three countries that assessed in English: England (539), the United States (540), and Singapore (558). The New Zealand mean was also significantly lower than the mean for Ontario (555), one of the Canadian benchmarking participants. New Zealand's

---

19 International results for New Zealand as reported by Chamberlain (2007b) and Mullis, Martin, Kennedy, and Foy (2007). National information specific to New Zealand is described in Chamberlain (2008).

20 Because children start primary school at five years of age, PIRLS involves New Zealand's Year 5 students.

average performance was similar to that of three countries, one of which was Scotland (527). There was no significant change in the New Zealand Year 5 students' mean achievement from 2001 (529) to 2006 (532). New Zealand also had a relatively wide range of performance (290 scale score points) compared with many other higher-performing countries.

Nationally, the wide range of performance was also observed within each of New Zealand's four main ethnic groupings. Of particular note, however, was the variation in average performance across these groupings. Pākehā/European (552) and Asian (550) students achieved, on average, at a much higher level than Māori (483)[21] and Pasifika (479) students.

PIRLS 2006 used four points on the achievement scale (625, 550, 475, and 400) to summarize the types of comprehension skills and strategies students employed in the assessment. These are described as the PIRLS *advanced, high, intermediate,* and *low* international benchmarks respectively. Compared with the students in many other PIRLS countries, a relatively large percentage of New Zealand students demonstrated strong reading comprehension skills, with 45 percent of the students reaching the PIRLS *high international benchmark* (c.f. the international median of 41%), while 13 percent scored at or above the PIRLS *advanced international benchmark*. This percentage ranked as one of the highest among the PIRLS countries and was almost double the international median of 7 percent. However, compared to students in other countries with similar characteristics, a slightly higher percentage of New Zealand students were found to have weaker reading comprehension skills; 24 percent of its students did not reach the PIRLS *intermediate international benchmark*, including 8 percent (c.f. the international median of 6%) who did not reach the PIRLS *low international benchmark*.

Pākehā/European and Asian girls were more likely to be in the higher-performing group; Māori boys, Pasifika boys, and Pasifika girls were the students most likely to be among New Zealand's lower achievers. The majority of learners who were assessed in the Māori language (2% of the Year 5 population) fell into this group of lower achievers. However, as already noted in Section 11.2.4, it is important to understand that while almost all of these students were themselves (ethnically) Māori, the Māori language for many of them was their second language, with English being their first.[22]

A significant finding from a New Zealand perspective concerned children's attitudes to and their self-confidence in reading. While New Zealand students' attitudes to reading were found to be moderately positive compared to the attitudes of their

---

21 This figure is the mean for all Māori Year 5 students, regardless of their language of instruction. Note that the majority of Māori students receive instruction in English, but almost all students who are in full immersion settings are themselves Māori.

22 Concerns had also been expressed during the administration of PIRLS 2006 by the translation reviewers and teachers as to the comparability and difficulty (length and vocabulary) level of the Māori language versions of the texts for Year 5 students in Māori immersion settings.

international counterparts, of concern was the fact that they were less positive in PIRLS 2006 than in PIRLS 2001. This observation was particularly apparent for New Zealand's Year 5 boys, and in particular Māori boys, and both Pākehā/European and Māori girls. Furthermore, New Zealand students were found to be a lot less confident about their reading ability when compared with both their international counterparts and their 2001 New Zealand counterparts. The lower level of self-confidence was evident for all subgroups, with the exception of New Zealand's Asian students.

11.4.2 Release of the PIRLS Results

To some extent, the *timing* of the international release of PIRLS 2006 made it slightly problematic for the Ministry of Education to prepare an announcement; it came just one week prior to the release of the OECD's PISA 2006 results. The two studies showed similar information for New Zealand in reading—the large spread of achievement, a relatively high proportion of readers with advanced comprehension skills, and the large gender differences in achievement that favored girls. However, New Zealand's ranking was much higher in PISA 2006 than it was in PIRLS 2006, even when countries common to both studies were compared. Thus, the release of PIRLS 2006 in New Zealand was relatively low key, with no official launch or announcement coming from the ministry. Instead, the international release was noted in a speech given by the then Minister of Education during his announcement of a new literacy resource for teachers (Carter, 2007).

11.4.3 Dissemination of the PIRLS Results

Dissemination of the PIRLS 2006 results in New Zealand has been multifaceted in that it has included reports, research seminars, presentations, and conference papers. On the day of the international release in November 2007, the PIRLS national research coordinator presented the results for New Zealand to Ministry of Education staff. In addition, the first of two descriptive national reports and a compendium in the form of a brochure summarizing the key findings were released into the public domain. The report provided a comprehensive overview of the New Zealand results in an international context (Chamberlain 2007b; Ministry of Education, 2007c). The second of the two reports, which focused on the results for New Zealand's subpopulations and included the summary compendium, were published the following year, in 2008 (Chamberlain, 2008, Ministry of Education, 2008b).

The timing of the release of both the PIRLS and PISA results also meant that the PIRLS 2006 national research coordinator and the PISA 2006 national project manager were able to deliver a joint presentation at the annual New Zealand Association for Research in Education (NZARE) Conference. The aim of the presentation was to highlight the findings that were common to both studies, given the difference in New Zealand's rankings on the two international achievement scales.

A paper titled "New Zealand Students' Engagement with the PIRLS 2006 Reading Passages" was also presented at IEA's Third International Research Conference in Taipei, Taiwan, in 2008. The paper summarized the findings of the qualitative research undertaken by the national research coordinator when PIRLS was administered in New Zealand. The research looked at whether or not the students engaged with the PIRLS 2006 reading passages, the reasons why, and the extent to which their engagement with the reading material related to their reading achievement (Chamberlain & Caygill, 2008).

Copies of the national reports and compendia were distributed to all schools that participated in PIRLS 2006. This material was sent out at the same time these publications were released into the public domain. They were also distributed to university libraries and the advisory services based within the universities, and they remain available in electronic form on the Ministry of Education's website: www.educationcounts.govt.nz/goto/pirls

11.4.3.1 New Zealand Educational Institute Te Riu Roa and the PIRLS Symposium

A significant feature of the dissemination of PIRLS 2006 was a symposium initiated by New Zealand's largest education union and professional institute, the New Zealand Educational Institute (NZEI) Te Riu Roa. The purposes of this event were for participants to have an "open and frank discussion" on the results from PIRLS pertaining to New Zealand, to consider the results in the context of current organizational and teaching practices in New Zealand, and to identify areas where further research was needed.

Representatives who attended were from diverse backgrounds and included education researchers, education school reviewers, education policymakers, reading researchers, primary school teachers and principals, and professional development providers.[23] Some of the areas that these participants identified as needing further investigation included improving the engagement, motivation, and achievement outcomes of our weakest readers, and providing ongoing support and professional development for teachers of literacy (NZEI, 2008).

11.4.3.2 New Zealand Educational Institute Te Riu Roa Focus Groups

Following on from the symposium, NZEI Te Riu Roa sponsored six teacher focus groups, with 10 to 12 teachers in each group, in different regions throughout New Zealand in October 2008 and June 2009. The aim of this work was to show teachers how the findings from a large-scale international study such as PIRLS could

---

23 The PIRLS 2006 national research coordinator presented at this symposium.

be relevant to their own practice. A senior representative from NZEI Te Riu Roa, the PIRLS 2006 national research coordinator, and a principal researcher with affiliations to NEMP facilitated each session. The program for each focus group discussion included:

- Reflections from the teachers on a key finding from PIRLS;
- Teachers' views of the PIRLS 2006 *Reader*[24] and the questions accompanying it in light of their own instructional practice;
- A technical exercise whereby teachers were asked to summarize information from a set of PIRLS 2006 international exhibits;
- A review and rating of the importance of the New Zealand literacy experts' priorities for literacy teaching and learning that had been identified at the symposium.

The focus-group work initiated and run by NZEI and supported by the Ministry of Education's Comparative Education Research Unit was a step toward achieving the aim of making the PIRLS information more relevant to teachers.

11.4.4 Impact of the Results

In order to understand the impact PIRLS has made on policy and research in New Zealand, it is first necessary to describe the reaction to the release, in 2003, of the PIRLS 2001 results.

The international release of the PIRLS 2001 results in April 2003 invoked strong comment from both media and education researchers in New Zealand, not all of which were favorable. For example, the media commentator Sumner Burstyn stated in the *New Zealand Herald* that "the data shows that something is profoundly wrong with reading here … [with New Zealand] significantly outranked by countries with comparable standards of living and lifestyles expectations" (Sumner Burstyn, 2003).

The reaction amongst the reading research community was mixed, with views ranging from reflective through indifferent to extremely critical. In December 2003, a number of New Zealand's reading "experts"[25] participated in a special symposium on PIRLS at the annual NZARE conference; the resulting papers were published in a special edition of the educational journal *Delta* in 2004.

The papers highlighted the polarization of views amongst New Zealand's reading researchers. Because the focus of most of the commentary from the media and some academics had been on New Zealand's apparent *drop* in ranking, some contributors put forward reasons relating to technical features of the study as to why this was so. These

---

24 The *Reader* attempts to present some of the reading material used in the assessment in an authentic format. It contained two texts (one literary text and one informational text) and was presented in color in a magazine format. The questions were presented in a separate booklet.

25 The invitation was not extended to any of the Ministry of Education researchers who had been directly involved in PIRLS.

reasons included countries' use of replacement schools to meet sampling requirements, the older average age of students in some countries, the exclusion rates for some countries, and the use of multiple-choice questions in the assessment (Elley, 2004; Limbrick, 2004). As well as this technical perspective, one researcher suggested that the drop was not unexpected, as New Zealand had lived on its reputation of being the "best readers in the world", as was suggested by the results of the first IEA study on reading in 1970/1971, and had not considered new research and new methods for teaching literacy (Greaney, 2004).

Despite the criticisms, all contributors were united in their concern about the large gap between New Zealand's higher and lower achievers, and the gender gap. However, there was little consensus amongst the experts on how to address these gaps (Clark, 2004; Openshaw, 2004).

In sharp contrast to PIRLS 2001, the reaction to the release of PIRLS 2006 was somewhat muted, probably because the release of the PISA 2006 international results ameliorated any criticism from the media and other commentators. An observation was made on the apparent decrease in New Zealand's ranking over the intervening years since 2001, but this interpretation was largely due to these commentators not taking account of new participating countries and the Canadian benchmarking provinces when they were making the comparisons across the cycles.

11.4.4.1 Impact of PIRLS on Policy

PIRLS is not the only source of evidence that would be, or has been, used for policy reforms in reading. Rather, as noted in Section 11.3.1, PIRLS is used alongside other research-based evidence for developing policy and for tracking change in achievement over time. At first, the use of PIRLS by policymakers was not obvious, with some of the technical issues raised by the academic community being the focus rather than the results per se. By being better informed about and having an understanding of the technical issues, policymakers have more readily accepted PIRLS 2006 and acknowledged its value with respect to monitoring and informing work in the Ministry of Education. For example, the ministry's annual report for the year ending 30 June 2009 to the House of Representatives cited data from PIRLS 2006 to highlight the inequitable outcomes for Māori and Pasifika students (Ministry of Education, 2009e).

PIRLS is also being used as part of a set of measures for evaluating the success of actions related to reading that are being implemented under the auspices of the Māori education strategy for 2008–2012, *Ka Hikitia: Managing for Success*. The strategy sets out goals and specific actions in order to "improve education outcomes for and with Māori" (Ministry of Education, 2009f, p. 5). Increasing "the mean reading scores in the Progress in International Reading Literacy Study (PIRLS) for Māori Year 5 students by 7 percent by 2011" (p. 31) was one of the specific, albeit ambitious, targets identified.

A program of work directed at improving educational achievement outcomes for Pasifika students was also put in place. The *Pasifika Education Plan 2006–2010* set out the goals for improving outcomes, with one of these goals focussed on improving Pasifika children's literacy and numeracy outcomes. One of the targets used to measure the success of the work in this area was "positive shifts in performance as measured by national and international assessments (PISA, PIRLS, TIMSS, and NEMP) by 2010" (Ministry of Education, 2007d, p. 16).[26]

In addition to being used for monitoring student outcomes, PIRLS has been used to aid understanding of *how* educational outcomes can be improved in New Zealand. One example is the best evidence synthesis[27] on school leadership commissioned by the Ministry of Education. This synthesis not only referred to the PIRLS 2006 achievement information but also used PIRLS 2006 international comparative data pertaining to school administration and leadership, and student safety (Robinson, Hohepa, & Lloyd, 2009).

While the Ministry of Education's policymakers and researchers refer to or use evidence from PIRLS, New Zealand's education research community seldom does, a pattern that is also evident with respect to data from other large-scale international studies. On the occasions PIRLS has been used, it has been for the purpose of challenging or, more often than not, criticizing current national literacy initiatives and the whole-language approach to teaching reading. Critics cite New Zealand's (apparent) drop in ranking, the large gender gap, and the relatively large range of performance as evidence (see, for example, Tunmer, Nicholson, Greany, Prochnow, Chapman, & Arrow, 2008).

11.4.4.2 National Standards

One of the key priority areas for the government is to improve students' foundation skills in literacy and numeracy. During 2009 and 2010, the development and implementation of national standards in literacy and mathematics for students at each year level of primary school (Years 1 to 8) in both English-medium and Māori-medium primary school settings became the focus for a significant amount of the education policy work in New Zealand.

While the NZC and TMoA give a broad overview of the learning in schools, the National Standards, which are directly aligned to the curriculum documents, make explicit the learning outcomes for New Zealand primary school students. The NZC National Standards for reading, writing, and mathematics were introduced at the same

---

26 An updated version of the plan for the period 2009–2012 released on 27 November 2009 states that National Standards (as noted in Section 11.4.4.2) are now used for setting targets for improvements in Pasifika children's literacy achievement. The international studies will continue to be used indirectly, although they are not explicitly mentioned in the revised plan.

27 The Iterative Best Evidence Synthesis Programme is a series of syntheses that draws international and national research evidence together with the aim of improving educational outcomes valued in New Zealand.

time the NZC was being fully implemented in English-medium settings in 2010.[28] TMoA *Ngā Whanaketanga Rumaki Māori*, the Maori-medium National Standards for *te reo matatini* (oral language, reading, and writing) and *pangarau* (mathematics) were implemented in Māori-medium settings during 2011 to coincide with the full implementation of TMoA.[29]

National Standards and *Ngā Whanaketanga Rumaki Māori* are underpinned by assessment for learning principles and practice. Thus, teachers do not rely on any form of national testing or additional assessments. Teachers are required to use a range of information, formal and informal, to make judgments about their students in relation to the standards.

To support teachers in making these judgments, a major undertaking by the Ministry of Education during 2010 was the alignment of a range of classroom assessment tools that teachers are expected to use in order to produce these judgments. The methodology employed to do the alignments was an adapted version of "script scrutiny" (Ministry of Education, 2010e). To understand how well a New Zealand standard for reading aligned with an internationally developed assessment, the ministry also conducted a separate standard-setting exercise to align the Year 5 English-medium reading standard with the PIRLS reading achievement scale (Lawes, 2010a).[30]

The implementation of PIRLS 2011 in New Zealand took place in late 2010. This latest iteration will be *one* of the sources providing baseline data for evaluating the extent to which the NZC and National Standards have enhanced reading achievement outcomes in New Zealand.[31]

11.5 Recent and Future Activities

As well as being responsible for implementing and reporting on the international studies, the Ministry of Education's Comparative Education Research Unit conducts a small secondary-analysis work program directed mainly at supporting in-house policy work. Two examples of such work are an examination of the practices of teachers according to whether or not their students were of *lower* reading ability as measured by PIRLS 2006, and a closer examination of achievement information for students assessed in the Māori language in the context of Māori-medium education in New Zealand.

---

28 The NZC National Standards for reading and writing are described in Ministry of Education (2009g); the mathematics standards are described in Ministry of Education (2009h).
29 The TMoA Māori-medium National Standards for oral language, reading, and writing are described in Ministry of Education (2010c); the mathematics National Standards are described in Ministry of Education (2010d).
30 In brief, it was found that the reporting bands used in the National Standards at Year 5 aligned well with the benchmarks used in PIRLS 2006.
31 The sample design in PIRLS 2006 enabled the achievement of students assessed in Māori to be reported separately from the achievement of students assessed in English. This is not the case in PIRLS 2011.

Several papers and presentations have and will continue to be made at annual NZARE conferences. Topics covered include the relationship between Pasifika students' reading achievement and their attitudes to reading (Lawes, 2009) and the importance of parents' engagement with their children's reading (Satherley, 2009). New Zealand PIRLS 2006 data were used as the basis of a paper presented at IEA's fourth International Research Conference in Gothenburg in 2010 (Lawes, 2010b). The particular focus of this paper was reading attitudes among low-ability students.

Given that the PIRLS 2011 data were collected at the end of 2010, the focus of any PIRLS-related activity will now probably move on from PIRLS 2006 to the scrutiny of these more recent data.

11.6 Concluding Comments

New Zealand has now participated in two cycles of PIRLS, and it embarked on the third cycle at the end of 2010. PIRLS plays an important role in monitoring the "health" of the New Zealand education system, particularly with reference to the international context, and its value is now generally accepted by policymakers, researchers, and practitioners. PIRLS provides the New Zealand education community not only with opportunity to reflect on and, to some extent, inform their literacy policies and practices but also time to learn from other countries. One of the challenges faced by the researchers who work on PIRLS (and, for that matter, the other international studies) is how to make the very rich information coming out of the study more accessible and relevant to teachers. The focus group work promoted by New Zealand's primary school teachers' union and professional organization, NZEI, has gone some way toward effectively addressing this issue.

References

Carter, C. (2007, November). *Literacy learning progressions: Keeping the focus on reading and writing*. Speech presented at Rata Street School, Naenae, Upper Hutt, Wellington, New Zealand. Retrieved from http:///www.beehive.govt.nz/speech/

Chamberlain, M. (2007a). New Zealand. In A. M. Kennedy, I. V. S. Mullis, M. O. Martin, & K. L. Trong (Eds.), *PIRLS 2006 encyclopedia: A guide to reading education in the forty PIRLS 2006 countries* (pp. 279–292). Chestnut Hill, MA: Boston College.

Chamberlain, M. (2007b). *Reading literacy in New Zealand: An overview of New Zealand's results from the Progress in International Reading Literacy Study (PIRLS) 2005/2006*. Wellington, New Zealand: Research Division, Ministry of Education.

Chamberlain, M. (2008). *PIRLS 2005/2006 in New Zealand: An overview of national findings from the second cycle of the Progress in International Reading Literacy Study (PIRLS)*. Wellington, New Zealand: Research Division, Ministry of Education.

Chamberlain, M., & Caygill, R. (2008, September). *New Zealand students' engagement with the PIRLS 2006 reading passages.* Paper presented at the Third IEA International Research Conference, Taipei, Chinese Taipei.

Clark, J. (2004). PIRLS: Explaining and closing the gaps in reading achievement. *Delta, 56*(2), 3–7.

Department of Education. (1978). *Educational standards in state schools.* Wellington, New Zealand: Author.

Elley, W. B. (2004). What wisdom can we draw from PIRLS? *Delta, 56*(2), 9–20.

Ewing, J. L. (1972). *The Currie Report: Ten years later.* Wellington, New Zealand: Department of Education.

Greaney, K. (2004). First to fourth to thirteenth and (in all probability) still dropping? New Zealand's international reading literacy results: Some personal thoughts about the reasons for the gap. *Delta, 56*(2), 53–64.

Hopeha, M. (2008). Reading comprehension in kura kaupapa Māori classrooms: Whakawhānuitia te Hinengaro. *New Zealand Journal of Educational Studies, 43*(2), 73–87.

Lawes, E. (2009, December). *Reading proficiency and enjoyment of Pasifika Year 5 students.* Paper presented at the New Zealand Association for Research in Education Conference, Rotorua, New Zealand.

Lawes, E. (2010a, December). *An alignment of the "by the end of Year 5" National Standard in reading with the PIRLS assessment.* Presentation of findings at the New Zealand Association for Research in Education Conference, Auckland, New Zealand.

Lawes, E. (2010b, June). *The varying relationship between New Zealand students' attitude to reading and reading literacy achievement.* Paper presented at the Fourth IEA International Research Conference, Gothenburg, Sweden.

Limbrick, L. (2004). The PIRLS survey 2001: What does it tell literacy educators in New Zealand? *Delta, 56*(2), 33–45.

May, S., Hill, R., & Tiakiwai, S. (2004). *Bilingual/immersion education: Indicators of good practice. Final report to the Ministry of Education.* Wellington, New Zealand: Ministry of Education.

May, S., Hill, R., & Tiakiwai, S. (2006). *Bilingual education in Aotearoa/ New Zealand. Key findings from bilingual/immersion education: Indicators of good practice.* Wellington, New Zealand: Ministry of Education.

McDowall, S., Cameron, M., Dingle, R., with Gilmore, A., & MacGibbon, L. (2007). *Evaluation of the Literacy Professional Development Project.* Wellington, New Zealand: Ministry of Education.

Ministry of Education. (1991). *Tomorrow's standards: The report of the Ministerial Working Party on Assessment for Better Learning.* Wellington, New Zealand: Author.

Ministry of Education. (1996). *Te Whāriki: He whāriki mātauranga mō ngā mokopuna o Aotearoa. Early childhood curriculum.* Wellington, New Zealand: Learning Media Ltd.

Ministry of Education. (1999). *New Zealand schools nga kura o Aotearoa 1998.* Wellington, New Zealand: Author.

Ministry of Education. (2002). *Excellence, relevance and access: An introduction to the new tertiary education system.* Wellington, New Zealand: Author.

Ministry of Education. (2007a). *The New Zealand curriculum for English-medium teaching and learning in Years 1–13.* Wellington, New Zealand: Learning Media Ltd.

Ministry of Education. (2007b). *Te reo matatini: Māori-medium literacy strategy.* Wellington, New Zealand: Huia Education.

Ministry of Education. (2007c). *Reading literacy in New Zealand: PIRLS 2005/2006. A summary of findings in New Zealand.* Wellington, New Zealand: Research Division.

Ministry of Education. (2007d). *Pasifika Education Plan monitoring report 2006.* Wellington, New Zealand: Author.

Ministry of Education. (2008a). *Te marautanga o Aotearoa.* [Māori-medium National curriculum]Wellington, New Zealand: Learning Media Ltd.

Ministry of Education. (2008b). *PIRLS 2005/2006 in New Zealand: A summary of national findings from the second cycle of the Progress in International Reading Literacy Study (PIRLS).* Wellington, New Zealand: Research Division.

Ministry of Education. (2009a). *Statement of intent 2009–2014.* Wellington, New Zealand: Author.

Ministry of Education. (2009b). *New Zealand schools nga kura o Aotearoa 2008.* Wellington, New Zealand: Author.

Ministry of Education. (2009c). *2010 school terms and holidays.* Retrieved from www.minedu.govt.nz/theMinistry/EducationInNewZealand/SchoolTermsandHolidays

Ministry of Education. (2009d). *Is there a place for you in primary teaching? Teacher education qualifications 2010.* Retrieved from www.TeachNZ.govt.nz/

Ministry of Education. (2009e). *Ministry of Education annual report 2009.* Wellington, New Zealand: Author

Ministry of Education. (2009f). *Ka Hikitia: Managing for success. Māori education strategy 2008−2012* (rev. ed.). Wellington, New Zealand: Author.

Ministry of Education. (2009g). *The New Zealand curriculum reading and writing standards for Years 1–8.* Wellington, New Zealand: Learning Media Ltd.

Ministry of Education. (2009h). *The New Zealand curriculum mathematics standards for Years 1–8.* Wellington, New Zealand: Learning Media.

Ministry of Education. (2010a). *20 hours ECE: Information for parents.* Wellington, New Zealand: Author.

Ministry of Education. (2010b). *New Zealand schools nga kura o Aotearoa 2009.* Wellington, New Zealand: Author.

Ministry of Education. (2010c). *Te marautanga o Aotearoa whanaketanga reo kōrero, pānui, tuhituhi* [Māori-medium national curriculum for oral languages, reading, and writing]. Wellington, New Zealand: Learning Media Ltd.

Ministry of Education. (2010d). *Te marautanga o Aotearoa whanaketanga reo pāngarau* [Māori-medium national curriculum for mathematics]. Wellington, New Zealand: Learning Media Ltd.

Ministry of Education. (2010e). *Methodology for aligning assessment tools to National Standards.* Retrieved from http://assessment.tki.org.nz/Effective-use-of-evidence/Alignment-between-National-Standards-and-assessment-tools

Ministry of Education. (2011). S*tatement of intent 2011/12–2016/17.* Wellington, New Zealand: Author.

Mullis, I. V. S., Martin, M. O., Kennedy, A. M., & Foy, P. (2007). *PIRLS 2006 international report: IEA's Progress in International Reading Literacy Study in primary schools in 40 countries.* Chestnut Hill, MA: Boston College.

New Zealand Education Institute Te Riu Roa (NZEI). (2008, May). *Report on the Symposium on the Progress in International Reading Literacy Study (PIRLS) 2005/2006.* Wellington, New Zealand: Author.

Openshaw, R. (2004). Is New Zealand's reading cup half full, or half empty? A final comment on the papers offered for the NZARE literacy symposium, 2003. *Delta, 56*(2), 109–118.

Organisation for Economic Co-operation and Development (OECD). (2009). *Education at a glance: OECD indicators.* Paris, France: Author.

Robinson, V., Hopeha, M., & Lloyd, C. (2009). *School leadership and student outcomes: Identifying what works and why. Best evidence synthesis iteration.* Wellington, New Zealand: Ministry of Education.

Satherley, P. (2009, December). *Parent–child reading engagement and students' reading skills: Findings from the 2005 Progress in International Reading Literacy Study.* Presentation of findings at the New Zealand Association for Research in Education Conference, Rotorua, New Zealand.

Statistics New Zealand. (2005a). *New Zealand in the OECD.* Retrieved from http://www.stats.govt.nz/products-and-services/nz-in-the-oecd/default.htm

Statistics New Zealand. (2005b). *Statistical standard for ethnicity 2005.* Wellington, New Zealand: Author. Retrieved from http://www.stats.govt.nz/analytical-reports/review-measurement-ethnicity/papers.htm

Statistics New Zealand. (2007). *QuickStats about New Zealand.* Wellington, New Zealand: Author. Retrieved from www.stats.govt.nz

Statistics New Zealand. (2011, February). *Hot off the press: Latest statistics from Statistics New Zealand.* Wellington, New Zealand: Author.

Sumner Burstyn, B. (2003, April 21). Teach the teachers and reading will improve. *New Zealand Herald* (regional edition).

Tunmer, W. E., Nicholson, T., Greany, K. T., Prochnow, J. E., Chapman, J. W., & Arrow, A. W. (2008). PIRLS before swine: A critique of New Zealand's national literacy strategy. *New Zealand Journal of Educational Studies, 43*(2), 105–119.

Walrond, C. (2008). Natural environment. *Te Ara: The encyclopedia of New Zealand.* Retrieved from http://www.TeAra.govt.nz/en/natural-environment

Wilson, J. (2008). Government and nation. *Te Ara: The encyclopedia of New Zealand.* Retrieved from http://www.TeAra/.govt.nz./en/government-and-nation

Chapter 12
The Impact of PIRLS in the Russian Federation[1]

Isak Froumin and Marina Kuznetsova[2]

12.1 The Russian Federation at a Glance[3]

Covering the eastern part of Europe and the northern part of Asia, the Russian Federation is the largest country in the world. It occupies one-seventh of the Earth's surface, with a territory of over 17 million square kilometers that includes a vast range of geographical, natural, and meteorological conditions. The country from east to west is more than 10 thousand kilometers in length; from north to south, it is more than 4 thousand kilometers.

The country's population of about 142.8 million people includes more than 100 ethnic groups, each possessing its own language. The majority of the population (about 81.5%) belongs to the Russian ethnic group. The overall population density is eight to nine persons per square kilometer. The urban population amounts to 104.1 million people, or 73 percent of the entire Russian population; 10.4 million people live in Moscow, the country's capital.

The living conditions of the Russian people have changed during the last 20 years due to the economic and social problems the country has encountered since the collapse of the Soviet regime. In 2005, infant mortality was 11 deaths per 1,000 live births. The average life expectancy is 65.3 years, with the average life expectancy of 72.4 years for females considerably higher than the 58.9 years for males.

Russia is a democratic federal parliamentary state with a republican form of governance. The state is ruled by the president and the Federal Parliament (comprising the Council of Federation and the Duma, Government, and the Courts of the Russian Federation). Legislative powers are exercised by the Duma.

In 2006, Russia's gross national product was about $USB1,000.00. The country's primary industries include oil, gas, and metal production as well as agriculture,

---

1   This publication was prepared as part of the project In-Depth Analysis of PIRLS-2006 Results.
    The project was administered by the Higher School of Economics, which received financial and methodological support from the Center of International Cooperation for Education Development of the Academy of National Economy, Government of the Russian Federation.
2   This publication is co-authored by Galina Kovaleva, Andrey Melnikov, Marina Pinskaya, Tatiana Timkova, Yulia Tumeneva, and Galina Zuckerman.
3   The introduction is based on the Russian Federation's country profile in the *PIRLS 2006 Encyclopedia* (Kennedy, Mullis, Martin, & Trong, 2007). The profile was written by Galina Kovaleva and Marina Kuznetsova from the Russian Academy of Education. Most of the statistical information given in this current chapter comes from the Russian State Committee for Statistics "Goskomstat": www.gks.ru/data

forestry, and fishing. Women and men were almost equally represented in the total workforce in 2005—49.4 percent and 50.6 percent respectively. The proportion of GDP given over to education from the consolidated budget of the Russian Federation and of the state extra-budgetary funding was 3.9 percent in 2006 (Institute of Statistical Studies and Economics, 2007).

Russian is the official language of the Russian Federation. The nation comprises 88 administrative regions, including autonomous districts, each with its own regional culture and community identity. Most students are taught in the Russian language; some, however, study one or more of the 79 languages of the national ethnic groups within the Russian Federation.

12.2 Russian Education System as a Context for PIRLS 2006

12.2.1 Structure and Governance of Education

Under the current Law on Education, passed in 1992, the Russian education system has become more decentralized in its decisionmaking and funding. Under the Law on Education, the state guarantees citizens of the Russian Federation free general education and, on a competitive basis, free vocational education at state and municipal educational institutions.

The Law on Education gives schools considerable autonomy and responsibility. Under this law, two main documents regulate school instruction. They are known as the *Educational Standard* and the *Educational Program*. The standard sets minimum curriculum requirements for schools and specifies the levels of achievement students should accomplish at each stage of their schooling. Each educational institution has the right to shape, within the requirements of the standard, its educational program. It thus has leeway in determining its curriculum, annual calendar study plan, and schedule of classes.

The tendency toward increasing variability of educational provision in Russia is evident in the growing financial and academic autonomy of educational establishments, the variety of the types and kinds of educational establishments in existence, the growth in number and diversity of educational programs, and the growing number of textbooks for school subjects written by different authors.

12.2.2 Structure of the Education System

The Russian Federation's education system includes preschool education, primary education, general secondary education, vocational training, higher education, postgraduate education, professional development, inservice training, and re-training education.

12.2.2.1   Preschool Education

Preschool education is optional. In 2006, preschool education encompassed 47,835 educational institutions catering for about 4.3 million children, a fifth of whom were living in rural areas. In 2005/2006, about 58 percent of all children of relevant preschool age (i.e., one to six years) were enrolled in preschools. This proportion has stayed relatively stable over the years since. During the last two decades of the 20th century, the number of children not attending preschool institutions increased (in 1985, the percentage of children attending a preschool educational facility was 68 percent).[4]

Since 1991, new types of preschool educational institutions have appeared in Russia. These include special education institutions. In line with past practice, preschool education programs focus not only on the physical health and development of children, but also on their general, or holistic, development.

12.2.2.2   General Education

General (school) education, the core of the Russian education system, includes three stages: primary education (Grades 1 to 4), basic or lower secondary education (Grades 5 to 9), and upper secondary education (Grades 10 to 11). Basic secondary education is compulsory under the Russian Constitution. Under the 1992 Law on Education, upper secondary education also became compulsory and free.

Primary education may be provided in primary schools and in secondary educational institutions. The classroom teacher usually teaches all subjects except music, and an experienced teacher, such as the deputy principal, is responsible for providing teachers across all subjects with instructional support. In Russia, teachers are responsible for choosing instructional materials according to professional preference, children's characteristics and interests, and parental opinion.

In the main, teachers work with the whole class during reading instruction. Students or the teacher read aloud to the class, and the teacher then facilitates class discussion about what has been read. In the first grade, where not all students can read, individual and group activities are also used. Teachers will sometimes place students who can read sentences at this stage into advanced learning groups.

Almost every classroom in Russian primary schools has a class library, which contains enough books and magazines to accommodate independent reading, according to children's interests, during lessons. Children can also take books home.

The average class size for the primary school is 24. However, some schools, particularly the rural ones, have only a few students in the class.

Formative and summative assessments are conducted to ensure that students' achievements comply with the curriculum requirements. They are also used to diagnose students' progress. As a rule, each school chooses the timing and form of its assessments. Summative assessment of student proficiency in each school subject

---

4   Statistics retrieved from http://stat.edu.ru/

generally takes place at the end of each school year. Assessment formats include oral examinations, short-answer, extended-response, and essay questions, and multiple-choice tests. Schools usually use individual teacher-made tests, locally developed tests, or tests developed centrally and published as special supplementary materials.

Innovations in assessment arising from reforms to general education include the introduction of a qualitative system of assessment without grades or marks at the end of primary school and a shift in the orientation of assessment to accommodate the changing nature of student learning and achievement throughout primary school.

12.2.2.3   Teacher Education

People wanting to become primary school teachers have several educational options:

- Five years of formal education at a higher education institution, majoring in the pedagogy, methodology, and instruction of primary education; or
- Four years of a Bachelor degree program at a higher education institution, majoring in pedagogy; or
- Two years at a pedagogical college, after graduation from high school; or
- Four years at a pedagogical college, after graduation from basic school.

In recent years, studying at a higher education institution has become more popular.

The five-year training program consists of about 9,000 hours of theoretical, practical, and research work, along with 24 or more weeks of teaching in schools. Theoretical and practical work make up 60 percent of all instruction time.[5]

The teacher-training curriculum includes four cycles of subjects and elective courses. One out of four cycles, referred to as the professional cycle, accounts for the largest block of time (55% of class time). It includes Russian, children's literature, introduction to the history of literature, mathematics, science, methodology, and instruction in teaching the Russian language and literature (570 hours); methodology and instruction in teaching mathematics (250 hours); science, technology, fine arts, and music. There is no separate specialization for teaching reading. Training in teaching reading is included in the methodology and instruction associated with teaching the Russian language and literature course.

As a rule, primary teachers take part in inservice training every five years. Inservice teacher training is no longer compulsory and is changing its orientation in order to align with the new goals of education, namely, a switch in emphasis from imparting subject content to fostering students' holistic development. Today, teachers electing to engage in in-service education find that the focus of this provision is on active learning strategies and child development.

---

5   State Educational Standard of Higher Professional Education, dated January 31, 2005, methodology and instruction in teaching State Registration No. 675.

12.3 Russia's Experience of National Large-Scale Assessment Programs

Over the last decade or so, the Russian education system's highest priority objective has been forming a national system for evaluating the quality of education.

Russia has had a long-term tradition of gathering comprehensive statistical data about the functioning of the general education system (school statistical reports). Also, until recently, students' successful graduation from basic (lower secondary) school was determined by their performance on annual, end-of-year examinations. These encompass particular subjects that were offered to students in some years and not others, at different levels of the school system, and in some schools and not others.

Choice of subjects and the examinations used to determine proficiency in those subjects also vary according to the entrance requirements of Russian tertiary education institutions. Russian students have always been expected, with rare exceptions, to sit state examinations at the end of both their basic and upper secondary schooling. Students successfully passing these examinations receive certificates of school completion. In 2009, with the aim of bringing some measure of national uniformity to the examination system, the government implemented the Unified State Examination in Russian language and mathematics in all regions of the Russian Federation.

Over the last 15 years, Russia has conducted a range of large-scale surveys and research projects designed to assess the quality of its education system. Some examples of these follow:

- *Assessment of Student Achievement in Mathematics, 1995:* The main aim of this assessment, which was conducted by the Center for Evaluating the Quality of Education of the Institute of Content and Methods of Education of the Russian Academy of Education (ICME RAE; see http://www.centeroko.ry/), was to survey basic school graduates' (Grade 9) achievement in algebra. Students were sampled from the Russian schools participating in IEA's Trends in Mathematics and Science Study (TIMSS) 1995.
- *Mathematics Achievement of Primary School Graduates:* This was carried out by the above-stated center jointly with the Department of Mathematics Education of ICME RAE. The main aim was to assess students' basic mathematical skills and to evaluate the findings against the particular context of the students' respective primary schools. About 2,400 students sampled from the TIMSS-Repeat 1999 schools participated in the assessment.
- *Quality of General Education, 2000–2001:* This, the first phase of an assessment designed to monitor the quality of general secondary education in Russia, targeted secondary education and was implemented by ICME RAE. The aim of this phase was to collect and analyze state compulsory examination papers completed by graduates of basic and upper secondary schools. The papers collected related to three subjects—Russian language, Russian literature, and mathematics—and came from Grades 9 and 11 students from a representative sample of schools.

- *Quality of General Education, 2000–2004:* This second phase of the national monitoring program focused on the educational achievements of primary school graduates. It began by assessing children's readiness for education on entering primary school. About 50,000 Grade 1 students were assessed at the beginning of the year and then again at the end of each subsequent academic year. They were assessed in mathematics, Russian language, and reading. At the end of their primary schooling, they were assessed in two additional subjects—English and ICT (information and communications technology).

- *The Unified State Examination (USE):* 2001 saw the implementation of a large-scale study that involved the participation of nearly all Russian regions. It was based on the introduction of the Unified State Examination (USE)—the main means of attesting student achievement at the end of upper secondary school and the main means for students to secure entrance to institutions of higher education or to vocational schools. On January 1, 2009, the government implemented the USE in two compulsory subjects—Russian language and mathematics—in all regions of the Russian Federation. The USE also offers attestation in nine other subjects, which students select on the basis of the requirements of the universities or the vocational schools they wish to attend.

- *"Reform of the Education System" Monitoring Study:* This study, conducted between 2004 and 2006, was designed to evaluate the availability of high-quality general secondary education in Russia as part of initiatives directed at reforming Russia's education system. The organization responsible for the study was the Institute of Sociology of the Russian Academy of Science. The study covered seven regions and 140 schools catering to 1,500 high school graduates, 1,000 secondary school graduates, and 800 students.

The Russian organizations best known for carrying out large-scale national assessments of the achievement of students in basic and upper secondary schools are the Center for Evaluating the Quality of Education of the Institute of the Content and Methods of Learning of the Russian Academy of Education, the Federal Institute of Education Development, the Federal Institute of Pedagogical Measurements, the Federal Testing Center, and the Higher School of Economics.

12.4   Russia's Experience of International Large-Scale Assessment Programs[6]

The Russian Federation has acquired considerable experience in participating in all kinds of international surveys related to assessment of student achievement and the quality of education, as is evident from Table 1.1 in Chapter 1.

---

6   Some of the information in this section was drawn from the official website of the Center for Evaluating the Quality of Education of the Institute of the Content and Methods of Education, Russian Academy of Education: http://www.centeroko.ru/

The first large-scale international survey in which Russia (the USSR) participated was the International Assessment of Educational Progress-II (IAEP-II), which was coordinated internationally by the American Educational Testing Service (ETS) in 1991. The survey assessed the knowledge and skills of 9- and 13-year-old students in mathematics and science, and it also focused on the factors that influence students' achievements in these subjects. The survey was carried out in Russia by ICME RAE.

IAEP-II represented a notable moment in the history of educational assessment in Russia (USSR). The study was the first to assess the achievement of a representative sample of students (approximately two million) against world standards and then to disseminate the findings publically. In 1991, Russia, as a subject state of the USSR, could not make independent decisions about education; its education system at that time can be characterized as closed and self-sufficient. It is therefore remarkable that the USSR allowed an international study on its territory, especially one that would see its education system compared with the education systems of the West. Even today, a common belief amongst people in the Russian Federation is that the USSR's education system was the best in the world.

Nowadays, the Russian Federation's participation in international comparative surveys plays a strong role in the Russian system of education. Russia actively participates in global integration processes, including those within the sphere of education. Implementation of long-term economic development plans as a part of the global economy requires, in the first place, investments in human capital. The degree to which education in the country is succeeding in this respect is evidenced by data from PIRLS and the many other international surveys of educational achievement in which Russia participates. Understandings gained from the results of these studies are helping Russia place its system of education on the "educational world map." The importance that Russia now attributes to these studies is evident in the priority given to them in its strategic education development plans and in corresponding policy documents put out by the government and the country's Ministry of Education and Science.[7]

The Russian organization with the primary responsibility for conducting large-scale international surveys (planning, implementation, and data collection) is ICME RAE, which, as we noted earlier in this chapter, has considerable responsibility for conducting national surveys and monitoring the effectiveness of Russia's education system. Over the years, the center has collected a considerable amount of data on how well Russia's education system is achieving its aims with respect to student performance.

---

7   See, for example, *Objectives of the Modern Model of Education of Current Importance*, an enclosure with a letter put out by the Ministry of Education and Science of the Russian Federation dated August 5, 2008. Also of relevance is the National Education Initiative No. 03-946, *Our New School: Education for Each and Every One of Us*, retrieved from http://mon.gov.ru

12.5 National Results, Impact, and Expected Long-Term Effects of PIRLS

12.5.1 PIRLS 2006 Results[8]

The performance of Russian students on PIRLS 2006 placed Russia amongst the top-performing countries on the international ranking scale. Russian primary school students achieved an average score of 565 on that scale. The difference between this outcome and the scores for Hong Kong and Singapore results was minimal and not statistically significant. The Russian score, however, was statistically considerably higher than the average scale scores of students from other participating countries.

Of the countries that participated in both PIRLS 2001 and 2006, Russia had the largest increase in average score (37) across the intervening years. In 2001, the average achievement score for the Russian primary school students was also higher than the international average score, but Russia ranked 12th on the international scale (out of 35 participating countries).

Another result of note for the Russian students across the two PIRLS surveys is the considerable growth in the students' average score for the group of skills delineated as retrieving information from the text and making straightforward inferences. The difference in the scores between 2006 and 2001 was 33 scale points (562 compared to 529). An even bigger improvement was evident with respect to Russian students' ability to interpret, integrate ideas and information, analyze, and evaluate the content, language, and elements of written text: the difference was 38 scale score points (563 in 2006 compared to 525 in 2001).

In 2006, 61 percent of the Grade 4 Russian primary school students demonstrated advanced levels of text comprehension. In comparison to 2001, the proportion of children with a very low level of achievement decreased from four percent to two percent.

12.5.2 Influence of PIRLS Results on Educational Policy and Pedagogical Practice

The improved performance of Russian fourth graders over the period between PIRLS 2001 and 2006 needs to be considered within the context of reforms made to primary education throughout the Russian Federation before and during the period encompassed by the two surveys. It is impossible, however, to identify any one factor accounting for the improvement. We consider the main reasons for the improvement to be the following:[9]

---

8   This section is based on work by Kovaleva, Zuckerman, and Kuznetsova (2007).
9   See also Zuckerman, Kovaleva, and Kuznetsova (2007).

- *Change in the average age of Russian primary-school graduates:* Russian school students who participated in the survey in 2006 were about half a year older than the children who participated in the same survey in 2001: the average age of primary school graduates in 2006 was 10.8 years while in 2001 it was 10.3 years. Given the rapid development of children in this age bracket, the difference is a considerable one (see Martin, Mullis, & Foy, 2011, in this regard).
- *Structural changes to the system of primary education:* In 2001, all Russian primary schools became four-year programs. Before that time, two systems of education co-existed: primary school Grades 1 to 3 and primary school Grades 1 to 4. In 2001, 63 percent of primary school students were taught under the Grades 1 to 3 configuration and thus only 37 percent under Grades 1 to 4. In 2006, almost all of the Russian students who participated in PIRLS were taught under the four-year pattern.
- *Rise in the level of school readiness of Grade 1 students and greater attention paid to pre-primary education:* According to data obtained from PIRLS questionnaires given to parents and principals, the number of children entering school in recent years who are deemed "school ready" is increasing. Between 2001 and 2006, the number of students whose parents described their readiness as "very good" increased by 15 percent. School principals reported an increase of 10 percent in the number of students they considered ready for school.
- *Qualitative changes in Russian primary schools:* During the mid 1990s, the Russian Federation formulated new aims for its education system. From here on, education would be directed not only at imparting skills and knowledge to students but also at facilitating their ability to direct their own learning. The most prominent feature of the innovations is the transfer from reproductive teaching methods, with knowledge and skills given to children in a "ready-made" form, to active and creative methods. The latter provide children with incentive to search independently for new knowledge that they need to answer their own questions. This change in emphasis has led to the implementation of new curricular programs and the publication of new textbooks that focus on developmental education. Although these changes have taken time to bed in, they appear to finally be having a positive influence on students' school achievement.
- *Changes in the socioeconomic status of families:* Today, many more Russian families than previously have in their homes books, magazines, computers, and separate desks for those of their children at school.[10] Between PIRLS 2001 and PIRLS 2006, the number of participating students identified as coming from socially and economically disadvantaged backgrounds decreased by 17 percent.

---

10 The presence of these items in homes was used as a de facto measure of socioeconomic status in PIRLS.

The list of indices of improvement could be continued here, but we consider that the above give a sufficient indication of positive changes in Russian school-students' abilities. It is obviously important that these improvements are ongoing.

Between 2001 and 2005, the reading comprehension ability of Grades 2, 3, and 4 students in about 2,000 Russian schools was evaluated as part of a study designed to assess the influence of reforms to the structure and content of general education. The survey was carried out in Russia by ICME RAE. The research team used PIRLS as their reference point when determining how to conduct the assessment and when developing test instruments. Research such as this, along with a considerably greater use of monitoring student achievement in general in schools, may also have had a positive influence on children's achievement in terms of them having become more accustomed to such activity.

Recently, the system for assessing students' educational achievement has been subject to another round of review. As a result, different types of tests as well as more "subtle" means of monitoring student achievement have appeared in schools. These enable teachers to check not only students' acquisition of knowledge but also their ability to apply acquired knowledge in new, atypical situations and to think critically and independently. We are sure that these developments have been prompted by Russia's participation in international comparative surveys such as PIRLS and PISA.

Changes to Russia's system of education over the last decade have involved both the particular (such as the developments in monitoring student achievement) and the general. Changes with respect to the latter involve a whole-scale program of modernization. At the end of 2000, the Russian Government began implementing wide-ranging changes that they signaled were to be in place by 2010. The government explained the main thrust of this program of reform as one directed at moving from a regime focused on functioning (maintaining the status quo) to a regime centered on continuous development. The program would thus involve an overhaul of the structure and content of educational provision, implementation of measures necessary for ongoing assessment of the quality and effectiveness of education, strategies to enhance equality of access to education, development of effective mechanisms to allow consideration of social directives and challenges, and a broadening of public participation in the governance and management of education.

The modernization agenda outlined in 2000 established a general framework that provided a reference point for programs and projects focused on achieving the educational developments (at both federal and regional levels) called for. Russia's participation in PIRLS 2001, PIRLS 2006, and other large-scale surveys of educational achievement directly influenced the content of these initiatives. For example, the Federal Program of Education Development for 2006–2010 established the following achievement indicator: "Raise Russia's ranking in international surveys of the quality of educational provision." The program has also paid close attention to putting in place means of decreasing the number of primary students whose level of achievement is such that they are "held back" (i.e., required to repeat a grade). The program was furthermore intent on raising the standard of reading literacy nationwide (Government of the Russian Federation, 2008).[11]

The important influence that preschool education tends to have on students' performance in primary school was also reflected in the government's educational reform policies. The Federal Program of Education Development for 2006–2010 again provides an example. It established measures to ensure that, by 2010, at least 85 percent of all five- and six-year-olds in Russia would be receiving preschool education, thereby bringing preschool enrollment of young children more in line with that of other developed countries. The federal program also set directions for the curriculum content of preschools. The aim was to have all children leaving preschool and entering primary school with the same level of readiness for school—a development that would, it was assumed, give children greater equality of access to all that the primary school has to offer.

12.6 Future Activities

12.6.1 Systemwide Reforms

Today, we can see within the Russian Federation's strategic documents pertaining to educational development a natural progression from the nation's previous programs of educational reform. For example, a current emphasis is on preparing as great a number of children as possible for school through widely accessible yet different (including independently provided) forms of preschool education.[12] To this end, the state now supports a variety of early childhood development programs offered by various organizations. (It is estimated that by 2016 almost 95 percent of five- and six-year-olds will be receiving some form of preschool education.[13]) The state is also mindful of the role that preschools can play in developing children's literacy and has either proposed or has in place means of providing each child with opportunity to develop skills in the language of education they will encounter on entering first grade.

Attention is also being given to bringing a changed orientation to the general education standards of 2004, in recognition that their focus on developing and then using learning skills in the worlds of work and the everyday is not enough. Educational policymakers and practitioners agree that it is necessary to keep what is deemed best practice within Russian education, but then orientate it so that student outcomes will reflect not only acquisition of curriculum-based requirements (knowledge and skills, creative experience) but also metacognitive skills that can be directed toward learning

---

11   Addition to the Resolution of the Government of the Russian Federation, dated December 23, 2005, No. 803: *Federal Program of Education Development for 2006–2010.*

12   At the time of PIRLS 2006, provision by independent preschool operatives was expected to increase from 1 percent in 2006 to 20 percent in 2010.

13   Enclosure with letter from the Ministry of Education and Science of the Russian Federation, dated May 8, 2008, No. 03-946: *Modern Model of Education Directed at Meeting the Challenges of Innovative Economic Development (Project).*

in general and solving "real-world" problems in particular. This changed orientation should enable schools and teachers to focus on developing students' interpersonal and intrapersonal abilities—their systems of values, interests, motivation, and the like.

The Russian Academy of Education has been actively pursuing these goals. In 2010, it implemented "second-generation" standards of education. These, it is believed, will bring a needed comprehensive nationwide approach to developing curriculum content, improving the learning process systemwide, and bringing greater standardization to the quality of educational provision and to the means used to assess students' achievement outcomes. The standards are also seen as one of the quickest means of achieving these aims right across the Russian Federation.

The improvements to the assessment system provide federal and local government agencies with an important framework within which to conduct and communicate their respective responsibilities for education. The reformed assessment system will, it is hoped, provide agencies with the feedback about the education system that they need to regulate it and to ensure it is meeting its objectives in terms of inter-disciplinary curricula acquisition (i.e., universal learning skills and activities) and subject-specific curricula acquisition.

The new system contains a number of special features (see also Kovaleva & Loginova, 2009, in this regard):

- A comprehensive approach within general education to assessment of students' subject-specific, metacognitive, and personal knowledge and skills acquisition;
- Standardized criteria for assessing whether educational programs are delivering the intended student achievement outcomes;
- A systematic means (such as evidence of ability to accomplish particular tasks) of ensuring that students have achieved proficiency in the subjects they are studying at school;
- Identification of changes in patterns of student achievement locally, nationally, and internationally;
- A combination of external and internal assessments as a mechanism for bringing a high standard of quality to the whole education system;
- Comprehensive use of and reference to formal assessments and attestation of knowledge and skills at particular stages of students' schooling (e.g., end of general education);
- Benchmarking of intended achievement outcomes, test instruments, and data presentation;
- Application of a cumulative assessment system (portfolio), which enables one to track and assess each student's learning needs and accomplishments;
- Use of, in addition to standardized written and oral tests, assessment methods such as projects, practical work, self-analysis, creative activity, self-assessment, and observations; and

- Gathering of data about factors (e.g., family background) known to influence learning, in order to provide contexts of understanding within which to interpret the outcomes of educational monitoring.

The assessment that students typically undertake shortly before leaving primary education (i.e., the examinations determining what course of action—tertiary education, employment—students will take on leaving school) generally still focuses on acquisition of subject-specific and metacognitive knowledge only. Efforts are being made to enlarge the scope of what is assessed so that it encompasses the other types of knowledge and skills emphasized in the second generation of educational standards.

12.6.2 Research Studies

Russia will continue to participate in international comparative studies, including PIRLS. This ongoing participation is stated as a priority for the nation's program of educational reform.[14] Publication of the PIRLS 2006 results led to various agencies in Russia undertaking a number of research studies devoted to in-depth analyses of the factors associated with students' success or failure in the assessment. The In-Depth Analysis of the PIRLS-2006 Results project implemented by the Higher School of Economics (with support from the Center of International Cooperation for Education Development of the Academy of National Economy) is an example of these studies. Some of the findings and conclusions of this project have appeared in this chapter. To date, the outcomes of the analyses have been published in Russian periodicals devoted to educational issues.[15] A book containing all papers, published or otherwise, devoted to secondary analyses of the PIRLS 2006 data for Russia and/or describing and discussing aspects of changes in education policy and practice relating to reading literacy was published in 2010 (Froumin, 2010).

12.7 Concluding Remarks

Without doubt, Russia's participation in PIRLS has been a very positive event. Russia's involvement established the country's place on the international scale of reading literacy, and it led to serious reflection on and debate about the strengths and weaknesses of how Russia teaches children to read and about the overall efficacy of the country's education system. Two questions continue to be at the heart of this debate:

- What are the weaknesses and strengths of Russia's education policy?
- What do we need to pay particular attention to with respect to the content of education and teachers' daily practice?

---

14 Enclosure with letter from the Ministry of Education and Science of the Russian Federation, dated May 8, 2008, No. 03-946: *Modern Model of Education Aimed at Meeting the Challenges of Innovative Economic Development (Project)*.
15 For an example, see *Voprosy Obrazovaniya* [Education Questions], Volume 1, 2009.

The strong performance of Russian students in PIRLS should not be taken as a sign that we can relax with respect to how we teach children to read. A closer analysis of the PIRLS data for Russia shows that this success is not shared by all groups of children. There are those who need to be mentored, using special methods for improving reading literacy. We need to improve our understanding of how schools can work to remediate the adverse influence of socially and economically disadvantaged home backgrounds on students' achievement at school. We need to give closer attention to the caliber of primary school teachers and to the suitability and usefulness of the textbooks being used. We need to develop a comprehensive understanding of successful pedagogical practices and to disseminate them to all schools. And we need to analyze what factors appear to lead to success for children in other countries and to determine how they intersect with our own understandings of the influence of such factors.

We would like to finish here by stating two other objectives—ones that are not directly connected with research interests. The first is to establish a sound understanding among all participants of the educational process—parents, teachers, administrators, educational policymakers, and politicians—of the importance and necessity of beginning the process of teaching reading skills at an early stage of children's lives (within the family and at preschool). The second is to continue our participation in large-scale international studies of educational achievement, such as PIRLS.

References

Froumin, I. D. (Ed.). (2010). *Neozhidannaya pobeda: rossiyskie shkolniki chitaut luchshe drugix* [The unexpected victory: Russian schoolchildren read better than others]. Moscow, Russian Federation: State University Higher School of Economics.

Government of the Russian Federation. (2008, November 17). *The main directions of the activities of the Government of the Russian Federation for the period up to 2012* (Decree No. 1663-p). Moscow, Russian Federation: Government of the Russian Federation.

Institute of Statistical Studies and Economics. (2007). *Education in the Russian Federation: 2007 statistical yearbook.* Moscow, Russian Federation: Author.

Kennedy, A. M., Mullis, I. V. S., Martin, M. O., & Trong, K. L. (Eds.). (2007). *PIRLS 2006 encyclopedia: A guide to reading education in the forty PIRLS 2006 countries.* Chestnut Hill, MA: Boston College.

Kovaleva, G. S., & Loginova, O. B. (2009). *Otsenka dostozenia planiruemych resultatov v nachalnoy schkole: Sistema zadany: Chast 1* [Assessment of achievement of the intended outcomes of primary-level schooling: System of tasks. Part 1]. Moscow, Russian Federation: Prosveshenie.

Kovaleva, G. S., Zuckerman, G. A., & Kuznetsova, M. I. (2007). *Isuchenie kachestva chteniya i ponimaniya* [A study of the quality of reading comprehension]. Retrieved from http://www.centeroko.ru/pirls06/pirls06_res.htm

Martin, M. O., Mullis, I. V. S., & Foy, P. (2011). Age distribution and reading achievement configurations among fourth-grade students in PIRLS 2006. *IERI Monograph Volume 4*, 9–34.

Zuckerman, G. A., Kovaleva, G. S., & Kuznetsova, M. I. (2007). Khorosho li chitayut rossiyskie shkolniki [Are Russian schoolchildren good readers?]. *Voprosy obrazovaniya, 4*, 240–267.

Chapter 13
The Impact of PIRLS in the Slovak Republic

Eva Ladányiová, Paulína Koršňáková, and Daniela Heldová

13.1 The Slovak Republic at a Glance[1]

The Slovak Republic is situated in central Europe. In area, it covers 49,034 square kilometers, and it borders five countries: the Czech Republic to the west, Poland to the north, Ukraine to the east, and Hungary and Austria to the south. The Slovak Republic offers a variety of landscapes, with fertile lowlands in the southern and eastern parts of the country and mountains spreading from the western part of the country through to its center and on towards the north-east, which boasts the best known of Slovakia's mountain ranges, the High Tatras.

Approximately 5.3 million people live in Slovakia; just over 51 percent live in villages with fewer than 10,000 people. The population density is 110 people per square kilometer. Slovakia is divided into eight regions that have gained a certain degree of autonomy since 2002. The capital and the largest city is Bratislava, with a population of 428,672. The Slovak Republic is a member state of the EU, NATO, OECD, UN, UNESCO, and other international organizations. On January 1, 2009, Slovakia adopted the euro currency, making it the 16th member of the Eurozone.

In 2008, the gross national product (GDP) per capita was estimated to be $US63,795. Slovakia's GDP comes mainly from the tertiary sector (services). However, the country's industrial sector also plays an important role within the country's economy. The main industries are car manufacturing and electrical engineering. Public expenditure on education in 2008 represented 2.9 percent of GDP.

13.2 The National Education System

The Ministry of Education is the central agency for state administration of Slovakia's education system. The ministry is responsible for developing unified educational policy and for creating educational laws, regulations, and documents. It devolves responsibility for implementation and administration of its policies to school authorities

---

1   This chapter is based on the Slovak Republic's country profile (Lukačková & Obrancová, 2007) in the *PIRLS 2006 Encyclopedia*, but it has been updated in order to cover the new Education Act (No 245) 2008. The statistical information presented in the chapter is drawn from these websites:
http://www.uips.sk
http://www.government.gov.sk/7887/slovensko.php?menu=1265
http://www.nbs.sk/sk/statisticke-udaje/vybrane-makroekonomicke-ukazovatele/zakladne-makroekonomicke-ukazovatele/u2008SOURCE

in the regions and municipalities. The work of these offices also includes supervision of school staff and professional advice. The municipal offices are responsible for preschools, primary schools, and educational facilities outside the formal primary school system. The regional offices are responsible for secondary as well as special schools and facilities.

State control is exercised through the State School Inspection, which conducts independent school inspections directed at monitoring and evaluating students' achievement in schools. Inspectors also collect information on the management, organization, and quality of the educational process. The majority of schools in Slovakia are public schools, run by municipalities and funded by the state. Non-public schools are private or church schools that are run by a person or legal entity. Private schools receive contributions from parents as well as subsidies from the state.

Compulsory education in The Slovak Republic lasts 10 years, from ages 6 to 16, and begins in primary school (*základná škola*). The education system comprises four main levels: preschool, primary, secondary, and higher education.

- *Preschool education* is voluntary, but is considered a part of the education system. It is designed for children two to six years of age. Preschools include kindergartens (*materská škola*) and special kindergartens (for children with special educational needs). The goal of preschool education is to complement family education, by providing activities that support the broader development of the child's personality, and to prepare the child for attendance in compulsory school. During the 2005/2006 school year, about 91 percent of children attended kindergarten in the year prior to compulsory school. In order to ensure that as many children as possible attend preschool, especially children from socioeconomically disadvantaged families, parents of children in the last year before compulsory school do not have to pay fees if their child is attending a public (state-supported) kindergarten.

- *Primary school* (*základná škola*), which begins for children when they reach six years of age, consists of two stages. The first (Grades 1 to 4) is comparable to ISCED Level 1, and the second (Grades 5 to 9) is comparable to ISCED Level 2. The Ministry of Education recently made provision for a "zero" grade for six-year-old children identified as not having sufficient maturity to benefit from school, perhaps because they come from a disadvantaged home background. However, not all schools are offering this option, and the extent to which it is being used and how it is being used differs from region to region. Where it is offered, parents can choose whether to enroll their child in this grade.

- During the first stage of primary school, a single teacher usually teaches all or almost all subjects. In the second stage, students are taught by several teachers who are specialists, generally in two subjects. After completing Grade 5,[2] students with special talents in academic subjects, the arts, or sports can apply for enrollment in

---

2   Grade 4 prior to 2009; this change was introduced by the Education Law of 2008.

an eight-year gymnasium, conservatory (art school), or sport school. At the end of their Grade 9 year, students take the national examination, called Testing 9, in both the language of instruction and mathematics. They may also, at this time, apply for further study at a secondary school, for which they are required to pass an additional entrance examination.[3] The majority of teachers in Slovak primary schools are female (88% in 2008).

- *Secondary schools* are of two types: general (the grammar school or *gymnázium*) and professional (secondary college or *stredná odborná škola*).[4] The grammar school offers academic courses in a variety of subjects and prepares students primarily for studies in higher education institutions. Students must study two foreign languages but can choose some optional subjects according to the school program. The period of study lasts from four to eight years. Students graduate from the gymnasium by passing the school-leaving examination called the *maturitná skúška*.

    Secondary colleges prepare students primarily for professional careers (e.g., in business or technical fields). Programs usually take four years to complete and end with the taking of a school-leaving (external) examination. Conservatories, a special type of secondary school, have six-year programs that prepare students for careers in singing, music, dance, or drama, and for higher education study. In addition to the study programs leading to the school-leaving examination, this type of school offers students the option of preparing for apprenticeships. Courses last two or three years and end with a final examination (the assessment is internal, not external). Students receive a certificate accrediting their professional skills.

- *Higher education* is conducted in three stages. The first stage (Bachelor's degree) lasts three years and is viewed mainly as preparation for the second stage of higher education. With respect to teacher education, teachers must complete the second stage of higher university education, with the exception of preschool teachers, who presently tend to be graduates of secondary pedagogical schools and social academies. Graduates of the first stage acquire qualifications that enable them to fill teacher-support roles, the exact nature of which depends on their subject specialization. During the second stage (Master's degree), which takes another two years to complete, students acquire their full teacher qualification. The courses include the pedagogy associated with teaching their specialist subjects. Students also experience teaching practice, which involves both observation and teaching in school classrooms. Students intending to become elementary teachers (i.e., teachers for the first stage of primary school) work toward a qualification that

---

3   Student achievement in both tests is one criterion for admission to an ISCED Level 3 school. Students who attain 90 percent or more for each test are admitted without having to sit any further examinations.

4   There used to be three types: grammar school (*gymnázium*), secondary college (*stredná odborná škola*), and secondary vocational school (*stredné odborné učilište*). This was another change brought in by the Education Law of 2008.

enables them to teach most curriculum subjects. Students wanting to teach at the second stage of primary school or at secondary school typically specialize in a combination of two subjects. In addition to studying at faculties of education, pre-service teachers can study at other faculties pertinent to their chosen subject areas.

On September 1, 2008, a new Education Act came into force. It set down changes to Slovakia's curricula in the first and fifth grades of the primary school, the first grade of the eight-year gymnasium, and the first grade of secondary school. Education in these grades is now based on a two-level model of curriculum. This consists of the national curriculum, which sets out the complement of subjects, compulsory and optional, from which schools create their own curricular program. Schools thus have autonomy in determining the program of study that they consider best suits the needs of their students and communities. Students in other grades have continued studying subjects under the old curriculum until they transfer to the next level of education.

13.3 Slovakia's Experience of Large-Scale Assessments

Slovakia's participation in large-scale assessments began with its involvement in *international* assessments after the country gained its independence on January 1, 1993. The country's experience of *national* large-scale assessments has evolved separately, however, with these being conducted in a manner distinct from that used for the international surveys. The national assessments focus, at the behest of educational policymakers, entirely on collecting achievement data (no contextual data) relating to core curriculum subjects and are conducted according to two-year cycles. Data are analyzed and reported only for the purposes of certification and school league tables.

13.3.1 National Large-Scale Assessments

Slovakia introduced its program of national large-scale assessments with the aims of monitoring the scholastic achievement of students at two ISCED levels, 2 and 3, and providing a mechanism for student certification.[5] This work was undertaken by a cooperative consisting of the National Institute for Education, which was responsible for the external portion of the school-leaving examination, the British Council, and the Open Society Foundation (headquartered in London). This cooperative was brought together with the aim of enhancing Slovakia's ability to develop assessments of student achievement in core subjects.

The program began with the administration of pilot assessments to representative samples of ISCED Level 3 students (Grades 12 to 13) during 2000 to 2004. The

---

5 The only exclusion from the assessments for student certification was the subject nutrition and health in education. However, the 2004 pilot assessment collected, from a representative sample of ISCED Levels 1 to 3 students, information on their knowledge, behaviors, and attitudes relating to nutrition and healthy lifestyles.

subjects assessed were language of instruction, foreign language, and mathematics, as well as subjects encompassed by the physical sciences and the social sciences. At the end of 2004, the entire ISCED Level 3 student population was required to sit external examinations in language of instruction (Slovak, Hungarian, and Ukrainian), foreign language(s) (English, French, German, Italian, Spanish, and Russian), and mathematics. A representative sample of ISCED Level 2 (Grade 9) students within the non-academic track was also required, at this time, to sit external examinations in language of instruction and mathematics.

Another important partner in the development of national assessments was the French Ministry of Education. It worked with Slovakia's National Institute of Education to conduct a large-scale assessment of primary education outcomes. In 2004, the two organizations conducted both the pilots and full-scale assessments of student achievement in two subjects—language of instruction and mathematics. The students assessed were a representative sample of ISCED Level 1 (Grade 4) students. This collaboration was not limited to test preparation and administration; it also involved statistical analyses and reporting.

Table 13.1 provides a summary of Slovakia's program of large-scale national assessments between 2000 and 2009. An important outcome for Slovakia of this program was the founding, on September 1, 2008, of a new institution—the National Institute for Certified Educational Measurements (NUCEM).

Table 13.1: Large-scale national assessments conducted by the Slovak Republic, 2000 to 2009

Year(s) of data collection	Name of assessment	Organization in charge	School subjects and student cohorts tested
2004 onwards	*Testing of 9** (series of external examinations taken by students at ISCED Level 2)	National Institute for Education[+]	External tests of students' achievement in language of instruction and mathematics, for entire population of ISCED Level 2 students (Grade 9, non-academic track), including students with special needs
2005 onwards	External part of the school-leaving examination *Maturitná skúška*	National Institute for Education[+]	External tests of achievement in language of instruction and foreign language (obligatory), as well as mathematics (obligatory) for all students taking the ISCED Level 3 school-leaving examination (Grades 12 to 14), including students with special needs

Notes:
* Tests assessing key competencies of reading and mathematical literacy (not used for grading) were introduced in 2008.
+ Became the National Institute for Certified Educational Measurements in September 2009 (www.nucem.sk).

13.3.2 International Large-Scale Assessments

Since participating in TIMSS 1995, Slovakia has taken part in all but a few of the large-scale international surveys of educational achievement. (One of the studies that the country did not participate in was TIMSS Advanced.) NUCEM has been responsible for conducting these studies in Slovakia. At first, responsibility for carrying out an international survey within Slovakia was given to the national project coordinator for that study rather than to a team of people. This approach resulted in delays in publication of national reports and thus a weak dissemination of the survey findings, a situation that limited the influence of the findings on educational and pedagogical reforms.

Recently, this work has been taken up by the Department for International Measurements within NUCEM (www.nucem.sk/sk/medzinarodne_merania). The department is made up of a unique interdisciplinary team, the members of which are open to networking as well as being competent practitioners with respect to all stages of comparative surveys (i.e., from design through implementation and analyses to reporting and dissemination).

13.3.3 Funding of Studies and Freedom of Expression

Most financial costs associated with large-scale assessments in Slovakia are covered by the Ministry of Education, given that the Institute for National Education was and NUCEM is a state-governed and state-financed public research institute within the educational sector. Agencies within the EU tend to meet remaining costs. For example, money from the European Social Fund was used to assist Slovakia develop its school-leaving examination while the Education, Audiovisual, and Culture Executive Agency (EACEA) has paid Slovakia's membership fee in the ongoing IEA International Civic and Citizenship Study (ICCS).

Generally, Slovakia spends more on the international costs of participation in the international surveys than on the costs associated with conducting these studies at the national level. For example, the national costs are usually about 80 percent of the study membership fee. Also, the expenses incurred by Slovakian schools that take part in these studies are generally not reimbursed. The only school costs that are covered are those for school staff who coordinate and administer the study within their school and who have to travel to receive face-to-face training in this work.

When implementing surveys, both national and international, Slovakia takes care to comply with the objectives, procedures, and quality controls stipulated within the design and administrative framework for each one. Slovakia considers adherence to quality parameters particularly important given that survey outcomes inform public perception of school efficacy and can be used for student accreditation. Slovakia is also mindful, with respect to quality adherence, of its obligation to the foreign institutions that help finance the country's participation in the studies.

The Slovakian national research coordinator for each study is required to prepare, prior to the release of the international report, a national report that is based on the format of the international report and the content of the international database and which covers matters considered important from the national perspective (e.g., major deviation in the Slovakian results from the international averages). After release of the international report, the national report is also published and made available in electronic form on NUCEM's website. The results of Slovakia's national examinations are also available on this website.

13.3.4 Reporting of Survey Results

The type of results of the large-scale surveys released to the media and the manner in which they are released are determined by the Ministry of Education. However, NUCEM's Department for International Measurements, which is usually also the national research center for the international studies, is free to communicate the results to members of the educational sector (e.g., teachers, teacher educators) as it sees fit.

During its first years of participation in the large-scale assessments, Slovakia tended, when reporting the results of these surveys, to focus on achievement data and outcomes, such as Slovakia's place on the country league tables. (For examples of this reporting, see that for TIMSS 2003 in Kuraj & Kurajová-Stopková, 2005, and for PISA 2003 in Koršňáková & Tomengová, 2004.) Although reporting of these outcomes continues to attract interest today (see, for example, Koršňáková & Kováčová, 2007; Ladányiová, 2007), considerable attention is now being given to the survey frameworks, research tools, and processes, as well as to contextual information (e.g., school climate, ethnicity).

Researchers, policymakers, and educators increasingly are seeing consideration of these matters as highly important because they acknowledge that the achievement results cannot be fully appreciated and understood without reference to this background information. That understanding, in turn, is vital for the drafting and implementation of effective national educational policy. Examples of reports taking what is known as a *thematic* approach are those by Koršňáková, Heldová, Kašiarová, Kuklišová, Swan, and Szobiová (2006) and Kubáček, Kosper, Tomachová, and Koršňáková (2004). Electronic media are also becoming an increasingly used means of disseminating information about the studies. For example, in addition to maintaining its official website with its links to the large-scale surveys and the institutions that have partnered Slovakia during work on these assessments,[6] NUCEM is supporting online networks

---

6   Refer, for example, to these websites:
     www.iea.nl
     www.pisa.oecd.org
     pisacountry.acer.edu.au

for social scientists conducting research on young people, including research relating to educational achievement.[7]

13.4 National Results, Impact, and (Expected) Long-Term Effects of PIRLS

13.4.1 National Results

Slovak students' average score on the PIRLS 2006 international reading scale of 531 points placed Slovakia in the top third of countries on that scale. All of these countries had average achievement scores significantly higher than the international mean of 500 points. Comparison of the Slovak students' achievement with the average achievement of the participating EU countries and the participating OECD countries positioned the performance of the Slovak students as average. However, the Slovak students' reading literacy ability was significantly better than it was in PIRLS 2001. The Slovak students were also relatively better at reading for literary purposes than reading for informational purposes.

Although the overall achievement of Slovak students between 2001 and 2006 improved, the percentage of students whose performance placed them below the lowest level of competency on the reading literacy scale (6%) did not change over this time period. Another 14 percent of Slovak students did not achieve above the lowest competency level of the scale. Thus, a fifth of the Slovak students who participated in PIRLS 2006 appeared to be functionally illiterate. This conclusion received support from the PISA 2003 and 2006 findings relating to Slovak students' achievement in reading literacy. In the 2003 survey, nearly 25 percent of the students were performing below Level 2. By 2006, this percentage had increased to nearly 28 percent.

Girls' reading performance in Slovakia was better than the boys', by 11 scale-score points. This difference, however, was lower than the international average difference. In general, a strong relationship was evident between students' attitudes toward reading and their level of achievement. A particularly interesting finding with respect to the gender results for Slovakia was the lack of significant difference between the achievement of girls and boys within the same categories of attitudes toward reading, even though the percentage of girls holding highly positive attitudes was considerably higher than the percentage of boys holding such attitudes.

As was the case in PISA, the PIRLS 2006 survey confirmed the strong relationship between students' socioeconomic backgrounds and their achievement. The difference in the achievement of students from homes with more than 25 books was considerably higher (65 points) than the achievement of students from homes with fewer than 25 books.

The larger number of sampled schools within the eight regions of Slovakia in PIRLS 2006 than in PIRLS 2001 gave greater scope for comparing the achievement of

---

7   See, for example, www.vyskummladeze.sk/index.php?lang=en

students across those regions. The difference between the best and the worst region was 40 scale score points. The lowest achievement scores were found in two eastern regions (Prešovský and Košický) and a region in the middle of the country (Banskobystrický). These regions were also those with the highest numbers of students either below or just at competency Level 1, a result that can be explained in part by the fact that the highest percentages of socially and economically disadvantaged students came from these regions.

The findings relating to how Slovak teachers teach reading are also particularly noteworthy, although not surprising. The teachers' responses on the PIRLS 2006 teacher questionnaire revealed that teachers were generally teaching their students in a relatively traditional way. They were using, as reading-source material, textbooks and workbooks, but usually only those containing literary content, such as stories and poems. Reading of informational texts, especially instructional manuals about how things work, and texts containing charts, diagrams, and graphs, was thus rare. In the main, students read aloud to the whole class, with teachers placing strong emphasis on each student's technique. The reading-related activities additional to reading aloud were, in order of frequency of use, students answering aloud questions from their teacher about what they had read, giving a summary of what they had read, and reproducing the content of a read text.

13.4.2 Publication of Results

The report detailing the Slovak Republic's PIRLS 2006 results (Ladányiová, 2007) was prepared and printed before the release of the international results to ensure that it would be ready for distribution on the day the international results were released. The national report covered information about the PIRLS study and its administration and presented a short review of the Slovak students' reading literacy within both national and international contexts. It also provided an account of the findings relating to how reading was being taught in Slovak schools. Policymakers and all schools that participated in PIRLS 2006 received a copy of the report, and it was made available on internet for all who might be interested in the results. A short "quick reference" summary of key results was also distributed to policymakers and journalists when the international results were released. Each school furthermore received, soon after release of the results, information about the performance of its students and how they had fared in comparison with students in the other participating Slovak schools. Schools also received some material indicating the implications of the findings for their teaching of reading.

Although the Ministry of Education had hosted a press conference at the time the PIRLS 2001 results were released, it did not do this for the 2006 results. Instead, the ministry released an official press statement about PIRLS 2006 and the results for the Slovak Republic. The National Institute for Education also, at this time, established a special committee responsible for communicating the results of studies and other matters to the media. Because the committee consisted of a small number of people, none of whom had been directly involved in administering the international studies, dissemination of information about PIRLS 2006 and its outputs was generally slow and limited. Consequently, only a few newspaper articles gave an account of the PIRLS 2006 results.

13.4.3 Impact of PIRLS 2001 and 2006

Since PIRLS 2001, awareness among educationalists and members of the general public of PIRLS has increased. Slovakia's participation in the PIRLS and PISA iterations has given greater prominence to issues associated with reading literacy in our country. This prominence is reflected in the increasing number of articles, books, and monographs dealing with reading literacy that have been published over the last few years.

Although the PISA and PIRLS studies tend to be mentioned together during consideration of the state of reading literacy in Slovakia, PISA usually attracts the greater degree of attention among members of the public and educational authorities. The reason why seems obvious. Slovak students' reading literacy skills emerged as much worse in PISA than in PIRLS. Whereas in PIRLS, the participating primary school students performed well above the international mean or on a par with the performance of the students in the EU and OECD countries, the secondary school students' average achievement score on the PISA reading literacy scale was considerably lower than the international (OECD) mean.

It is this poorer performance that has caused consternation, particularly among educational policy- and decisionmakers. It has led to criticism of Slovakia's traditional mode of educational provision and underscored the importance of educational reform. Various educational experts have examined and discussed the possible reasons for the poor reading achievement of our 14-year-old students. They have also emphasized the need for more in-depth analyses of both the PIRLS and PISA databases, given that little such work has been done. This lack is probably because Slovakia has only a few people with expertise in reading literacy and in the sophisticated statistical methodology used in the large-scale international studies. Those people with expertise in either or both of these fields also have limited time to do this work because of their commitments to other research activity. Nevertheless, the Ministry of Education, now highly mindful of the need for this work, has initiated further analysis directed at explaining our students' achievement in PIRLS and PISA. Time will show if this initiative is effective. The ministry is also looking to implement, within Slovakia's national assessments, elements of the frameworks and modes of administration used in the international studies.

To a certain extent, the impact of PIRLS is evident in the new curriculum documents that are gradually being prepared for the grades involved in the above-mentioned educational reform. The document setting out the state program of education for language and communication is just one that highlights new thinking about the teaching and attainment of reading literacy. The document states that the development of reading competencies goes beyond the traditional focus on reading technique. There is a need, for example, to ensure children gain literacy in informational as well as literary texts. (The PIRLS 2006 data revealed that 64 percent of students had teachers who had never used texts containing graphs, charts, and the like.) One of the new basal readers for the first grade of primary school explicitly states that some of the comprehension questions in it are based on questions used in PIRLS.

The new Education Act of 2008 introduced a very important shift in terms of educational achievement. It has positioned students from underprivileged backgrounds as students requiring specialized educational interventions involving professional and financial support. The Education Act also provides support for teachers and schools catering to these students. However, at the time of writing, the education reform was at an early stage of implementation, and it was agreed that its success would depend on how well teachers and schools could accommodate it. Also, some of the reform work (including preparation of curriculum documents) relating to the upper grades of the compulsory school system had yet to be prepared, let alone implemented. As such, it will be some time before we can ascertain how well these changes, some of which have been prompted by Slovakia's participation in PIRLS and other large-scale international assessments, are having an impact on Slovak students' reading proficiency.

13.5 Expected Future Activities

The Slovak Republic is participating in the next iterations of PIRLS and TIMSS. PIRLS 2011 will thus allow us, at the national level, to conduct deeper analyses of students' reading achievements across time and within particular contexts, while our involvement in TIMSS will allow us to explore whether and how reading abilities hinder or promote achievement in science and mathematics. We also intend to use the findings from these studies to gain a clearer picture of how equity within our schooling system is influenced by the languages of instruction, and to identify good pedagogical practices common to all. This endeavor is being made possible by slightly oversampling the target school and student population, and by making language of instruction an explicit variable.

We also, with respect to future publications, intend to provide a compendium of blocks of released PIRLS test items. These will be accompanied with clear notes for teachers on how to use the items with their students and on how the items might inform changes to their teaching practice. We also plan to publish a monograph devoted to reading literacy within the context of Slovak education. Issues will be considered from both theoretical and practical perspectives, and effort will be made to describe and discuss how schools can use ensuing understandings to tailor the new state program of education for use in their own teaching and learning programs.

13.6 Concluding Remarks

Participation in PIRLS is important for Slovakia for several reasons, including the fact that the country no longer conducts national assessments of Grade 4 (the PIRLS target grade) students' educational achievement. PIRLS offers the participating schools and teachers a benchmarking activity and a means of keeping informed about the overall achievement of their students within both national and international contexts. To a much greater extent than we have done in the past, we want to exploit the potential that our participation in PIRLS affords us (e.g., study framework, released test items, contextual information) to support and facilitate innovation in reading education in the Slovak Republic.

References

Koršňáková, P., Heldová, D., Kašiarová, N., Kuklišová, M., Swan, M., & Szobiová, E. (2006). *Čitateľská gramotnosť slovenských žiakov v štúdii PISA 2003: Správa* [Reading literacy of Slovak students in PISA 2003: Report]. Bratislava, Slovakia: ŠPÚ.

Koršňáková, P., & Kováčová, J. (2007). *PISA SK 2006: Národná správa* [PISA 2006: National report]. Bratislava, Slovakia: ŠPÚ.

Koršňáková, P., & Tomengová, A. (2004). *PISA SK 2003: Národná správa: Učíme sa pre budúcnosť* [PISA 2003: National report. Learning for the future]. Bratislava, Slovakia: ŠPÚ.

Kubáček, Z., Kosper, F., Tomachová, A., & Koršňáková, P. (2004). *PISA SK 2003: Matematická gramotnosť: Správa* [PISA 2003: Report on numeracy]. Bratislava, Slovakia: ŠPÚ.

Kuraj, J., & Kurajová-Stopková, J. (2005). *TIMSS 2003: Národná správa* [TIMSS 2003: National report]. Bratislava, Slovakia: ŠPÚ.

Ladányiová, E. (2007). *Čitateľská gramotnosť žiakov 4. ročníka ZŠ. Národná správa zo štúdie PIRLS 2006* [Reading literacy of Grade 4 school students: National study report PIRLS 2006]. Bratislava, Slovakia: Štátny pedagogický ústav.

Lukačková, Z., & Obrancová, E. (2007). The Slovak Republic. In A. M. Kennedy, I. V. S. Mullis, M. O. Martin, & K. L. Trong (Eds.), *PIRLS 2006 encyclopedia*. Chestnut Hill, MA: Boston College.

Chapter 14
The Impact of PIRLS in South Africa

Sarah Howie and Elsie Venter

14.1 South Africa at a Glance

The Republic of South Africa is located at the southern point of Africa. The Atlantic and Indian oceans surround the country on the western and eastern coastlines, which stretch almost 3,000 kilometers in length. South Africa borders a number of other African countries, namely Botswana, Namibia, and Zimbabwe in the north and Mozambique and Swaziland to the east, as well as the independent Kingdom of Lesotho, which is surrounded by South African territory. South Africa comprises an area of 1.2 million square kilometers, roughly three times the size of Germany. The landscape varies greatly, with desert conditions in the north-west (the Kalahari), dry highveld in the central to northern area, bushveld in the far north, dramatic mountains in the east (the Drakensberg mountain range), tropical forests and beaches on the north-eastern coasts, and Mediterranean conditions in the unique ecosystem of the Western Cape.

The country comprises nine provinces with six major cities—Bloemfontein (the judicial capital), Cape Town (the legislative capital), Durban, East London, and Port Elizabeth (all three are important sea ports together with Cape Town), Johannesburg (the hub of business and industrial activity in the country), and Pretoria (the administrative and ultimate capital of the country).

Prior to the advent of Europeans, the land area encompassed by South Africa was home to many African tribes. South Africa was a Dutch colony (settled in 1652). As a result of developments in Europe, the British took the Cape over from the Dutch in 1795. Seven years later, the colony was returned to the Dutch government, only to come under British rule again in 1806, recaptured because of the alliance between Holland and France (under Napoleon). South Africa exhibited many of the characteristics of colonial settlements. By the second half of the 18th century, the colonists, mainly of Dutch, German, and French Huguenot origin, had begun to lose their sense of identification with Europe, and the Afrikaner nation was conceived.

South Africa is a nation of approximately 48 million people of diverse origins, cultures, languages, and religious beliefs. About 79 percent are African, 9 percent white, 9 percent colored (people of mixed African, Asian, and white descent), and 2.5 percent are Indian.

South Africa is a multilingual country that recognizes 11 languages as official; most of these are indigenous to South Africa (South Africa.info, 2006). English is the most commonly spoken language in government and commercial environments.

South Africa has the most advanced, broad-based industrial sector on the continent of Africa (South Africa.info, 2009), but it is still behind other developing countries such as Chile (UNESCO, 2007). The gross national product (GNP) per capita is US$3,690, which is considerably higher than the GNP per capita of most other African countries: 34 percent of South Africans live on less than US$2 per day (UNESCO, 2007, p. 229). During the past decade, South Africa experienced a huge migration to the cities. Today, almost 60 percent of the population is urban-based. Mortality rates are very high. Life expectancy is 46 years on average, and the infant mortality rate is 53 per 1,000 live births (Mullis, Martin, Kennedy, & Foy, 2007, p. 26).

Poverty and HIV/AIDS are widespread in South Africa. Poverty is particularly acute among people living on the urban fringes and in the rural areas. The profile of the rural areas consists increasingly of households headed by elderly women or by teenage children, and containing young children and older relatives. These people are very poor, surviving on pensions and child grants, and for the most part lack formal schooling (OECD, 2007).

14.2 South Africa's Education System as a Context for PIRLS

In 1994, a change of government brought in an inclusive and democratic political system. Three overlapping principles regulate access to education:

- Access with no discrimination;
- Physical accessibility in terms of distance and safety while traveling to school; and
- Affordability for all, including free primary education (Department of Education, 2006b, p. 665).

There have been serious challenges to implementing these principles, particularly free primary education.

During the 2000s, the South African Qualifications Authority (SAQA) implemented a 10-level education and training framework, with Level 1 the least complex level and Level 10 the most complex (see Figure 14.1). The 10 levels are grouped into three bands:

- *General education and training (GET)*, comprising Level 1 and early childhood development (Grades R to 9)[1] and including the foundation phase (Grades R, 1 to 3), intermediate phase (Grades 4 to 6), and senior phase (Grades 7 to 9);
- *Further education and training (FET)*, comprising Levels 2 to 4 (Grades 10 to 12); and
- *Higher education and training (HET) and research*, covering Levels 5 to 10 (undergraduate to postgraduate degrees) (SAQA, 2005).

---

1   R refers to reception year; before learners enter Grade 1.

Figure 14.1: The South African Qualifications Authority 10-level framework

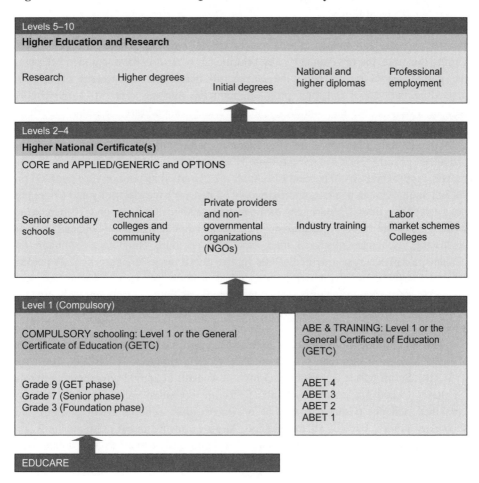

Source: SAQA (2000, 2005).

No formal requirements, other than appropriate age and parents' financial ability, exist with respect to children's progress from Educare to GET Level 1. (Educare is pre-primary education. It comprises one to three years of preschooling and is identified as Grades 000, 00, and 0.) While all children of appropriate age (i.e., ages 7 to 15; Grades 1 to 9) must attend school, many children do not benefit from pre-primary education because it is neither compulsory nor subsidized by government and because many parents cannot afford this level of education. Preschool provision is also scarce in many areas. Internal school examinations provide an avenue for learners to progress from Level 1 to the next level. At the end of Grade 12, learners who obtain a university exemption pass after taking the National Senior Certificate examinations are eligible to access tertiary institutions.

Education spending has grown by approximately 14 percent a year over the past four or so years and totaled approximately US$B19 during school year 2008/2009. During this time, the government's key priorities in education have included extending the no-fee school policy from the current 40 percent to 60 percent of schools, expanding the school nutrition program, reducing average class sizes in schools, serving lower-income communities, and increasing expenditure on school buildings (South Africa.info, 2009).

Even though education is the single largest category of the combined national and provincial government's spending (about 24%), poverty-related educational challenges remain. Approximately 40 percent of schools are classified as poor or very poor. Of the 26,292 South African schools, approximately 60 percent have electricity and 67 percent have telephone lines (Department of Education, 2006a). Only around 20 percent of schools meet the three basic prerequisites of telecommunications—connectivity-grid electricity, exchange telephone lines, and two or more computers—although the percentage varies across provinces; 2004 figures give a range of 1 percent to 38 percent (Holcroft, 2004). South African independent schools (private schools) are well resourced and often use cutting-edge technology in their educational delivery and community engagements. Independent schools comprise only 2.3 percent of the education system.

The net enrolment rate in South Africa at the primary level is 89 percent, which is a higher enrolment rate than that of most developing countries (UNESCO, 2007, pp. 255–320). South Africa has about 12.3 million students at 26,592 government schools. Of these, 19,260 are primary schools, 5,851 are secondary schools, and 1,481 are combined schools (Grades 1 to 12) or intermediate schools (both primary and secondary grades, but not all the grades). In government-funded public schools, the average ratio of students per educator is 31 to 8, compared to 17 to 5 in independent schools. However, various studies reveal that class sizes regularly exceed 40 students in a class (Howie, 2002; Howie et al., 2009).

14.3 South Africa's Involvement in International and National Large-Scale Assessments of Education

South Africa is one of 20 countries in Africa that have participated in major international studies organized under the auspices of the International Association for the Evaluation of Educational Achievement (IEA) and the Southern African Consortium for Monitoring Education Quality (SACMEQ). The last decade saw a significant increase in the number of large-scale studies of education being conducted internationally; it also saw an increase in the number of African countries participating in such studies. South Africa has participated in three out of the four Trends in International Mathematics and Science Study (TIMSS) surveys (1995, 1999, and

2003), one out of the two SACMEQ studies (SACMEQ II), and one of the two Progress in International Reading Literacy Study surveys (namely, PIRLS 2006). All of these are studies of student achievement. South Africa has also participated in all three Second International Technology in Education Studies (SITES M1, M2, and 2006), all of which are achievement based.

Participation in these international studies has not been an easy task for South African researchers. They experienced various obstacles during the country's participation in studies preceding PIRLS 2006. For instance, South Africa was the only African country to participate in TIMSS 1995 (see Howie, 1997; Howie & Hughes, 1998), but in 1999 the country was joined by Morocco and Tunisia (Howie, 2001) and then, in 2003, by Botswana, Egypt, and Ghana. However, in 2007, the government announced that South Africa would not be joining the TIMSS 2007 assessment. Controversy surrounded this announcement, and a number of different reasons for this decision emerged from the national organizers of the study and from the government. The lead research organization suggested that the reason for non-participation was that the timing of the research "clashed" with implementation of the interventions:

> The South African education system has undergone radical restructuring in its recent past, as several initiatives and interventions have been introduced—each one sharing the common objective of improving teaching and learning in all areas of the curriculum, but especially in mathematics and science. Bearing in mind the strain this intervention has put upon the education system (and more pertinently, the educators themselves), it is recommended that South Africa does not participate in TIMSS 2007, but rather does so in 2011 as this will allow the interventions to become embedded within the education system. This achieved it would then be more reasonable to measure South African performance in TIMSS 2011 to see how far the country has progressed. (Reddy, 2003, p. 120)

In a second instance, South Africa participated in SACMEQ's second study in 2001 (for more details, see Moloi & Strauss, 2005; Passos, 2009; Van den Berg & Louw, 2007). Seven African countries participated in the first study (implemented in the mid 1990s). They published their findings in individual reports (see more details in Kulpoo, 1998; Machingaidze, Pfukani, & Shumba, 1998; Milner, Chimombo, Banda, & Mchikoma, 2001; Nassor & Ali Mohammed, 1998; Nzomo, Kariuki, & Guantai, 2001; Voigts, 1998). South Africa was only able to participate in the second study (as one of 14 countries) after a quality assurance unit had been established within the Department of Education, the reason being that only government-related organizations can participate in SACMEQ studies.

With respect to national large-scale education-based studies, the legislative framework of the National Education Policy Act 27 of 1996 and Section 48 of the Assessment Policy for General Education and Training makes provision for conducting systemic evaluations of nationally representative samples of learners. The aim of these studies is to assess the degree to which the goals (access, equity, redress, and quality) of South Africa's educational transformation process are being accomplished and maintained. Numeracy, literacy, and life skills as well as the teaching and learning context were the focus of the first administration of the systemic evaluation in 2001, conducted at Grade 3. During 2004, a similar study was conducted at Grade 6 in language, mathematics, and natural science. A second round of implementation of the systemic evaluation program occurred at the Grade 3 level during 2007, while a Grade 9 systemic evaluation took place during 2009.

In 2010, a new set of Annual National Assessments (ANAs) for Grades 1 to 6 was implemented in all schools across the country. Both the national government and the Department of Basic Education had identified the ANAs as one critical lever for monitoring and improving the quality of education in South Africa. The first major step in this regard was the launch of the Foundations for Learning Campaign in 2008, which is designed to improve literacy (Grade 3), language (Grade 6), numeracy (Grade 3), and mathematics (Grade 6) in primary schools. An important aspect of the campaign has been administering standardized tests of literacy and numeracy to all Grades 1 to 6 learners. The assessments are based on test frameworks derived from the learning outcomes specified in the National Curriculum Statement of 2003 (Department of Education, 2003). Student performance in all learning areas was generally very low, and concerns exist about the quality of the assessments in terms of their design and implementation.

14.4 National Results and the Impact of PIRLS

14.4.1 National Results

PIRLS 2006 permitted South Africa to review the quality of reading literacy across all of its 11 languages for the first time and furthermore to have international benchmarks against which to compare the relative standing of each language nationally and internationally (Howie et al., 2009). The results revealed that the overall performance of South Africa's Grades 4 and 5 learners[2] was not comparable to the performance of the Grade 4 learners in the other 39 countries that participated in the study. The South African learners achieved the lowest mean performance in the study—approximately 200 points below the international average score of 500 fixed for the reading literacy achievement of Grade 4 learners internationally. Furthermore, the South African learners achieved lower scores than the participating students in other developing countries, including Iran, which was facing very difficult conditions at the time.

The South African learners were 11.9 years on average, which made them the oldest cohort in the study, although it has to be remembered that these were Grade 5

---

2   South Africa tested about 16,000 learners in Grade 4 and 14,000 in Grade 5. Learners in both grades could be tested in all 11 languages. The Grade 5 results are included in the international report.

learners who were compared to Grade 4 learners in other countries and therefore would have been about a year older.

PIRLS required that testing be undertaken in the language used in the respective schools that students had been attending for the past four years. In South Africa, language in education is a complex matter. Children have the right to be educated in any of the 11 languages. However, for a number of reasons, many African children experience little of their schooling in their home language. Those children speaking African languages at home are schooled in an African language for the first three years and then switch, in Grade 4, to English or Afrikaans. From Grade 4 onwards, the language of teaching and learning is, depending on the school, one or the other of these two languages, but students typically still have, as a subject, the language of the first three years. For the PIRLS tests, children wrote the test in the language that they had experienced during their first three years at school.

An analysis of student performance per language of all of South Africa's 11 official languages revealed that the learners who responded to the assessment in Afrikaans achieved the highest scores. Girls, on average, outperformed boys. Across all languages, Grade 5 learners achieved higher scores on average than the students in Grade 4.

Another analysis, this time between the students who completed the test in a language other than the one they primarily spoke at home and students for whom the test and home language were the same, revealed that English home language learners who wrote the assessment in English were the best-performing group, with an average achievement score of 458 (19.0) in Grade 4 and 513 (13.6) in Grade 5. Afrikaans home-language learners who wrote the test in their home language achieved an average score of 364 (13.5) in Grade 4 and 430 (14.1) in Grade 5.

Second-language English or Afrikaans learners also gained higher achievement scores than students learning in other official languages. Where the test was administered in English and in Afrikaans, the difference between first- and second-language learners was the most pronounced of any of the between-language comparisons conducted. The achievement distinction between home language as test language and home language as different from the test language was much smaller for all the African languages; in fact, no substantial differences in achievement were found (Howie et al., 2009).

In general, countries with the highest average achievement had greater percentages of learners reaching the higher benchmarks than countries with lower overall achievement. Only two per cent of South African Grade 5 learners and one per cent of Grade 4 learners were able to attain the advanced international benchmark. Of particular concern was the realization that almost half of the learners tested in English and Afrikaans and more than 80 percent of learners tested in African languages did not have "basic reading skills and strategies", an outcome that positioned the performance of these students at the lowest international benchmark.

14.4.2 Publication of Results

The national PIRLS 2006 results were released to coincide with the international press conference in November 2007. A summary report on the South African Grade 5 results was presented at a national press conference to which strategic stakeholders were also invited. The press release was followed by a day-long seminar presenting more detailed analyses of the results to more than 50 academics, policymakers, and practitioners in the field. The press release was extensively covered and made headline news in all the daily newspapers around the country as well as on the national television and radio stations. The interest was enormous, with the national research coordinators being invited onto talk-shows and news broadcasts on radio and television. Business media in particular followed the study in detail and covered it in a number of issues of their respective newspapers and periodicals. A year of presentations followed around the country to government, business, and the education communities. The old adage that "bad news is always news" and the fact that South Africa had the lowest ranking of all the participating countries kept the story in the media over a number of months. Even at the time of writing, we have noted new articles referring to the PIRLS 2006 results. A few international articles on the South African PIRLS 2006 findings have also been published, further disseminating the results.

14.4.3 Impact of PIRLS 2006

What have we learnt about the state of health of South African education from a decade of international studies and, in particular, PIRLS 2006? And what impact has PIRLS 2006 had on South African education? The "mirror" (see Howie & Plomp, 2005) presents the country with an "ugly face" of systematic and systemic failure in education. The problems of the past still haunt the present, and the new government has yet to see positive effects (on educational achievement) of the policy developments since 1994. Perhaps the conventional wisdom that it takes 20 years to change an education system is valid for South Africa. Maybe our expectations have not been realistic enough, and perhaps we have been too impatient. What we should be seeing, however, are indicators that the basic and essential conditions of an effective education system are firmly in place, thereby assuring us that learners' achievement will improve.

Monitoring of our education system through these international studies has failed to reveal any improvement in student achievement despite all the activities since 1995, hence the comment above about the time needed to observe change in an education system. What the monitoring has made transparent (from the time of TIMSS 1995 through to the latest study, PIRLS 2006) is the "Two Nations" of South Africa (Fleisch, 2008) and the bimodal distribution of the achievement data (Howie, 2002), where there is a small group of high-achieving learners and a second larger group of low-achieving learners. A small cluster of learners achieved the highest international benchmarks in each study, while the majority (80% and more) did not achieve the lowest. In PIRLS 2006 (and SACMEQ II), South African learners generally did not perform beyond the lowest benchmarks. It is therefore very important that studies such as PIRLS 2011 be undertaken to fulfill this monitoring function, which is the reason for South Africa's commitment to participate in the 2011 iteration.

Decisionmaking based on the international studies has been difficult to discern. While decisions and events follow release of information about the international studies and their outcomes, it is not always easy to categorically link these to the studies themselves (Beaton, Postlethwaite, Ross, Spearritt, & Wolf, 2000). For example, the curriculum revision was underway when the TIMSS 1999 results were released. Those involved in the curriculum revision process requested the reports and findings and fed these into the decisions made regarding the GET-band curricula for mathematics and science. This has also been the case with respect to the Foundations for Learning Campaign for literacy and numeracy,[3] where the PIRLS results and contextual information informed the design and implementation of this national initiative.

Dissemination of the national reports and the subsequent secondary analyses in particular serve the purpose of "enlightenment." The broader community, politicians, the business community and industry, the media, education organizations, and non-governmental organizations as well as the education system have all become involved in discussion about the results in particular and about education in general. As noted earlier, the PIRLS 2006 national research coordinators and other researchers on the team travelled around the country presenting the PIRLS 2006 findings to leading universities and provincial government departments as well as non-governmental agencies, businesses, and industry representatives.

The impact of the international studies on educational stakeholders in South Africa has differed over the years as has the reaction from various parts of the country's broader society. The results from the first international study in which South Africa participated (i.e., TIMSS 1995) led to nationwide concern and were interpreted as a problem emanating from secondary schools (Howie, 2000). The results were seen as a weakness in secondary school mathematics and science teaching rather than as a problem stemming from primary education (Fleisch, 2008). The results also saw the Department of Education recognizing the benefits of such large-scale assessments; their initial rejection of the role of international studies converted to acceptance and a collaborative stance (Howie, 2000; Howie & Plomp, 2005).

Findings from TIMSS 1999 revealed an enormous variation in the number of school days across South Africa (between 120 and 280 days depending on the school) and in the length of school days, with some as short as four hours (Howie, 2002). The government subsequently gazetted 200 school days per year, and stipulated that teachers must be on school premises for seven hours a day. Also, because the TIMSS 1999 data became available at the time when South Africa's national curricula for science and mathematics were being revised, the committees responsible for this work

---

3   We provide more information about this campaign later in this chapter.

were able to use the findings to inform their work on the revised national curriculum statements (see Howie, 2008).

We consider the third Minister of Education after 1994, Naledi Pandor, to be the government official who has thus far most recognized the value of South Africa's participation in large-scale assessments, whether conducted regionally, nationally, or internationally. She not only lent her support to these assessments but also recognized the difficulties associated with their implementation and the generally negative publicity that participation in them was receiving. The reaction of the minister brought about positive changes with respect to the implementation of the international studies and the use of the resulting data. The National Department of Basic Education now manages the SACMEQ studies directly, and it also supported PIRLS 2006.

The much-worse-than-predicted results of PIRLS 2006 for South Africa prompted Minister Pandor to introduce important changes to the education system; a particular focus was reading literacy. However, these initiatives need to be monitored to determine if they are achieving the aims driving them. The PIRLS 2006 data now serve as a critical external baseline for reading literacy achievement for Grades 4 and 5. Responding to questions raised in parliament about the poor quality of literacy and numeracy among primary school learners (National Assembly, Internal Question Paper 9/5/2008), Minister Pandor alluded to the initiatives that she had implemented to address these matters. She implied, and we concur, that the initiatives can be viewed as a direct or indirect consequence of South Africa's participation in PIRLS 2006.

Researchers nationwide have increasingly come together in order to improve the quality of the large-scale studies. PIRLS 2006, for example, was overseen by a national committee comprising leading organizations in the field and experts in reading and assessment. In addition, organizations such as the Joint Education Trust, the Human Sciences Research Council, and the University of Pretoria are now working more closely with the Department of Education during all phases—design, implementation, dissemination of the findings—of the international, national, and regional studies of educational achievement and quality.

The various initiatives that have been put in place include a variety of programs. For example, the Drop All and Read Campaign welcomes Grade R and Grade 1 learners into education by providing them with their own branded bags containing a selection of books that the children can read by themselves or that parents and caregivers can read to them. The program was implemented in 2008. Another program, launched two years later, is the aforementioned Foundations for Learning Campaign, a four-year initiative designed to improve the reading, writing, and numeracy skills and abilities of all South African children. The campaign, which has provided teachers and schools with clear directives on expected levels of learner performance, has centered its efforts on the foundation and intermediate phases of primary schooling in order to ensure that learners acquire and sustain a solid foundation for learning.

The Department of Education meanwhile has become strongly committed to providing schools with literacy resources. Over the last four or so years, for example, the department has sent engaging story books, written in all official languages of South Africa, to over 11,000 primary schools. The distribution of these books has allowed many schools to establish classroom libraries for the first time.

Other resources and documents that the department has distributed to schools in recent years include the following:

- The national reading strategy document, which outlines activities and approaches designed to promote and develop the reading skills of learners.
- A handbook for teachers titled *Teaching Reading in the Early Grades*, the purpose of which is to assist teachers to develop methods, approaches, and activities that will improve their teaching of reading.
- A "toolkit" for teachers that contains both reading resources and guidelines. At the time of writing, 1,000 had been sent to pilot schools countrywide.
- An early grades reading assessment that is currently being used by teachers in selected districts as part of a program to monitor progress across different schools. By 2010, the assessment had been written in Sepedi, Xitsonga, Tshivenda, isiXhosa, and English, and it has since appeared in the remaining five languages (isiNdebele, isiZulu, Sesotho, Setswana, and siSwati).

The recently implemented National Policy Framework for Teacher Education and Development addresses the issue of poor teacher development brought to light by studies such as PIRLS. Its position in South Africa's inservice and continuous training programs should ensure that teachers are now being trained to teach effectively.

To monitor whether learners' competencies are improving, the Department of Education is establishing baseline data on learners' achievement literacy and numeracy in the early grades. As part of the Foundations for Learning Campaign, primary school learners have been assessed annually via standardized tests. The resultant data are being compared against the established baselines.

The PIRLS 2006 data also revealed that more than half of the primary schools assessed in 2005 had no school libraries or classroom libraries and that just over 50 percent of children had no access to books at home. In the first quarter of 2008, the government announced that it was doubling the public library budget. The extent to which the PIRLS 2006 findings contributed to this development is uncertain, but the timing of this announcement suggests PIRLS did have an influence. The same could be said for the Ithuba Writing Project, which has distributed, since 2008, 2.3 million books in all 11 languages to schools. In 2009, a national weekly newspaper launched another national, large-scale initiative to collect and distribute books to children in need. Even if PIRLS did not have a direct impact on the advent of these developments, there is certainly a heightened awareness throughout South Africa today of the country's problems and needs regarding literacy.

14.5 Future Activities

14.5.1 Research and Publications

PIRLS 2006 was part of the Reading Literacy Research Programme, which was launched at the Centre for Evaluation and Assessment and funded by the Royal Netherlands Embassy. This program includes investigations into teacher education and adult literacy education as well as the conducting of a number of case studies of reading literacy practices in schools and classrooms at Grade 4 level (Zimmerman, 2011). The first phase of the program was completed in 2009, and several other case studies are taking place during 2011 and 2012. Master's and doctoral students are conducting secondary analyses of the PIRLS data, while members of the PIRLS research team are addressing key questions related to literacy-based policy (and implementation thereof).

Publication of the national summary report for PIRLS 2006 (Howie et al., 2009) is being followed by a comprehensive report containing all the components of the Reading Literacy Research Programme. Reports relating to data derived from all 11 language assessments will be published alongside nine provincial-level reports. These are targeted at policymakers at both provincial and national levels and will provide each province and each language with benchmarks against which to evaluate the impact of the Foundations for Learning Campaign.

Two doctoral studies were completed in 2011 (Van Staden, 2011; Zimmerman, 2011). The first study examined the factors affecting the performance of South African students across the five major language groupings. Van Staden's analyses employed multilevel modeling, and the theoretical underpinning for this study was based on Creemers' framework for school effectiveness (see, for example, Creemers & Reezigt, 1999). The second study was a set of case studies of schools, the students of which achieved each of the international benchmarks. However, because so few schools representing "typical" schools in South Africa met these benchmarks, Zimmerman (2011) established a number of South African benchmarks. The aims of the study were to identify effective classroom practice and to explain the type of performance found in PIRLS across all of the benchmarks. All funding for this research was secured during Phase 1 of the Reading Literacy Research Programme. It came from the Royal Netherlands Embassy; no funding was received from the South African government.

PIRLS 2011 is being undertaken in South Africa with very limited funding. Some funding has been received from the National Research Foundation, the SANPAD organization, and the Zenex Foundation. Another challenge facing administration of PIRLS 2011 in South Africa is the moratorium that has been placed on international testing to allow for the education initiatives to take effect before the country enters another round of assessment. This situation has delayed the PIRLS data collection by about a year and has put great pressure on the South African team to deliver the data according to the international deadlines.

14.6 Concluding Comments

If we fail to provide relevant and effective education to the poorest and youngest citizens of our country, we will likely doom them to an almost unbreakable cycle of poverty from which only the very brightest will escape. As Taylor (2007) observes, "... not only does a lack of skills put a ceiling on economic growth of the country, but poor communities are able to make little more progress under a democratic government than they were under apartheid" (p. 24). He attributes this situation to "inappropriate policies and an inability of a weak state to effectively implement its policies at the school level" (p. 24).

International comparative education studies use the world as an educational laboratory (Keeves, 1996) to broaden national perspectives and to raise expectations about what might actually be possible. They provide researchers in education with a means of supporting policymakers and others in the education system. Although education systems are embedded in national cultures and histories, they increasingly are being subjected to the same global forces transforming many other aspects of national life.

While exposing national achievements through comparison with other countries that have done better might bring discomfort, surely this can be borne knowing what is at stake and by appreciating that the knowledge can be used constructively for national reforms. Now that access to education and the right to learn have been established for the majority in South Africa, it is time to set key priorities for the country's future. If South Africa wants to succeed in a rapidly changing and competitive technological world, it will need to concentrate on developing its capacity to produce well-qualified human resources.

References

Beaton, A. E., Postlethwaite, T. N., Ross, K. N., Spearritt, D., & Wolf, R. M. (2000). *The benefits and limitations of international educational achievement studies.* Paris, France: International Institute for Educational Planning/International Academy of Education.

Creemers, B. P. M., & Reezigt, G. J. (1999). The concept of vision in educational effectiveness theory and research. *Learning Environments Research, 2,* 107–135.

Department of Education. (2003). *National curriculum statement.* Pretoria, South Africa: Author.

Department of Education. (2006a). *Education statistics in South Africa at a glance in 2005.* Pretoria, South Africa: Government Printing Works.

Department of Education. (2006b). *South African country paper.* Paper presented at the 16th Conference of Commonwealth Education Ministers: Access to Education for the Good of All. Retrieved from http://www.16ccem.com/

Fleisch, B. (2008). *Primary education in crisis.* Cape Town, South Africa: Juta.

Holcroft, E. (2004). *SchoolNet South Africa*. Retrieved from http://www.idrc.ca/en/ev-71274-201-1-DO_TOPIC.html

Howie, S. J. (1997). *Mathematics and science performance in the middle school years in South Africa: A summary report on the performance of the South African students in the Third International Mathematics and Science Study*. Pretoria, South Africa: Human Sciences Research Council.

Howie, S. J. (2000). TIMSS in South Africa: The value of international comparative studies for a developing country. In D. Shorrocks-Taylor & E. W. Jenkins (Eds.), *Learning from others* (pp. 279–301). Boston, MA: Kluwer Academic.

Howie, S. J. (2001). *Mathematics and science performance in Grade 8 in South Africa 1998/1999: TIMSS-R 1999 South Africa*. Pretoria, South Africa: Human Sciences Research Council.

Howie, S. J. (2002). *English language and other factors influencing Grade 8 pupils' achievement in mathematics*. Enschede, the Netherlands: University of Twente Press.

Howie, S. J. (2008). *Measuring the health of the education system: Lessons from international studies for South Africa*. Keynote address, presented at the Association for the Study of Evaluation and Assessment national conference, Pretoria, South Africa, July 2008.

Howie, S. J., & Hughes, C. A. (1998). *Mathematics and science literacy of final-year school students in South Africa: Third International Mathematics and Science Study*. Pretoria, South Africa: Human Sciences Research Council.

Howie, S., & Plomp, T. (2005). International comparative studies of education and large-scale change. In N. Bascia, A. Cummings, A. Datnow, K. Leithwood, & D. Livingstone (Eds.), *International handbook of educational policy* (pp. 75–100). Dordrecht, the Netherlands: Kluwer Press.

Howie, S., Venter, E., van Staden, S., Zimmerman, L., Long, C., Scherman, V., & Archer, E. (2009). *PIRLS 2006 summary report: South African children's reading achievement*. Pretoria, South Africa: Centre for Evaluation and Assessment, University of Pretoria.

Keeves, J. K. (1996). *The world of school learning: Selected key findings from 35 years of IEA research*. Amsterdam, the Netherlands: International Association for the Evaluation of Educational Achievement.

Kulpoo, D. (1998). *The quality of education: Some policy suggestions based on a survey of schools in Mauritius*. Paris, France: International Institute for Educational Planning.

Machingaidze, T., Pfukani, P., & Shumba, S. (1998). *The quality of education: Some policy suggestions based on a survey of schools in Zimbabwe*. Paris, France: International Institute for Educational Planning.

Milner, G., Chimombo, J., Banda, T., & Mchikoma, C. (2001). *The quality of education: Some policy suggestions based on a survey of schools in Malawi*. Paris, France: International Institute for Educational Planning.

Moloi, Q. M., & Strauss, J. (2005). *The SACMEQ-II Project in South Africa: A study of the conditions of schooling and the quality of education* (South Africa working report, SACMEQ Educational Policy Research Series). Paris, France: SACMEQ.

Mullis, I., Martin, M., Kennedy, A. M, & Foy, P. (2007). *PIRLS 2006 international report: IEA's Progress in International Reading Literacy Study in primary schools in 40 countries.* Chestnut Hill, MA: Boston College.

Nassor, S., & Ali Mohammed, K. (1998). *The quality of education: Some policy suggestions based on a survey of schools in Zanzibar.* Paris, France: International Institute for Educational Planning.

Nzomo, J., Kariuki, M., & Guantai, L. (2001). *The quality of education: Some policy suggestions based on a survey of schools in Kenya.* Paris, France: International Institute for Educational Planning.

Organisation for Economic Co-operation and Development (OECD). (2007). *Country background report: South African education.* Paris, France: Author.

Passos, A. (2009). *Teacher competence and pupil performance in Mozambican and SACMEQ upper primary schools.* Unpublished doctoral dissertation, University of Pretoria, South Africa.

Reddy, V. (2003). *Mathematics and science achievement at South African schools in TIMSS 2003.* Pretoria, South Africa: Human Sciences Research Council.

South Africa.info. (2006, December). *South Africa: Fast facts.* Retrieved from http://www.southafrica.info/ess_info/sa_glance/facts.htm

South Africa.info. (2009). [Website]. Retrieved from http://www.southafrica.info/about/history/history.htm

South African Qualifications Authority (SAQA). (2000). *The National Qualifications Framework and standards setting.* Pretoria, South Africa: Author.

South African Qualifications Authority (SAQA). (2005). *Draft level descriptors for a 10-level NQF* (Government Notice No. 28141). Pretoria, South Africa: Government Gazette.

Taylor, N. (2007). Equity, efficiency and development of South African schools. In T. Townsend (Ed.), *International handbook of school effectiveness and improvement* (pp. 523–540). Dordrecht, the Netherlands: Springer.

UNESCO. (2007). *Global monitoring report.* Paris, France: Author.

Van den Berg, S., & Louw, M. (2007). *Lessons learnt from SACMEQ II: South Africa student performance in regional context* (Stellenbosch Economic Working Papers 16/07). Stellenbosch, South Africa: University of Stellenbosch.

Van Staden, S. (2011). *Reading between the lines: Contributing factors that affect Grade 4 learner reading performance.* Unpublished doctoral dissertation, University of Pretoria, Pretoria, South Africa.

Voigts, F. (1998). *The quality of education: Some policy suggestions based on a survey of schools in Namibia.* Paris, France: International Institute for Educational Planning, UNESCO.

Zimmerman, L. (2011). *The influence of schooling conditions and teaching practices on curriculum implementation for Grade 4 reading literacy development.* Unpublished doctoral thesis, University of Pretoria, Pretoria, South Africa.

Chapter 15
The Impact of PIRLS in 12 Countries: A Comparative Summary

Anke Barbara Liegmann and Isabell van Ackeren

15.1 Nature and Structure of the Comparative Analysis

In the previous chapters, the impact of PIRLS 2006 was presented from national points of view. Although the authors followed, to a considerable extent, a given outline, they were also free to consider country-specific features in their presentation. As a consequence, the reports reflect some degree of heterogeneity. In this chapter, we endeavor to draw from these chapters both commonalities and differences across the countries with respect to the impact of the PIRLS 2006 findings on educational stakeholders, the media, and educational policymaking.

Five of the 12 countries included in this publication also took part in the study examining the impact of the findings of PIRLS 2001 (reported in Schwippert, 2007). These countries were England, Germany, Hong Kong, Hungary, and Slovakia. The authors of the reports for these countries were therefore able to consider the impact of both studies and how that impact had played out over time. Austria, Belgium (Flemish),[1] and South Africa took part in PIRLS for the first time in 2006, so their national reports naturally focus on the impact of that assessment. The remaining four countries participated in PIRLS 2001 and 2006, but not the impact study. Some authors also mentioned in their reports the impact of other large-scale studies in which they have participated, notably PISA and TIMSS.

Other than these differences, the structure and focus of each country chapter aligns with the approach taken in the first impact publication, thereby allowing comparability across time. For the same reason, this synthesis chapter also ties in with the approach of the corresponding chapter (van Ackeren, 2007) in the earlier publication. In format, the chapter follows the structure of the country chapters, and the information that we have drawn from these chapters is complemented with information from the international report on PIRLS 2006 (Mullis, Martin, Kennedy, & Foy, 2007), the country reports of the previous impact study (Schwippert, 2007), and the United Nations Development Programme's 2009 country by country human development report (UNDP, 2009).

---

1   Hereafter in this chapter referred to as Belgium.

15.2 General Context Data: Countries at a Glance

We begin by setting the 12 countries in context through brief accounts of their respective demographic and geographic characteristics as well as their political orientations. Eight of the countries are entirely European with regard to their geographical and political positions. The Russian Federation encompasses both European and Asian geopolitical orientations. Asia and Africa are represented by the Russian Federation, Hong Kong, and South Africa. The remaining country, New Zealand, is not easy to assign both geographically and culturally, but it tends to affiliate itself geographically with Australia and the islands of the Southwest Pacific, and it has its roots in Europe and the island nations of the Pacific.

15.2.1 Geography, Demography, and Politics

The countries involved in the impact of PIRLS project clearly differ with respect to their geographic and demographic conditions. The Russian Federation is not only the largest of the participating countries but is also, in terms of land mass, the biggest country in the world. Hong Kong is the smallest of the participating countries, with a land mass of only 1,104 square kilometers, yet it is also one of the most populated regions in the world (see Table 15.1). Countries with a low population density are the Russian Federation and New Zealand. Approximately 100 inhabitants or fewer per square kilometer are found in Austria, Hungary, Latvia, Slovakia, and South Africa. The remaining European countries have a population density of between 229 (Germany) and 486 (the Netherlands) inhabitants per square kilometer.

Politically, four countries of the former "Warsaw Pact" are represented, each of which is today governed as a parliamentary democracy. The breakdown of the Soviet Union led, for these countries, to a process of political restructuring at the beginning of the 1990s that affected most aspects of their public life and their education systems. Hungary, Latvia, and Slovakia are now members of the European Union, and the Russian Federation has been admitted to the circle of the world's leading industrial nations (G8).

The political demarcation against the NATO states from the end of the Second World War until the beginning of the 1990s is the reason why there was a poor participation of these countries in international large-scale assessments of educational achievement. Nevertheless, Russia participated in the IAEP-II study in 1991.[2] The authors of the chapter on the Russian Federation underline it as a "notable moment." They observe, "It is ... remarkable that the USSR allowed an international study on its territory, especially one that would see its education system compared with the

---

2 International Evaluation of Educational Progress; this study assessed the mathematics and science skills of samples of 9- and 13-year-old students from the United States and 19 other countries, using technology developed for the National Assessment of Educational Progress (cf. Board on International Comparative Studies in Education, 1995).

education systems of the West. Even today, a common belief amongst people in the Russian Federation is that the USSR's education system was the best in the world." These comments are also valid for Latvia, which was part of the USSR until 1991. However, Hungary has been taking part in IEA studies since 1970. At almost the same time that the Eastern Bloc states were liberating themselves from communist dictatorship, South Africa dismantled its system of apartheid government in the interests of democratic government, the establishment of which was formally marked in 1994 when all adult South Africans gained the right to vote in general elections for national government. Today, these countries, formerly diverse in their forms of politics and governance, are united by the principles of democracy, a change that naturally has a bearing on their education systems.

15.2.2 Economic Well-being

The United Nations Development Programme (UNDP) distinguishes the nations of the world by means of its Human Development Index (HDI), which includes gross domestic product, life expectancy, and educational level in its classifications. The index groups countries according to four categories: those with "very high human development," those with "high human development," those with "medium human development," and those with "low human development." Seven of the "Impact of PIRLS" countries belong to the very high category. They are, in descending order, the Netherlands, Austria, Belgium, New Zealand, Great Britain (UK), Germany, and Hong Kong. Slovakia, Hungary, Latvia, and the Russian Federation belong to the high category, while South Africa belongs to the medium grouping (see Table 15.1). Within the scope of school achievement studies, researchers also consider the extent to which the peoples within a country share in its relative prosperity, in terms of ease of access to educational opportunities and educational attainment.

15.3 Countries' Education Systems as a Context for PIRLS

The results of former large-scale assessments of educational achievement show that the structure and governance of education systems are relevant context variables for the differentiated evaluation of domain-specific performance. The results of comparative large-scale assessments also provide knowledge about the effectiveness of education systems—knowledge that can be used to inform educational policy- and decisionmaking. While the synthesis of this information in this publication might hint at reasons for variation in student achievement across and within countries, it is not possible to derive cause-and-effect chains from the reports presented. We ask readers to keep this caution in mind when considering background (contextual) variables as mediating influences on the impact of PIRLS within and across the 12 countries.

Table 15.1: **Landmass, total population, population density, and HDI of the 12 Impact of PIRLS countries**

Country	Population density (population number per km^2)	Population (in millions)	Size (km^2)	HDI 2007
Austria	99	8.3	83,879	**0.955**
Belgium (Flemish)	344	10	30,582	**0.953**
England	395	51	130,422	**0.947 (UK)**
Germany	229	82	357,000	**0.947**
Hong Kong SAR	6,320	7	1,104	**0.944**
Hungary	108	10	93,036	0.879
Latvia	35	2.3	64,600	0.866
Netherlands	486	16	41,526	**0.964**
New Zealand	15	4.1	271,000	**0.950**
Russian Federation	8–9	142.8	17,000,000	0.817
Slovak Republic	110	5.3	49,034	0.880
South Africa	40	48	1,200,000	*0.683*

Note: Human Development Index, bold print = very high human development (HDI ≥ 0.900), normal print = high human development (HDI 0.800–0.899), italic print = medium human development (HDI 0.500–0.799).
Sources: National reports in this publication; United Nations Development Programme (2009, p. 12).

15.3.1 Governance of the Education System

The interests of the different stakeholders in the various levels of the education system are coordinated in diverse ways internationally. Political structures and cultural traditions play an important role. Generally, the relationship between the education system and the individual school can be characterized, on the one hand, by schools having a strong measure of autonomy with respect to their administration and curricular programs. This development can be connected to quasi-market elements (designed to reap the supposed efficiency gains of free markets without losing the equity benefits of traditional systems of public administration and financing). On the other hand, a stronger accentuation of central governance strategies can be observed. Here, only a few competencies are decentralized.

This second model applies to (for example) Austria, which has a comparatively strongly regulated hierarchical school governance model, although there appears to be a trend toward reinforcement of the (partly) autonomous school. The same is true for England, where the majority of decisions regarding educational policies are also a matter for central administration. However, this form of centralization is combined with the transference of particular competencies to local administration and to school administration, respectively, as well as the generating of competition among schools (e.g., with regard to extended parental choice and examination "league tables", cf. 15.4.3 below).

This tendency is also described for Hong Kong, where strict centralization has been abandoned with the aim of achieving greater diversity in the educational infrastructure. Structures have been established that simulate elements of the market economy. Keywords are parental choice of school and privatization of educational domains.

As a final regulation system, the Dutch governance model is named, which is traditionally characterized by schools having a high degree of autonomy. The Ministry of Education, Culture, and Science ensures the financing of the educational establishments and determines standards in the core subjects. It also places certain controls on educational provision through regulations and legislation. Educational facilities and their maintenance are assigned to communal, regional, church, or other private school boards, which have further liberties with respect to the configuration of the curricula, the selection, advanced training, and recruitment of educational personnel, and the design of lessons.

In the federal states of Belgium and Germany, cultural sovereignty lies at the level of the member states (16 federal states in Germany and 3 regions in Belgium). Despite the states and regions being subject to fundamental centralized regulations, this form of governance has enabled the development of diverse education systems in the administrative areas.

Overall, the national reports show a growing tendency toward granting more autonomy to local units, right down to individual schools. This is evident, for instance, in the reports of the former Eastern Bloc countries Hungary and the Russian Federation. The authors of the Slovak Republic report describe these decentralization processes as being largely completed. This greater degree of autonomy now presents these countries with the challenge of ensuring comparability across schools.

15.3.2 Structure of the School System

The structure of a school system can be essentially characterized with regard to how and at which time in the school career students are allocated to different types of schools according to performance criteria. Germany and Austria both follow a tracked school system, which selects students at a very early stage of their schooling (Grade 4 or age 10) and assigns them to schools that require different performance levels. In the German *Bundesländer*, students have recourse to two to five different types of school. In Austria, students are offered two types that differ with regard to their focus.

The Dutch education system can also be regarded as selective, although the selection takes place later, after seven to eight years of comprehensive schooling or when children reach 12 years of age.[3] In Slovakia, children with outstanding academic or artistic talents or those who are especially gifted in sports can change to specific schools after Grade 4. Although, in Belgium, schooling for students after Grade 6 is also differentiated, all of the country's ensuing courses of education can lead to the acquisition of higher qualifications.

In the remaining countries, students receive joint schooling for a minimum of eight years. New Zealand stands out because students with special needs are integrated into the regular school system to the greatest extent possible.

In Germany, serious discussion about the problems (e.g., for educational equity) thrown up by selective school structures prevails. This discussion is made more cogent by the results of international comparative studies. This situation has recently led to a number of federal states reorganizing their school systems.

15.3.3 Particular Aspects of Educational Provision

Comparison of information in the national reports concerning selected aspects of educational provision—notably pre-primary facilities, age of enrollment, afternoon care, and language advancement programs—is difficult because not all authors gave detailed accounts of these matters. Therefore, the following provides only generalized descriptions; no effort is made to offer comprehensive cross-country comparisons.

- *Pre-primary education:* The facilities and institutions of pre-primary education are realized in various ways. While, in the Netherlands, for example, the "kindergarten" is integrated into the system of primary education and the final year is obligatory for all children (this equates to the second year of *basisschool*), most other countries *appear* (given the lack of mention of this matter) to have in place state-independent provision of pre-primary education. These facilities differ with regard to fees, age groups, length of attendance, and enrollment numbers. The authors from Latvia and Hungary were the only other authors besides the Dutch author to mention obligatory attendance at pre-primary facilities.

- *Age of enrollment:* In most countries, the age of compulsory school enrollment is six years. Exceptions can be found in the Netherlands and England, where the age

---

3   In the Netherlands, children can be sent to school as early as four years of age, where they attend the first year of *basisschool*. Compulsory school attendance begins at age five in Grade 2.

of enrollment is five years, and in Latvia and the Russian Federation, where the age of enrollment is seven years.

- *Afternoon care:* In countries where the school day ends at noon, an additional school-based care system is needed during the afternoon (e.g., in Austria and Germany). During the last 15 years, the care system in primary and secondary education in Germany has been continuously expanding, but its realization has not been uniform across the schooling system. In some places, additive and facultative care is offered; in others, children experience a "genuine" all-day school system. This kind of all-day school is obligatory for children in primary education in most countries and is mentioned in the reports from England and New Zealand.
- *Language advancement programs:* Mention is made in several of the country reports of special programs geared toward language advancement. In England, for instance, language and mathematical competencies are already evident within the preschool curriculum, and the country's National Literacy Strategy, which focuses on providing strategies for language teaching, has been in place for several years. In Belgium, preschool education concentrates on eliminating socially related barriers to educational opportunity, while in Germany there are various programs directed at supporting students with deprived as well as migrant backgrounds.

15.3.4 Experience of Large-Scale Assessments

Large-scale assessments provide a means of monitoring the efficiency of education systems, and their findings not only offer important hints about the effects of reforms on those systems but also give impetus to future innovation. In this section, we outline the diversity of developments relating to system monitoring and reform among the 12 countries since the 1960s. The impact of PIRLS 2006 must be seen with regard to this background of experience, as the extent of that impact in any one country is mediated by the country's familiarity with the kind of survey that PIRLS represents.

15.3.5 International Surveys

The 12 countries compared in this report can be divided into two groups on the basis of their degree of participation in international comparative studies (see Table 15.2).

The first group is made up of the "experienced," which are those countries with a rich tradition of participation in international studies. This group includes Belgium, England, Hong Kong SAR, Hungary, the Netherlands, and New Zealand. Since the 1960s, these countries have continuously participated in the numerous large-scale international studies relating to various areas of education conducted by the OECD and IEA.

The second group—the "newcomers"—includes those countries that began participating in international comparative studies within the last two decades. As we mentioned previously, the comparatively late participation of Latvia, the Russian

Federation, Slovakia, and South Africa is due to historical and political reasons. After implementing democratic government, these countries also set about democratizing their education systems.

Table 15.2: Overview of countries' participation in international comparative studies and implementation of national comparative studies

Country	International studies			National studies			
	Regular		Long tradition but irregular	Long tradition	Since 1990s	Last decade	No tradition
	Long tradition	Since 1990s					
Austria		Irregular				░	
Belgium (Flemish)	░						
England	░			░			
Germany			░		No consistent pattern		
Hong Kong SAR		░					
Hungary	░			░			
Latvia		░		▓			░
Netherlands	░						
New Zealand	░					░	
Russian Federation		░		▓			
Slovak Republic		░		▓		░	
South Africa		Irregular				░	

░ Applicable   ▓ Performance data without contextual information

Austria also belongs to this second group of countries. However, its tradition of participation in international studies needs to be seen in relation to its efforts to give schools autonomy, a process that did not begin until the mid 1990s. During this process, Austria implemented several means of assessing the quality of its educational provision, one of which is its participation in international comparative studies. However, as the Austrian authors report, this participation has been somewhat sporadic. The South African authors report a similar pattern of participation.

Germany cannot be readily assigned to either of the two groups, for two reasons. First, because the work of the Ministry of Education is exercised locally by the federal states, each state can decide whether or not to have its schools participate in the international studies. That said, a general agreement to participate has evolved throughout Germany over time. The second reason resides in Germany's long-term, strong focus on a humanistic (qualitative) tradition in educational research. It was not until the 1990s that Germany began amplifying its research endeavor by focusing on empirical methods of data collection and analysis.

15.3.6 National Surveys and School-Exit Examinations

The 12 countries also have diverse traditions of national monitoring of their students' educational achievement as well as a plurality of state-held school-exit examinations. Among the *experienced* are countries that have long conducted national assessments alongside the international comparative studies. This is the case for England, Hungary, and the Netherlands. The two other internationally test-experienced countries—Belgium and New Zealand—began conducting their national assessments during the last decade or two.

Nearly all of the newcomers (i.e., Austria, Hong Kong, the Russian Federation, Slovakia, and South Africa) established their national assessments when they began participating in the international studies. Latvia has refrained from conducting national assessments up to this day. However, it uses data from its state-directed nationwide school exit examinations as a means of feedback about the efficiency of its education system.

Germany is again the exception. Some of the federal states (e.g., Hamburg) regularly perform comparative monitoring studies, others (e.g., Brandenburg, Rheinland-Pfalz) carry out these studies on an occasional basis, and some have never conducted studies of this kind. However, all federal states use national data from the PISA and PIRLS iterations to monitor their students' achievement.

15.3.7 Quality-Monitoring Agencies and Feedback Systems

In order to conduct large-scale assessments at both national and international levels, most of the 12 countries have in place special institutions charged with carrying out this work. The only reports where no mention is made of specially established quality agencies are those for Belgium and Latvia. The ministries of education in these two countries take sole responsibility for educational monitoring.

The establishment of specialist agencies can be regarded as a general impact of large-scale assessments on countries' approaches to testing their students, in particular, and monitoring the quality of the education system, in general. As the authors of the country reports articulate, these institutions are entrusted with various tasks in addition to those associated with their large-scale assessment responsibilities. These additional tasks include development of national performance standards, preparation and conducting of school-exit examinations, and development and implementation of methods designed to monitor students' learning needs.

Data collected through large-scale assessments can help administrative agencies and policymakers develop and establish measures directed at improving their respective education systems. These data also offer practitioners (i.e., teachers and school managers) valuable information about the quality of their work. In order for insights drawn from the data to have a positive impact on schooling, countries must have in place a means of providing all relevant stakeholders with that information. As is evident from the country reports, the strategies being used to do this vary considerably.

The authors of the Belgium report, for example, reported a university-based initiative known as the Flemish School Feedback Project. Initiated in 2006, it assesses secondary school students in mathematics and language with the aim of developing a confidential feedback system for schools.

In England, the results of national tests are generally used with the objective of making them publically accessible for accountability reasons; the media publishes the results in the form of league tables. The controversy surrounding this approach is evident in England's recent attempt to bring in alternative means of performance review. Teachers can now request and conduct tests themselves in order to assess the performance of their students and, where necessary, instantly implement remedial strategies. However, as is occurring elsewhere in the world, strains on the public purse have led to increasing demand for accountability for money spent on education.

This conflict between autonomy and accountability has produced a "cooperative" or "blended" approach in Hong Kong and the Netherlands. In these two countries, assessment agencies forward the results of performance reviews to the schools. They also send selected results to individual students and parents. This approach not only helps schools develop diagnostic and remedial strategies for their students and tailor their curricula to suit their students' needs but also provides parents with accountability information.

In Germany, the manner in which agencies responsible for the large-scale assessments usually provide teachers and other educational stakeholders with feedback deriving from the studies has been criticized for its lack of accessibility. The typically complex statistical and linguistic presentations produced by these agencies have been seen as oriented more to the needs of educational scientists (researchers) than of educational practitioners (teachers). Teachers' associations have therefore, not surprisingly, been at the forefront of these criticisms. The presentation of the German results has furthermore been seen as "too general," meaning that teachers and school managers have rarely been able to derive "concrete" advice from this information on how they might improve their pedagogical practice and school ethos. Germany therefore has implemented a publication strategy that produces reports tailored to (and that are therefore accessible to and useful for) specific groups of educational stakeholders.

The experience in Germany makes clear the importance of quality, accessible feedback. Without it, stakeholders are unlikely to accept the findings of the large-scale assessments let alone use them to effect improvements in their educational jurisdictions, schools especially.

15.4 National PIRLS Results at a Glance

15.4.1 Reading Proficiency

Synthesis of the data on student reading competence revealed, yet again, marked differences across the 12 countries. Of the 40 countries that participated in PIRLS 2006, the two that gained the highest average scores on the international reading literacy achievement scale were also two of the countries involved in this impact study, namely, the Russian Federation and Hong Kong. The Russian students' score on the scale was 565; the score for the Hong Kong students was 564. The country with the lowest average score on the international scale was South Africa (302), which, of course, also took part in this present study.

With the exception of South Africa, the scores for general reading capacity in the considered countries sat significantly above the international average. Statistically significant improvements were observed in the performance of the Hong Kong, Hungarian, German, Russian, and Slovakian Grade 4 students between PIRLS 2001 and 2006. The opposite was the case for the Grade 4 students in England and the Netherlands (see Table 15.3).

Differences between students' average achievement scores on the two purposes for reading scales (i.e., informational and literary) were most pronounced in Hungary. There, students were substantially poorer readers of informational than of literary texts. Although no other country showed such a demarcation between ability to read one type of text over the other, the students in South Africa were also clearly better at reading informational than literary texts.

The authors of the national reports for Belgium and the Netherlands pointed out that these two countries experience considerable difficulty providing the type of support that strong readers need to become exceptional readers. However, in general, the Dutch students were a comparatively homogenous group with respect to their reading ability. This meant there were only a few students at the extremes of the proficiency scales. The country reports for Germany and Slovakia contain evidence of a comparatively large at-risk group, the members of which are described as "functional illiterates." In New Zealand, although an impressively large number of students were reading at peak levels, there was also a relatively large group of students with low levels of reading competence.

Table 15.3:   Summary of reading achievement of PIRLS 2006 students within the 12 Impact of PIRLS countries

Country	Average scale score	SE	Literary average scale score	SE	Informational average scale score	SE	Overall difference between 2001 and 2006 scores		Years of formal schooling	Average age
Russian Federation	565	3.4	561	3.3	564	3.3	37	▲*	4	10.8
Hong Kong SAR	564	2.4	557	2.6	586	2.3	36	▲*	4	10.0
Hungary	551	3.0	557	2.9	541	3.1	8	▲*	4	10.7
Germany	548	2.2	549	2.2	544	2.3	9	▲*	4	10.5
Netherlands	547	1.5	545	1.8	548	1.6	-7	▼*	4	10.3
Belgium (FL)	547	2.0	544	1.9	547	2.0	-		4	10.0
Latvia	541	2.3	539	2.4	540	2.4	-4		4	11.0
England	539	2.6	539	2.6	537	2.5	-13	▼*	5	10.3
Austria	538	2.2	537	2.1	536	2.3	-		4	10.3
New Zealand	532	2.0	527	2.1	534	2.2	3		4.5–5.5	10.0
Slovak Republic	531	2.8	533	2.9	527	2.6	13	▲*	4	10.4
PIRLS Avg.	**506**	**0.5**	**506**	**0.5**	**506**	**0.6**	-		-	
South Africa	302	5.6	299	5.2	316	5.1	-		5	11.9**

Notes:
* Difference was statistically significant.
** Tested grade was Grade 5.
Sources: National reports in this publication; Bos et al. (2007, p. 110ff.).

15.4.2 Factors Mediating Reading Competence

Educational literature has long identified several key factors that influence students' ability to achieve scholastically. Several of the factors given particular credence within the context of the PIRLS program of assessments are gender, language spoken at home, migration background, attitudes toward reading, self-perception of reading ability, and family-based reading habits.

- *Gender differences:* The authors of the country reports for Austria, Germany, Hong Kong, Latvia, and the Netherlands all reported gender differences in favor of girls. However, reference to contextual data makes clear that the reasons for this pattern of difference are country-specific. The Austrian and German authors attributed the difference to gender-specific reading attitudes. The Latvian author attributed the difference not only to gender-based attitudes toward reading but also to urban versus rural effects. She noted, for example, that the gap between boys' and girls' reading proficiency in rural areas has widened since PIRLS 2001 in favor of the girls. In the Netherlands, the gap between the performance of girls and of boys has lessened since PIRLS 2001. The explanation, however, resides in girls' weaker performance in reading literary texts.

- *Language groups:* In Latvia, New Zealand, and South Africa, lessons are conducted in various languages, which led to the PIRLS test in these countries being presented in more than one language (South Africa conducted 11 language versions of the test). Statistically significant relationships were found in all three countries between test performance, home language, and the language used in the test or during lessons. In New Zealand and South Africa, these differences were particularly noticeable. The other nine countries reported differences in performance when the language used during lessons varied from the language spoken at home. This association was most evident in the countries with a high ratio of immigrants (Belgium, England, and Germany). The authors of the Belgium report ascribed the weaker performance of children with immigrant backgrounds to the generally higher incidence of socioeconomic deprivation among migrant groups relative to non-migrant groups.

- *Reading attitudes:* Reference is made in the reports from Austria, Germany, and Slovakia to students' attitudes toward reading. In all three countries, the better readers amongst the girls tended to be those who held positive attitudes toward reading—who said they read for pleasure during their free time. The girls in these countries also read for pleasure more often than the boys did. In Slovakia, the performance of girls and of boys who held positive attitudes toward reading was highly similar.

- *Reading ability self-concept and family reading habits:* In the Hong Kong report, the author pointed out that the children who did not perform well on the reading literacy test were also the children who saw themselves as poor readers. PIRLS findings relating to the influence of family reading habits on students' reading competency also caught the eye of the educational and research communities as well as of members of the public in Hong Kong. Means of facilitating and supporting positive family reading habits have since been implemented with the aim of improving students' overall performance. This development aligns with recommendations arising out of the PIRLS 2001 findings. These strongly emphasized the need for schools and parents to work collaboratively to enhance children's reading skills.

15.4.3 Comparison with PIRLS 2001 and Other Countries

Differences in reading performance between PIRLS 2001 and 2006 received some attention in Sections 15.4.1 and 15.4.2. We refer readers not only to those sections but also to discussion in the national reports from England, the Netherlands, and New Zealand. The national reports for PIRLS 2001 and 2006 from these countries questioned the validity and comparability (England and New Zealand) and the objectivity (Netherlands) of large-scale assessments, both national and international. In their respective chapters in this current volume, the Belgian and New Zealand authors insinuated, amongst other things, that the differences across countries in the chronological and school-entry ages of the students who participated in PIRLS 2006 compromised the cross-country comparability of the results.

The German and Latvian authors drew comparisons between the PIRLS and PISA achievement results. These results made apparent that secondary school students in these countries were not, on average, reading as well as their primary school counterparts. Both countries have not yet been able to satisfactorily explain the reasons for the different performance of the 10- and 15-year-olds. In the Netherlands, the various datasets emerging from large-scale assessments confirm this decline across the two main schooling levels, a decline that has attracted a great deal of educational stakeholder and public attention.

The South African authors stated that results from TIMSS showed a small number of students performing at the high end of the achievement scales and the majority of students positioned at the lowest levels. The performance of the South African students in PIRLS 2006 confirmed this pattern.

Those conducting international assessments work hard to ensure that data can be validly compared across countries. However, there are inevitably country-specific conditions that lead some researchers and educational stakeholders to question the validity of these comparisons.

15.5 Reporting of PIRLS Results and the Impact of that Reporting

15.5.1 Reporting Strategies

The authors of the national reports described, in varying detail, how their countries published the results of PIRLS. Evaluation of the level of public interest in PIRLS across the countries is difficult because of the different measures the authors used to determine this. Although this diversity means that tendencies in publishing strategies can only be tentatively elucidated, two main strategies do seem apparent from the country reports. The first is that publication is positioned as a media event on a given day and time. The national research centers accordingly prepare reports, press releases, and packets of information and then present this material to media representatives. This approach seems to be the one most preferred by countries with little experience of international comparative studies. The second "strategy" involves information about PIRLS being released as a "piece of news amongst many", which then tends to go unheeded.

The country reports all mentioned efforts to bring the results of PIRLS to the attention of the research community, educational policy- and decisionmakers, school teachers and managers, and members of the general public. The publications produced generally varied in format and content in order to accord with the perceived needs of the group being targeted. Brochures and abstracts or summaries, detailed reports of the study, and news releases were also issued. In Latvia, the national coordinator of PIRLS held seminars for secretaries of education, school principals, and primary school teachers in order to present and explain the PIRLS results. South Africa also conducted extensive activities directed at having the results presented and discussed on radio and television. The South African national research center followed these efforts with presentations for government officials, business and industry representatives, and members of the education community.

Some countries (e.g., Belgium, Hong Kong, Germany, and Slovakia) stated that their national centers sent reports containing detailed presentation and analyses of the results to participating schools. Countries also made available websites providing information on the study design and the results and (in some instances) outlining for teachers the implications of the findings for teaching reading.

Table 15.4 provides a summary of the methods the countries used to disseminate the PIRLS findings. We again emphasize that the reports varied considerably in the amount and nature of the information on this matter. The table therefore displays *reported* activities; the likelihood that countries engaged in other dissemination activities cannot be ruled out.

The authors' comments in the previous chapters of this book suggest that media interest is not influenced by the quality or quantity of the activities. Rather, the nature of educational discussion about the results in each country seems to influence media responses. Some authors cited the principle of "best news is bad news" to explain why PIRLS seems to attract the most media response when students' performance is considered less than satisfactory. In England, for example, media interest in PIRLS focussed mostly on the growing number of children deemed functionally illiterate.

Several countries that participated in both PIRLS and PISA in 2006 noted that the results for the two studies were released almost simultaneously. The extent to which the findings of each attracted media interest seemed to relate to national student rankings on the respective assessment scales. It is striking that, in the Hungarian press, PISA attracted more attention due to *poor* results while in New Zealand the results of PISA were emphasized because of students' *high* ranking on the achievement scales. The Netherlands' authors also reported that the Dutch Ministry of Education took a substantially greater interest in the PISA than in the PIRLS results. In Austria, PISA's "recognition value" was seen as the reason for the greater attention paid to it in the media.

Most country authors reported efforts to make the PIRLS results known within a broad public context. However, only a few reported an advanced feedback culture with respect to the schools that participate in large-scale assessments such as PIRLS. The only countries in which schools were said to receive detailed reports and explanations of the results were Belgium, England, Germany, and Slovakia. The German authors explained that the emphasis on feedback is a deliberate effort to garner practitioner support for participation in large-scale assessments. As the report's authors pointed out,

Germany has only relatively recently begun participating in such studies, which means that many practitioners are still somewhat unfamiliar with them and so need to have the benefits of participation illustrated for them. However, a feedback culture is also reported in Belgium and England, where participation in and the value of large-scale assessments have long been widely accepted.

Overall, no clear cross-national pattern can be discerned with respect to reporting the results of PIRLS and other large-scale assessments. It seems that neither a country's ranking on achievement scales nor its experience of large-scale assessments offers factors prompting specific reporting strategies.

Table 15.4:   Strategies countries reported using to disseminate PIRLS findings

Country	Web-site**	Press confer-ences/ press release	Symposia with explana-tions for stake-holders, the educational community, etc.	Publications for the broader public (jour-nalists, par-ents, educa-tional practi-tioners)	Publica-tions for research commu-nities	School feed-back	Public interest (media)
Austria	■	■	■	■	■		Low
Belgium (FL)	■					■	Low
England		■			■		Low
Germany		■		■			Low
Hong Kong SAR	■	■	■	■			High
Hungary					■		Low
Latvia		■	■	■		***	High
Netherlands		■	■	■			Low
New Zealand			■			***	Low
Russian Federation*							Not specified
Slovak Republic	■	■		■			Low
South Africa		■	■	■	■		High

Notes:
* The Russian report did not mention activities.
** Most country reports refer to summaries or full versions of the national reports available as a web resource. Mentioned here are only those countries that describe websites covering the PIRLS survey.
*** National report was sent to the participating schools.

■ Reported   □ Not reported; cannot be ruled out

15.5.2 Impact on Educational Policymaking

The decisions that educational policymakers and government politicians make about reforms to an education system cannot be said to be informed by the results of just one study. The influences on policy decisions are, of course, much more complex than that, and each decision will be a product of particular socio-political and educational contexts. However, the national reports reveal that all countries were endeavoring to determine policy with the support of research evidence. Doing this is more easily accomplished for some types of policy than others, and likewise with respect to different research outcomes. Single reform measures, such as those directed at improving reading abilities in elementary and primary schools, may be more readily attributable to PIRLS than to other studies, such as TIMSS or PISA, which focus on broader spheres of educational competency.

The Netherlands' authors ascribed the general lack of interest among policymakers in the results of PIRLS to an overly large amount of data accruing out of numerous detailed comparisons of performance. Germany and New Zealand tell of little acceptance due to the complexity of the design of the study and its reports. Both countries have therefore invested considerable effort in simplifying the accessibility of the data and explaining their implications in more, but clearer, detail.

Russia and South Africa essentially agreed to participate in PIRLS 2006 because they wanted to assess if previous reforms to their education systems were having the desired effect. In Russia, the PIRLS results were interpreted as a confirmation not only of successful restructuring of the education system (e.g., extending primary education from three to four years' duration) but also (and more importantly) of efforts to enhance the quality of primary education: more self-directed and active learning on the part of students, less reproduction of teacher-fed knowledge, and greater adherence to creativity-enhancing pedagogy and discovery learning.

The authors of the South African national report, in contrast, described bitter disappointment. The restructuring of the education system since 1995 had raised hopes of improved socioeconomic standing among impoverished demographic groups occasioned by greater equity of student access to higher educational levels. However, the PIRLS 2006 data revealed little evidence of this. The authors of the South African report concluded: "The problems of the past still haunt the present, and the new government has yet to see positive effects (on educational achievement) of the policy developments since 1994. Perhaps the conventional wisdom that it takes 20 years to change an educational system is valid for South Africa."

Generally, those countries that had only very recently begun participating in large-scale assessments perceived a relatively high degree of public interest in the outcomes of PIRLS. That interest seemed to focus primarily on educational problems made apparent by the results and on whether the aims driving prior reforms to the education system were being realized.

15.6 Impact of PIRLS

Considerable variation was again evident in the country reports. Some authors detailed nearly all reforms to their country's education system and educational policy of previous years; others listed only those changes perceived as directly influenced by the findings of PIRLS. Commentary on the extent to which PIRLS had influenced educational "inputs" and "outputs" strategies was also variable, as were reports of intentions to engage in further reading-related research. Therefore, once more, what we offer here is a cross-national summative account that presents tendencies rather than sureties. (For a country by country detailing of the authors' perceived impacts of PIRLS and other large-scale assessments on their countries' education systems and schooling, on the inputs and outputs of those systems, and on future research initiatives, see Table 15.5.).

15.6.1 Impact on Schools' Context and Input Quality

- *Quality of instruction:* In many countries, the impact of the PIRLS results was interpreted as an indication of the need to improve the quality of reading instruction. The Austrian, Hong Kong, and Latvian authors all wrote of the need for schools to have a standardized understanding of best practice with respect to reading-related pedagogy and for teachers to have at hand strategies that would enable them to tailor reading approaches to the needs of individual children.
- *The curriculum:* The Austrian, English, Hong Kong, Hungarian, New Zealand, and Slovakian authors all pointed to changes to the curriculums of their countries that they considered had been influenced by PIRLS. Some of the changes had already been implemented at the time of writing, others were to be implemented, and others again were being mooted. In Hungary, for example, from the start of school year 2008/2009, reading lessons were extended into Grades 5 and 6 classroom programs. Critics, however, fear that this change is disadvantaging strong readers. Hong Kong was aiming at improving the reading abilities of children across all subjects of the curriculum. In New Zealand, a revised national curriculum was implemented in 2010, and by 2011 an equivalent curriculum had been introduced in schools where Māori is the language of instruction.
- *Structure of the education system:* In some countries, the PIRLS results led to discussion about and implementation of changes to the structure of the education system. Extending the duration and therefore influence of pre-primary education was being sought in Austria (an obligatory free year at preschool for five-year-olds), Germany, and Russia. Latvia, meanwhile, was planning to lower the compulsory school-entry age from seven to six years. The Hungarian authors reported discussion about shortening joint primary education (i.e., the period before students enter different educational tracks) from eight to six years in order to give students opportunity to develop stronger skills in the various tracked courses of education on offer. In contrast to this, German politicians and researchers were discussing extending the period of joint schooling.

Table 15.5: Summary of impact of PIRLS 2006 on policy decisionmaking in the 12 countries

Country	Context and input qualities					Process- and output-centered strategies				
	Quality of instruction	Curriculum	Structure of the school system/ education system	Teacher education and/or pedagogical recommendations for teachers	Resources	Quality agencies	Monitoring	Reading programs	Programs for special groups	Standards
Austria	Concept for individualization of instruction	Planning "reading education" as a cross-sectional topic	One obligatory year of kindergarten beginning in 2010; evaluation of the school entrance age	Intention to have PIRLS-related topics part of in-service training		Establishment of the Coordination Center for Reading	Assessment of school readiness every three years	Early reading socialization, reading partnerships, school libraries, development of a diagnostic tool (start of primary education)	Strategies for supporting children with German as a second language and all children with problems, deficits, learning disorders, etc.	Development of linguistic competencies at the beginning of primary education; educational standards for Grade 4 in German and mathematics
Belgium (Flemish)									Support of children performing well is planned	
England		Revision of the national curriculum for primary schools		Modifying the National Literacy Strategy to give greater flexibility to schools to organize their teaching; programs for increasing teachers' knowledge of books and enjoyment of reading and of extending the creative use of children's literature				Designated 2008 as the National Year of Reading; "book gifting" programs run by a national charity	Initiatives such as Every Child a Reader to reduce social inequalities in education, and Boys into Books to foster positive attitudes toward reading among boys	

Country	Context and input qualities					Process- and output-centered strategies				
	Quality of instruction	Curriculum	Structure of the school system/ education system	Teacher education and/or pedagogical recommendations for teachers	Resources	Quality agencies	Monitoring	Reading programs	Programs for special groups	Standards
Germany	Programs to enhance reading instruction (e.g., Pro.Lesen)		Expanding of all-day schooling; fostering the quality of preschool education, child care, and advancement	Implementing within teacher education (pre- and inservice) programs featuring strategies on how to teach according to competency-based educational standards; development of diagnostic competencies and ability to deal with heterogeneity and promote students' individual learning		Founding of the Institute for Educational Progress (IQB)	Comparative assessments at Levels 3 to 8; introduction of a biennial national education report		Programs focused on low-performing students	Implementation of National Standards
Hong Kong SAR	Emphasizing the task of the 2000 Education Reform, which focuses on variety and high-quality teaching methods	"Reading to learn" as a key learning objective for students		Programs to update teachers' knowledge with regard to developing students' reading skills, attitudes, and habits	More resources in primary schools to help promote reading abilities			Guidebook for parents to support children's positive reading attitudes; reading activities for the public supported by HK Education City	Reading programs for boys and for children with disabilities	
Hungary		Extending official teaching of reading into Grades 5 and 6 (instead of until Grade 4)		Development of a web-based formative assessment for Grades 1 to 6			Annual national assessment focussing on skill development (competency-based programs)			

| Country | Context and input qualities | | | | | Process- and output-centered strategies | | | | |
	Quality of instruction	Curriculum	Structure of the school system/ education system	Teacher education and/or pedagogical recommendations for teachers	Resources	Quality agencies	Monitoring	Reading programs	Programs for special groups	Standards
Latvia	Pedagogical recommendations for teachers in Grades 1 to 4 on how to unify instruction of spoken and written language		Closing of very small schools; lowering the school-starting age							
Netherlands				Policy initiatives on the topics of teachers and school leadership			Annual monitoring of students' performance in mathematics and reading		Policy initiatives on the topics of special education and advanced readers	Development of standards at the end of primary education
New Zealand		Development and implementation of the New Zealand Curriculum		Targeting teacher-focus groups with the aim of making PIRLS information more relevant to teachers' practice			Annual monitoring of students' performance in Years 1 to 8		Development of the Māori Education Strategy and the Pasifika Education Plan to improve educational outcomes for Māori and Pasifika*	Development and implementation of the National Standards
Russian Federation	Transfer from reproductive teaching methods to active and creative methods		Changing primary education to a four-year program (instead of both four- and three-year programs); creating a preschool system	Introducing different programs and textbooks at schools			Review of the system for assessing students' achievements			

Country	Context and input qualities						Process- and output-centered strategies			
	Quality of instruction	Curriculum	Structure of the school system/ education system	Teacher education and/or pedagogical recommendations for teachers	Resources	Quality agencies	Monitoring	Reading programs	Programs for special groups	Standards
Slovakia		Development and implementation of The State Program of Education with regard to reading competencies			Professional and financial support for students with special needs and underprivileged backgrounds as well as for their teachers, and schools					
South Africa				Providing teachers and schools with clear directives on expected levels of learner performance; teachers handbook to assist teachers with respect to methods, approaches, and reading activities	Supporting schools to establish classroom libraries; school bags with a selection of books for Grade R and Grade 1 learners; doubling of the public library budget		Development of an early grade reading assessment instrument and establishing baseline data on learners' achievement in the early grades; annual assessment of primary school learners	National Reading Strategy that outlines activities for and approaches to developing reading skills		Development and implementation of clear directives on expected levels of learner performance

Note: * Pasifika refer to people who come from or identify with the island nations of the South Pacific.

- *Teacher education:* Measures designed to enhance the quality of teacher education were reported in the chapters on England, Germany, and Hong Kong. Particular aims were improving teachers' understanding of how children learn to read and helping teachers design lessons conducive to improving and assessing students' reading abilities. Other countries (e.g., Russia, South Africa) were developing programs or handbooks directed at helping teachers enhance their reading instruction.

- *Resourcing:* In Hong Kong, the PIRLS results were said to have had a direct influence on the government's decision to increase its funding of primary education. Slovakia was committed to increasing the resources necessary to support children from disadvantaged home backgrounds or with special educational needs. South Africa had begun supporting schools and primary students by providing gratis copies of books, while in Hong Kong a public awareness campaign was stressing the need for parents to support their children's learning, especially their reading endeavor, both at school and at home.

15.6.2 Impact on Process and Output-Centered Strategies

- *Process factors:* Many countries reported having in place programs promoting reading abilities or developing programs in response to the PIRLS results. These kinds of overarching programs are examples of process factors because their aim is to facilitate appreciation of reading not only in schools but also throughout society. These initiatives are either directed at all students (e.g., in Hong Kong) or are especially designed for certain groups of students, as in England, which targets, via initiatives such as "Every Child a Reader", students considered at risk of educational under-achievement or failure. Austria has reading partnerships (adults reading aloud to students) as well as support for teachers of a kind that helps them use different types of reading materials when teaching.

- *Outputs:* Discussion about the results of large-scale comparative studies led to several countries either developing and strengthening or reviewing existing and often long-extant means of evaluating the performance of their education systems. (The first group of countries included Austria, Germany, and South Africa; the second England, Hungary, New Zealand, and Russia.) These output strategies embraced system monitoring, educational reporting, and the development and inspection of educational standards. Austria had developed standards against which to monitor, every three years, the language competency of children in preschools. In the Netherlands, the PIRLS results were being seen as an ancillary means of tracking the reading achievement of students during their primary schooling. This is because the cohort of primary school students targeted by the PIRLS assessments (fourth-graders) does not correspond to the cohort of primary school students assessed against Dutch national standards of competency. This assessment takes place toward the end of *basisschool* (Grade 8), when most children are around 12 years of age. With data from both the international and national assessments showing a decline in reading performance between Grades 4 and 8, Dutch students in every grade of primary education are now being assessed against national standards.

- *Further research:* Nearly all of the 12 countries were engaged in some form of secondary analyses of the PIRLS data and most were either committed to or interested in participating in PIRLS 2011. The Belgium author advised that Belgium would not take part in PIRLS 2011 because of the current financial crisis, and South Africa questioned future participation for the same reason. The Hong Kong authors signaled Hong Kong's intention to engage in extensive research on teaching quality, the Belgian authors said Belgium intended to analyze the extent to which individual schools had used the results to inform pedagogical practice and classroom reading programs, and the Hungarian author reported that Hungary was implementing a large-scale evaluation of a web-based program designed to assist teachers monitor their students' reading abilities.

15.7 Concluding Comments

The comparative study presented in this chapter has focused on the impact of the PIRLS 2006 results on education as perceived and described by the authors of the 12 country reports. More specifically, we have, in this chapter, endeavored to provide an overview of the similarities and differences in impact across the participating countries on various levels of educational policy, educational administration, and educational research. Given the different geographical, historical, political, and educational contexts evident in each country, effort to draw conclusions from this synthesis of cross-country experience must always be seen and interpreted with reference to the specific situation of each country.

The extent to which reactions to the results of PIRLS can differ across countries and how they are characterized by the above-mentioned contexts can be briefly summarized by bringing to the fore the reports from Hong Kong and the Russian Federation. The students in both countries who participated in PIRLS 2006 achieved, on average, outstanding results on the PIRLS assessment. Both countries moreover saw a marked increase in their students' average literacy-scale score points between PIRLS 2001 and PIRLS 2006. However, while the authors from Hong Kong described numerous additional research projects and reported administrative measures aimed at further improving the reading abilities of their students, Russia seemed content with the results, an attitude that the authors of the Russian chapter appeared to view as unwise complacency. They argued that Russia's educational policymakers and administrators seem to regard the PIRLS results as a verification of the educational reforms initiated since 1995 and therefore see no need to further consider what lessons for educational improvement might be drawn from the results.

The perceived responses to PIRLS in these two countries also suggest that different patterns of reaction can be identified. For some countries, the results of PIRLS appeared to be serving as a means of legitimating policy implementations and/or providing a measure of accountability for investment in educational programs and interventions directed at producing certain outcomes (tactical interest). Other countries, however, were apparently using the data to monitor the quality of their schools and were then using the information derived from that process to effect improvements to their systems and practice of education. It thus seems that the results of large-scale assessments not only have direct or indirect effects on the processes of quality development of education systems but also deliver important information on how well those developments are achieving their intended purpose.

We consider that our comparative analysis has highlighted (just as the corresponding analysis in the PIRLS 2001 impact report did) the interplay of research tradition, controversy over research methodology, and the need to interpret results within the current sociopolitical contexts of the respective countries. Although no causal connections can be made on the basis of this study, the factors that appear to mediate the impact of PIRLS on educational policy and practice also align with those elucidated in the previous impact study (see Figure 15.1). This alignment points to the necessity and fruitfulness of engaging in ongoing research into the influence of the results of large-scale assessments on education systems worldwide.

Figure 15.1: Selected factors possibly influencing the impact of PIRLS in the 12 participating countries

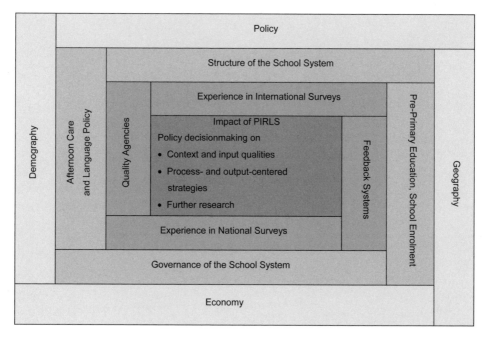

References

Board on International Comparative Studies in Education (BICSE). (1995). *International comparative studies in education: Descriptions of selected large-scale assessments and case studies*. Retrieved from http://www.nap.edu/openbook. php?record_ id=9174&page=R1

Bos, W., Hornberg, S., Arnold, K.-H., Faust, G., Fried, L., Lankes, E.-M., Schwippert, K., & Valtin, R. (Eds.). (2007). *IGLU 2006: Lesekompetenzen von Grundschülern in Deutschland im internationalen Vergleich* [IGLU 2006: Reading competencies of primary students in Germany in international comparison]. Münster, Germany: Waxmann.

Mullis, I. V. S., Martin, M. O., Kennedy, A. M., & Foy, P. (2007). *PIRLS 2006 international report: IEA's Progress in International Reading Literacy Study in primary schools in 40 countries*. Chestnut Hill, MA: Boston College.

Schwippert, K. (Ed.). (2007). *Progress in reading literacy: The impact of PIRLS 2001 in 13 countries*. Münster, Germany: Waxmann.

United Nations Development Programme (UNDP). (2009). *Human development report 2009: Summary*. New York: Author.

van Ackeren, I. (2007). Comparative synthesis. In K. Schwippert (Ed.), *Progress in reading literacy: The impact of PIRLS 2001 in 13 countries* (pp. 243–264). Münster, Germany: Waxmann.

Chapter 16
Concluding Remarks

Jenny Lenkeit and Knut Schwippert

One of the main aims underpinning the accounts presented in this volume was to provide insights into the impact of PIRLS 2006 on the systemic, governmental, and administrative systems and the schools of different education systems around the world as well as on public opinion and the work of educational researchers. As is evident from the country chapters, the conducting of the study and its results met with different responses ranging from public uproar to minimal interest. Restructuring, modification, and/or the development of new systemic structures and educational programs were also important direct or indirect consequences of the study.

Another goal with respect to this publication was to contribute to one of the purposes of international achievement studies, that is, to enable people to gain a better understanding of their own education systems by viewing them against the systems of other countries (Porter & Gamoran, 2002). The project thus attempted to bring together, in a systematic way, the breadth of reactions that PIRLS 2006 appears to have caused in the different countries which participated in this impact study. It also sought to underline how such information can be used to inform change (where thought necessary) in those systems.

The authors of the 12 country chapters were equipped with an analytical framework that provided a basis for the anticipated cross-national comparison, and they were asked to address some overall aspects of the possible impacts we anticipated the study might have had. We also intended that the framework would provide readers with information about each country that would allow them to bear in mind national contexts when considering and interpreting the authors' descriptions and perceptions of PIRLS impacts. However, although we also designed the framework as a structuring orientation for the single chapters, we had no intention of it serving as a restraint on what the authors could write; we made clear to them that we wanted them to focus on aspects they considered relevant within their countries.

We were furthermore interested in having authors from countries that also participated in the impact study associated with PIRLS 2001 (Schwippert, 2007) give a longitudinal perspective on the impact of PIRLS assessments. We assumed that the passage of time in those countries would have bedded in, to varying degrees, any transformative processes initiated after the first PIRLS cycle. We also knew that the different institutional associations of the authors, as well as their positions within the education system of their respective countries, would yield a variety of perspectives not only on the utility of the PIRLS program per se but also on its relative impact in societal and research spheres.

To give a sense of this volume's comparative utility, we consider it relevant to refer to the four different functions of comparative research as stated by Hörner (1997, 2010). These functions are located along two comparison-based axes: the "practical" versus the "theoretical", and the "universal" versus the "distinctive." The *idiographic function* of a comparison (i.e., identification of what is individual or particular) is located at the intercept of theoretical interest and distinctiveness. Its usefulness lies in the ability it gives us to identify the features within a given system that are unique to it. The *melioristic function* (i.e., identification of what can be used for the benefit of society) is located at the intercept of distinctiveness and practical interest. Both *evolutionistic* and *experimental functions* are positioned on the universality attribute. The former, however, allows us to seek out developmental trends within a specific feature (the *practical* considerations), while the latter enables us to acquire knowledge that informs *theoretical* positions.

Understanding which of these functions is served by the study documented in this book requires us to trace back over what we have learned from this exercise. First, the information provided in this volume has given us insight into the impact of PIRLS on different spheres of the respective education systems, with that insight carefully tempered by appreciation of the countries' societal, political, and educational contexts. Second, the comparative nature of the study has allowed us to identify from the distinctive inquiries of the single chapters differences and similarities across the participating countries in the perceived impacts of PIRLS. However, as is apparent in the comparative summary (Chapter 15), explanations for these differences and similarities are not easy to obtain. It is this limitation—difficulty of advancing our theoretical knowledge or understanding (the idiographic function of comparative research)—that classes the comparative potential of the presented volume as melioristic. The value of this study thus lies primarily in enabling us to identify those features, aspects, and strategies that we can most appropriately use for the betterment of our own education systems (Hörner, 2010).

But, as Ginsberg (1997, p. 47) reminds us, "... comparative analyses have the possibility of shrouding the 'truth' as well as shedding new light on previously ignored or misinterpreted phenomena (Eckstein, 1986), [and] we must be cautious to avoid the 'abuses'—exaggeration, over-emphatic conclusions, decontextualization, and ego-centrism ..." (p. 47). His caution has even more cogency when we acknowledge that (education) systems are not constituted by the addition of single characteristics but rather their systemic combination (Hörner, 2010). However enriching it may thus be to use the developments of other countries to advance our own educational transformation processes, *educational borrowing* and its transfer of concepts and programs from one system to another is, as Fuchs (2005) demonstrates, rarely fruitful. The potential for successful change lies in carefully considering how well any proposed change is likely to fit into the particular cultural and structural realities of our own education system.

Despite the need to keep these limits in mind, we are confident that this impact of PIRLS study, like its predecessor, still offers the various stakeholders within any education system valuable information and insight. The conducting of assessments such as PIRLS and the analysis and discussion of the resultant data give government officials and agencies, policymakers, and educators opportunity to identify, discuss, and address education-based problems and challenges. Exchanging experience and ideas across countries adds to this benefit, and even more so when the countries being compared have similar systemic and cultural structures. We consider that placing greater emphasis than has been the case to date on the cultural and historical contexts of countries participating in cross-national assessments of educational achievement will enable a more straightforward and useful comparison across those countries. This approach, in turn, should allow clearer understanding of what changes (inputs) to an education system are most likely to have the desired outcomes on student achievement (outputs).

The findings outlined in the comparative summary of this volume are also valuable in terms of delineating challenges for further research. So far, the methodology and design of the PIRLS program has not allowed us to draw associative or causal inferences with respect to factors influencing the impact of PIRLS. As such, we suggest that the time has come to determine whether the systemic, economic, historical, structural, and cultural characteristics of the countries assumed to mediate the stature and the strength of the impact of both PIRLS 2001 and 2006 on the countries' respective education systems (see Chapter 15, Figure 15.1, p. 251) hold up when put to empirical scrutiny. We suggest the need to test whether and to what degree the identified factors are systematically associated with the varying impacts across countries.

Bulgaria, Canada, England, France, Germany, Hong Kong SAR, Hungary, Iran, Israel, Italy, Kuwait, Lithuania, Morocco, the Netherlands, New Zealand, Norway, Romania, the Russian Federation, Singapore, the Slovak Republic, Slovenia, Sweden, and the United States participated in the third iteration of PIRLS, that is, PIRLS 2011. For these countries, 10 years have passed since their primary students were assessed during the first PIRLS assessment of 2001. This time interval offers enticing opportunity for researchers and educational stakeholders to further identify not only the long-term impacts of PIRLS but also the respective effects on student achievement of educational programs, modified structures, pedagogical strategies and the like that are fed back into education systems as an explicit or implicit response to the findings of this large-scale assessment study and others like it.

References

Eckstein, M. A. (1986). The comparative mind. In P. G. Altbach & G. P. Kelly (Eds.), *New approaches to comparative education* (pp. 167–178). Chicago, IL: University of Chicago Press.

Fuchs, H.-W. (2005). Leistungsmessungen und Innovationsstrategien in Schulsystemen. Zur Einleitung in den Band [Assessments of achievement and innovation strategies in educational systems: An introduction to the book]. In H. Döbert & H.-W. Fuchs (Eds.), *Leistungsmessungen und Innovationsstrategien in Schulsystemen: Ein internationaler Vergleich* [Assessments of achievement and innovation strategies in educational systems: An international comparison] (pp. 9–14). Münster, Germany: Waxmann.

Ginsberg, M. B. (1997). The limitations and possibilities of comparative analysis of education in global context. In C. Kodron, B. van Kopp, U. Lauterbach, U. Schäfer, & G. Schmidt (Eds.), *Vergleichende Erziehungswissenschaft: Herausforderung, Vermittlung, Praxis* [Comparative education: Challenge, mediation, practice] (pp. 46–51). Frankfurt am Main, Germany: Böhlau.

Hörner, W. (1997). "Europa" als Herausforderung für die Vergleichende Erziehungswissenschaft: Reflexion über die politische Funktion einer pädagogischen Disziplin ["Europe" as a challenge for comparative education: Reflections on the political function of a pedagogic discipline] (pp. 65–80). Frankfurt am Main, Germany: Böhlau Verlag.

Hörner, W. (2010). Die Bildungssysteme Europas: eine Einführung [The educational systems of Europe: An introduction]. In H. Döbert, W. Hörner, B. van Kopp, & L. R. Reuter (Eds.), *Die Bildungssysteme Europas* [The educational systems of Europe] (pp. 1–10). Hohengehren, Germany: Schneider.

Porter, A. C., & Gamoran, A. (2002). Progress and challenges for large-scale studies. In A. C. Porter & A. Gamoran (Eds.), *Methodological advances in cross-national surveys of educational achievement*. Washington, DC: National Academy Press.

Schwippert, K. (Ed.). (2007). *Progress in reading literacy: The impact of PIRLS 2001 in 13 countries*. Münster, Germany: Waxmann.

Bibliography of International PIRLS Publications 2001

Campbell, J. R., Kelly, D. L., Mullis, I. V. S., Martin, M. O., & Sainsbury, M. (2001). *Framework and specifications for PIRLS assessment 2001* (2nd ed.). Chestnut Hill, MA: Boston College.

Gonzalez, E. J., & Kennedy, A. M. (Eds.). (2003). *PIRLS 2001 user guide for the international database*. Chestnut Hill, MA: Boston College.

Martin, M. O., Mullis, I. V. S., Gonzalez, E. J., & Kennedy, A. M. (Eds.). (2003). *Trends in children's reading literacy achievement 1991–2001: IEA's repeat in nine countries of the 1991 Reading Literacy Study*. Chestnut Hill, MA: Boston College.

Martin, M. O., Mullis, I. V. S., & Kennedy, A. M. (Eds.). (2003). *PIRLS 2001 technical report*. Chestnut Hill, MA: Boston College.

Mullis, I. V. S., Kennedy, A. M., Martin, M. O., & Sainsbury, M. (2006). *PIRLS 2006 assessment framework and specifications* (2nd ed.). Chestnut Hill, MA: Boston College

Mullis, I. V. S., Martin, M. O., & Gonzalez, E. J. (2004). *International achievement in the process of reading comprehension: Results from PIRLS 2001 in 35 countries*. Chestnut Hill, MA: Boston College.

Mullis, I. V. S., Martin, M. O., Gonzalez, E. J., & Kennedy, A. M. (2003). *PIRLS 2001 international report: IEA's study of reading literacy achievement in primary schools in 35 countries*. Chestnut Hill, MA: Boston College.

Mullis, I. V. S., Martin, M. O., Kennedy, A. M., & Flaherty, C. L. (Eds.). (2002). *PIRLS 2001 encyclopedia: A reference guide to reading education in the countries participating in IEA's Progress in International Reading Literacy Study (PIRLS)*. Chestnut Hill, MA: Boston College.

Bibliography of International PIRLS Publications 2006

Foy, P., & Kennedy, A. M. (2008). *PIRLS 2006 user guide for the international database.*Chestnut Hill, MA: Boston College.

Kennedy, A. M., Mullis, I. V. S., Martin, M. O., & Trong, K. L. (Eds.). (2007). *PIRLS 2006 encyclopedia: A guide to reading education in the forty PIRLS 2006 countries*. Chestnut Hill, MA: Boston College.

Martin, M. O., Mullis, I. V. S., & Kennedy, A. M. (Eds.). (2007). *PIRLS 2006 technical report*. Chestnut Hill, MA: Boston College.

Mullis, I. V. S., Kennedy, A. M., Martin, M. O., & Sainsbury, M. (2006). *PIRLS 2006 assessment framework and specifications* (2nd ed.). Chestnut Hill, MA: Boston College

Mullis, I. V. S., Martin, M. O., Kennedy, A. M., & Foy, P. (2007). *PIRLS 2006 international report: IEA's Progress in International Reading Literacy Study in primary schools in 40 countries*. Chestnut Hill, MA: Boston College.

Information on the Contributing Authors

INTRODUCTION

Professor Knut Schwippert holds the chair of International Comparative Education and System Monitoring at the University of Hamburg, Faculty of Education, Psychology and Human Movement. During PIRLS 2001, he was jointly responsible for coordinating Germany's involvement in this assessment, and is currently a member of the PIRLS 2011 national steering committee for Germany. His main areas of research interest are methods in international large-scale assessments, heterogeneity in schools, and organizational development.

Jenny Lenkeit holds a Master of Arts in international educational research from the Humboldt University of Berlin. She is writing her doctoral thesis on educational effectiveness measures in large-scale assessments and works as a research assistant at the University of Hamburg for the Department of Education.

Address for correspondence: Department of Education, Section I: General, International Comparative and Intercultural Education, University of Hamburg, Binderstrasse 34, 20146 Hamburg, GERMANY
(knut.schwippert@uni-hamburg.de; jenny.lenkeit@uni-hamburg.de)

PIRLS IN BRIEF

Professor Wilfried Bos holds the chair for Educational Research and Quality Assurance at TU Dortmund University and is director of the Institute for School Development Research. He has been chair and national research coordinator of past iterations of TIMSS and PIRLS in Germany and of PIRLS in Luxembourg and the German-speaking community of Belgium. Currently, he is the national research coordinator for both PIRLS and TIMSS 2011 in Germany. Wilfried Bos has been involved in international large-scale assessments since the mid-1990s, when he was the project coordinator for TIMSS 1995 (Pop. III) in Germany. His main research interests are research methods in education, quality assurance and improvement in education systems, international educational research and comparative education, evaluation and large-scale assessments, and research on education in China.

Address for correspondence: Institute for School Development Research, Vogelpothsweg 78, D-44227 Dortmund, GERMANY
(officebos@ifs.tu-dortmund.de)

Martin Goy works as a researcher at the Institute for School Development Research at TU Dortmund University, where he is a doctoral candidate under the supervision of Professor Wilfried Bos. He is a member of the research staff of the National Educational Panel Study (NEPS), and was a member of the research staff for PIRLS

2006 in Germany. He also worked as a student research assistant for Professors Wilfried Bos and Knut Schwippert during PIRLS 2001. His main research interests are international and comparative education, large-scale assessments, self-concept and motivation in school contexts, and the development and facilitation of reading literacy.

Address for correspondence: Institute for School Development Research, TU Dortmund University, Hauert 14a, D-44227 Dortmund, GERMANY (goy@ifs.tu-dortmund.de)

Irmela Tarelli works as a researcher at the Institute for School Development Research at TU Dortmund University. She recently completed her doctoral thesis on home literacy environments within the context of PIRLS 2006. She has been involved with PIRLS since 2001. She worked as a student research assistant with the German PIRLS 2001 team and as a member of research staff for PIRLS 2006. Since 2010 she has been the project coordinator for PIRLS 2011 in Germany. Her main research interests are national and international school achievement studies and cross-cultural comparisons. A particular focus is the impact of the home literacy environment on students' achievement.

Address for correspondence: Institute for School Development Research, TU Dortmund University, Vogelpothsweg 78, D-44227 Dortmund, GERMANY (tarelli@ifs.tu-dortmund.de)

AUSTRIA

Dr. Birgit Suchań works in the area of psychology at the University of Salzburg, but is also involved, through the Federal Institute for Educational Research, Innovation, and Development of the Austrian School System (BIFIE), as a researcher on IEA's PIRLS and TIMSS programs.

Christina Wallner-Paschon is also affiliated with the University of Salzburg, where she is involved in the field of education. She, too, is a researcher with the IEA PIRLS and TIMSS programs.

Cornelia Rieß's area of expertise is economics and social economics. She is engaged in the former at Johannes-Kepler University, Linz (Austria), and at Charles-University, Prague (Czech Republic). She is involved in the latter at Johannes-Kepler University, Linz (Austria). Her research interests include educational standards in primary schools. She has conducted much of this work at BIFIE.

Address for correspondence: BIFIE, Salzburg, Alpenstr. 121, 5020 Salzburg, AUSTRIA (b.suchan@bifie.at; c.wallner-paschon@bifie.at; c.riess@bifie.at)

BELGIUM

Jan Van Damme is a professor at the Katholieke Universiteit Leuven in Belgium and head of the Research Center for Educational Effectiveness and Evaluation. He was responsible for the Flemish participation in PIRLS 2006 and has been involved in several iterations of TIMSS. Most of his publications relate to longitudinal studies of students in primary and secondary education and to multilevel studies focusing on class, teacher, and school levels. His more recent topics of interest are school feedback on student achievement, change in education systems, and the effect of that charge at the country level. He is one of the founders of the EARLI SIG on educational effectiveness.

Dr. Heidi Knipprath is engaged on the School Feedback Project at the Center for Educational Effectiveness and Evaluation, which is affiliated with Katholieke Universiteit Leuven. She has analyzed various international databases on educational achievement, including PIRLS 2006. Her main areas of research interest are school effectiveness, value-added models, Japanese education, and lifelong learning.

Hongqiang Liu is a doctoral researcher under the supervision of Professor Jan Van Damme at the Research Center for Educational Effectiveness and Evaluation. His research focus is educational quality and equity, as evidenced in international data from studies such as PIRLS, TIMSS, and PISA.

Address for correspondence: Department for Educational Sciences, Center for Educational Effectiveness and Evaluation, Katholieke Universiteit Leuven, Dekenstraat 2, 3000 Leuven, BELGIUM
(Jan.VanDamme@ped.kuleuven.be; heidi.knipprath@ped.kuleuven.be; Hongqiang.liu@ped.kuleuven.be)

ENGLAND

Liz Twist is a principal research officer at the National Foundation for Educational Research in England. Her work within the foundation's Department for Research in Assessment and Measurement includes her role as national research coordinator for PIRLS 2011. She was also the national research coordinator of the first two PIRLS surveys. In addition to her work with PIRLS, Liz directs the development of the national tests in English (reading and writing) taken by all students at the end of primary school and undertakes a range of other assessment research. Previously the deputy head-teacher of a primary school, her research interests include special educational needs, assessment of reading attainment, and measurement of reading attitudes.

Address for correspondence: Department for Research in Assessment and Measurement, National Foundation for Educational Research, The Mere, Upton Park, Slough, Berkshire, SL1 2DQ, ENGLAND
(l.twist@nfer.ac.uk)

GERMANY

Knut Schwippert (see under Introduction above)
Martin Goy (see under PIRLS in Brief above)
Jenny Lenkeit (see under Introduction above)

HONG KONG SAR

Professor Shek Kam Tse is director of the Centre for the Advancement of Chinese Language Education and Research and is currently serving as associate dean of the University of Hong Kong's Faculty of Education. During the 2001 and 2006 PIRLS surveys, he was responsible for coordinating the Hong Kong SAR elements of the project, and he is serving as the Hong Kong SAR national research coordinator during PIRLS 2011. His main areas of research interest are methods of large-scale international assessment surveys, organizational and methodological developments in reading and writing literacy, innovative methods of teaching Chinese language, teaching and learning of Chinese as a second language, the composing process used when writing Chinese, and the medium of instruction in schools where students and staff are from bilingual backgrounds.

Dr. Elizabeth Ka Yee Loh is an assistant professor within the University of Hong Kong's Faculty of Education. During the 2001 and 2006 PIRLS iterations, she was a member of the research team managing Hong Kong SAR's participation in the study. She is presently a member of the Hong Kong PIRLS 2011 research team. Her main research interests are the teaching and learning of Chinese characters, reading and emotive writing, assessment of Chinese reading and writing, innovative Chinese language pedagogy, the Chinese language education of students with special educational needs, and the teaching of Chinese as a second language to non-Chinese learners.

Address for correspondence: Faculty of Education, Room 405, Runme Shaw Building, The University of Hong Kong, Pokfulam Road, HONG KONG SAR
(sktse@hkucc.hku.hk; ekyloh@hkucc.hku.hk)

HUNGARY

Péter Balkányi works within the Ministry of Education as a reading expert. Much of his work there involves coordinating Hungary's participation in PIRLS assessments. He also oversees the development of items and scoring guides for the reading portion of

Hungary's National Assessment of Basic Competencies, and scoring of the PISA assessment. His research interests focus on exploring reasons behind the achievement of Hungarian students on the PIRLS assessments and scoping these against national and international contexts. He is also interested in the relationship between the teaching of reading in Hungary and reading performance at home and in school.

Address for correspondence: 1054, Budapest; Báthory u. 10. HUNGARY (Balkanyi.Peter@oh.gov.hu)

LATVIA

Antra Ozola was the PIRLS 2006 national research coordinator. She works as a full-time researcher and lecturer within the University of Latvia's Faculty of Education, Psychology, and Art. She is also a doctoral student of administration sciences; her particular focus is educational management.

Address for correspondence: Faculty of Education, Psychology, and Art, Jurmalas Gatve 74/76, Room 218A, University of Latvia, Riga LV-1083, LATVIA (antra.ozola@lu.lv)

NETHERLANDS

Andrea Netten works as a research associate at the National Center for Language Education, an institution that aims to improve the teaching and learning of Dutch language arts in schools. Andrea was the Netherlands' national research coordinator for PIRLS 2006, and she has reprised this role for the 2011 PIRLS survey. She is currently writing her doctoral dissertation, which focuses on reading achievement and second language learning.

Address for correspondence: Expertisecentrum Nederlands, Postbus 6610, 6503 GC Nijmegen, THE NETHERLANDS (a.netten@taalonderwijs.nl)

NEW ZEALAND

Megan Chamberlain is a principal research analyst in the Ministry of Education's Comparative Education Research Unit. Her working career in the ministry involved her in a number of national studies before she began working on the IEA studies. She has been the national research coordinator for SITES-Module 1, TIMSS 1999, TIMSS 2003, and PIRLS 2006. She will continue in the NRC role for PIRLS 2011. Her current area of interest is integrating information across the international studies in order to provide better understanding of New Zealand students' reading outcomes.

Address for correspondence: Comparative Education Research Unit, Ministry of Education, PO Box 1666, Wellington 6140, NEW ZEALAND (Megan.chamberlain@minedu.govt.nz)

RUSSIAN FEDERATION

Dr. Isak Froumin is the scientific supervisor of the Institute of Education at the National Research University Higher School of Economics and is a leading expert at the World Bank. His research activities focus on improvement of Russia's educational system, educational reform, educational policy, and comparative international studies.

Address for correspondence: The National Research University Higher School of Economics, Myasnitskaya 20, Moscow, RUSSIAN FEDERATION (ifroumin@hse.ru)

Dr. Marina Kuznetsova has worked since 1995 as a senior researcher within the Center of Primary Education, Institute of Content and Methods of Learning, Russian Academy of Education, and is a reading expert on the Russian Federation's national PIRLS team. Her research interests include methods of teaching reading, assessment in primary education (native language and literature), and development of assessments related to national standards and national monitoring systems.

Address for correspondence: 18-214, Tsentralnaya str, Chernogolovka, Moscow distr, RUSSIAN FEDERATION 142432 (bernin@mail.ru)

Galina Kovaleva is head of the Center for Evaluating the Quality of Education, Russian Academy of Education.

Andrey Melnikov is a child psychologist at the Educational Program Department.

Marina Pinskaya is senior researcher at the Institute for Educational Studies of the University Higher School of Economics.

Tatiana Timkova is a researcher at the Institute for Educational Studies of the University Higher School of Economics.

Yulia Tumeneva is director of the Center for Monitoring the Quality of Education within the Institute for Educational Studies of the University Higher School of Economics

Galina Zuckerman is a leading researcher within the Psychology Institute, Russian Academy of Education.

SLOVAK REPUBLIC

Eva Ladányiová (previously Obrancová) works at the National Institute for Certified Educational Measurements, Department of International Measurements. She was the national research coordinator for PIRLS 2006. She has also been involved in PISA as part of the team developing the Slovak version of the tools used in the assessment, and as overseer of coding the assessment's reading items. Her main area of research interest is the reading literacy performance of students in international large-scale assessments.

Address for correspondence: Nobelova 46, 831 02 Bratislava, SLOVAK REPUBLIC (Eva.Ladanyiova@gmail.com)

Paulína Koršňáková works as a senior administrative officer at the IEA Secretariat. Prior to this, she led the Department of International Measurements, located within the National Institute for Education, and later within the National Institute for Certified Educational Measurements, which serves as the national research center for IEA studies in Slovakia. Dr. Koršňáková is a member of the editorial board of the e-journal *Pedagogika*, published by the Slovak Pedagogical Society. Her main areas of interest relate to using the outcomes of comparative and applied research to inform education policy development.

Address for correspondence: IEA Secretariat, Herengracht 487, 1017 BT Amsterdam, THE NETHERLANDS (p.korsnakova@iea.nl).

Dr. Daniela Heldová works at the National Institute for Certified Educational Measurements, which is situated within the Department of International Measurements. During PIRLS 2001, she was involved in developing the Slovak language version of the assessment tools. She was also involved in quality monitoring, scoring procedures, and the interpretation and reporting of findings. Her research interests relate to reading literacy, as measured by the IEA PIRLS and OECD PISA surveys, and to the sorts of changes that need to be made to how reading is taught in Slovakia in order to improve students' reading literacy.

Address for correspondence: Odd. medzinárodných meraní, Národný ústav certifikovaných meraní vzdelávania, Pluhová 8, 831 03 Bratislava 3, SLOVAK REPUBLIC (daniela.heldova@nucem.sk)

SOUTH AFRICA

Professor Sarah Howie joined the Faculty of Education at the University of Pretoria in 2002 as the director of the newly established Centre for Evaluation and Assessment and as programme manager of the M.Ed programme in assessment and quality assurance. She has extensive experience in large-scale assessment studies such as TIMSS–R, PIRLS 2006, and SITES 2006, and has also contributed to a number of publications in this research domain. Professor Howie serves *inter alia* on the South African ministerial committee on learner retention as well as on the statistical committee for the South African Quality Assurer for Further Education and Training, Umalusi.

Address for correspondence: Room 30, Library Building, Faculty of Education, Groenkloof Campus, University of Pretoria, Pretoria 0002, SOUTH AFRICA (Sarah.Howie@up.ac.za)

Elsie Venter is data manager at the Centre for Evaluation and Assessment. She has extensive experience as a data manager responsible for large-scale databases, such as TIMSS 1999 and 2003, PIRLS 2006 (of which she was a co-national research coordinator), the National Census of South Africa Community Profiles, and provincial and national systemic evaluation studies. She has lectured in the fields of physical science, biology, and mathematics, and currently teaches on the M.Ed programme in assessment and quality assurance at the Centre for Evaluation and Assessment.

Address for correspondence: Centre for Evaluation and Assessment, Groenkloof Campus, University of Pretoria, Pretoria 0001, SOUTH AFRICA
(elsie.venter@up.ac.za)

COMPARATIVE SUMMARY

Professor Isabell van Ackeren holds the chair of Research on Educational Systems and School Development within the Faculty of Educational Sciences, Institute of Pedagogy, at the University of Duisburg-Essen. She is the principal of the research group "Educational Research". Her main areas of research interest are school quality and development, evaluation of school programs and organization, and comparative studies.

Address for correspondence: Faculty of Educational Sciences, University of Duisburg-Essen, Berliner Platz 6-8, 45117 Essen, GERMANY
(isabell.van-ackeren@uni-due.de)

Dr. Anke B. Liegmann works as a researcher (postdoctoral) within the research group "Educational Research," which is situated within the Faculty of Educational Sciences, Institute of Pedagogy, at the University of Duisburg-Essen. Her main areas of research interest are school development, teacher training, students' careers, and heterogeneity in schools.

Address for correspondence: Faculty of Educational Sciences, University of Duisburg-Essen, Berliner Platz 6-8, 45117 Essen, GERMANY
(anke.liegmann@uni-due.de)

Studies in International Comparative and Multicultural Education

Volume 7

Knut Schwippert (Ed.)

Progress in Reading Literacy

The Impact of PIRLS 2001 in 13 Countries

2007, 280 pages, pb, € 29,90
ISBN 978-3-8309-1759-5

I n 2001, the International Association for the Evaluation of Educational Achievement (IEA) conducted the Progress in Reading Literacy Study (PIRLS), designed to assess the reading literacy achievement of students in two age cohorts within and across 35 countries. This present volume explores the impacts that participation in and the findings of the study have had within 13 of those countries.

The book also provides a brief overview of PIRLS 2001 and its international findings. The final chapter of the book presents a synthesis of the findings of the country chapters.

Knut Schwippert's book accumulates and synthesizes international experiences and therefore, the book is a unique source to gather information on the impact of PIRLS from an international perspective.

http://www.j-e-r-o.com/index.php/jero/issue/current

WAXMANN
Münster · New York · München · Berlin

Studies in International Comparative and Multicultural Education

Volume 10

Hans-Georg Kotthoff, Stavros Moutsios (Eds.)

Education Policies in Europe

Economy, Citizenship, Diversity

2007, 240 pages, pb, € 29,90
ISBN 978-3-8309-1918-6

National education systems across Europe are being brought into the service of a 'competitive knowledge-based economy' and of 'social cohesion'. Moreover what it is to be a citizen and how the new citizens should be educated are issues subject to research and educational initiatives in many European countries. The European Union is now, directly or indirectly, shaping the major orientations of European education systems. This book is the result of a Socrates/ Erasmus 'Intensive Programme' on contemporary European education policies. It brings together contributions which address the above themes from a variety of standpoints.

WAXMANN
Münster · New York · München · Berlin

Studies in International Comparative and Multicultural Education

Volume 11

Sabine Hornberg

Schule im Prozess der Internationalisierung von Bildung

2010, 266 Seiten, br., 29,90 €
ISBN 978-3-8309-2259-9

*Der Autorin gelingt eine theoretisch an-
spruchsvolle und methodisch disziplinierte
Darstellung, die als aktuelles deutsch-
sprachiges Standardwerk zur Internationalisierung
der Schule angesehen werden kann. Das Buch ist
ferner – nicht zuletzt wegen des umfangreichen
und systematisch zusammengefassten faktischen
Materials, insbesondere zu schulorganisatorischen
und curricularen Aspekten, – den Lehrkräften und
Schulleitungen als Referenzquelle für die Schulent-
wicklungsarbeit im Bereich der Internationalisierung
zu empfehlen.*

Bildung und Erziehung, 4/ 2011

WAXMANN
Münster · New York · München · Berlin

Studies in International Comparative and Multicultural Education

Volume 12

Bianca Roters

Professionalisierung durch Reflexion in der Lehrerbildung

Eine empirische Studie an einer deutschen und einer US-amerikanischen Universität

2012, 328 Seiten, br., 34,90 €
ISBN 978-3-8309-2662-7

In einer vergleichend angelegten Studie werden die Professionalisierungsdiskurse in Deutschland und den USA anhand von Dokumentenanalysen, Interviews mit Lehrerausbildern und dokumentierten studentischen Reflexionen untersucht. Ihr spezifisches Erhebungsfeld stellt dabei die Ausbildung angehender FremdsprachenlehrerInnen dar. Zentrales Ergebnis der Studie sind sechs empirisch nachweisbare Reflexionsniveaus, durch die in Form einer Typologie eine Charakterisierung studentischer Reflexionsfähigkeit vom deskriptiv-pauschalisierenden bis hin zum transformativ-reflexiven Novizen möglich ist. Anhand der empirischen Befunde werden hochschuldidaktische Empfehlungen für ein reflexives Professionalisierungskonzept in der Lehrerbildung ausgesprochen.

Münster · New York · München · Berlin